Finch

Regional Integration

Regional Integration: The Latin American Experience

Edited by
Altaf Gauhar

Third World Foundation
for Social and Economic Studies
London

THIRD WORLD FOUNDATION
New Zealand House
80 Haymarket, London SW1Y 4TS

© Third World Foundation 1985

British Cataloguing in Publication Data

Regional Integration: The Latin American Experience
1. Latin American-Economic Integration
1. Gauhar   2. Third World Foundation
337.1'8   HC 125

ISBN 0 907962 31 9

Filmset in 10/12 point Monophoto Photina by
Northumberland Press Ltd, Gateshead
Tyne and Wear
Printed in Great Britain by
Richard Clay (The Chaucer Press) Ltd,
Bungay, Suffolk

Contents

Contents

Introduction

Cartagena 1984 was the second in the series of South-South conferences initiated by the Third World Foundation to enable Third World statesmen and scholars to meet in their personal capacities, for an intensive exchange of views on important issues relating to the social and economic development of the Third World. The theme of South-South One, held in Beijing in April 1983, was 'Strategies of Development, Negotiations and Cooperation'. It involved a critical and objective appraisal of development strategies, the causes of the stalemate in North-South negotiations and prospects and opportunities for effective South-South cooperation.

At the conclusion of South-South One it was decided that a summit of Third World statesmen, policymakers and academics should be convened every three years and the intervening period used for a thorough examination of specific regional issues and problems. This volume comprises the papers presented at the first regional conference under the Beijing programme and marks an important step towards South-South Two scheduled for 1986. Sixty delegates from Latin America, Africa, Asia and the Caribbean and a dozen observers from Europe, US and Canada participated in the conference, held in Cartagena, Colombia.

It is essential to assess the results of regional integration, wherever it has been attempted, so that the mistakes of the past do not remain the obstacles of the present only to become the lost opportunities of the future. The Cartagena conference was unique in the sense that the theoreticians who formulated models of regional cooperation confronted for the first time those who make and implement policies only to discover that the failure of nearly every initiative towards regional integration was as much the result of flawed conception as defective policy formulation and haphazard execution. Together they considered the consequences of the global economic crisis on the countries of Latin America and critically assessed their experience in regional integration. This collection of thirteen papers was presented at the conference by scholars and officials representing the three groups who emerged considerably chastened from three days of gruelling but objective introspection and self-criticism.

Does regional economic cooperation and integration present a way out of the current economic crisis for the developing countries who are the hardest hit by it? Regional integration remains an appealing concept but one is less certain whether it is practicable for it may fail to withstand the challenges posed by the vagaries of international finance markets, chronically unstable state structures, and an increasingly polarised system of international relationships. But in the context of economic cooperation among developing countries (ECDC), it offers a glimmer of hope for unity. The South's heterogeneity is repeatedly underlined by detractors of South-South cooperation but homogeneity is not necessarily a precondition for unity. Nevertheless, a measure of unity is vital if the countries of the South are to succeed in restructuring the international economic order.

Latin America provides an excellent case-study of how the international economy has impinged upon development policies geared to promote formal schemes of regional integration. Despite nearly three decades of formal regional integration, the countries of Latin America are amongst those most adversely affected by the present crisis in the world economy.

The need for hard foreign currency has led to a deterioration in intra-regional trade, accentuating the contraction of Latin American economies even further. Regional integration, far from providing a safety-net for the external balance of payments, has been dealt a bitter blow by an involvement in the international economy that exceeds the resource capacity of Latin American countries. A process of gradual disengagement from the international economy and a greater reliance on the regional economies has been suggested often enough but it has as many critics as it has supporters. The critics argue that delinkage would make Latin America permanently economically backward and even less able to compete on the international market.

With a debt burden of US $350 billion the countries of Latin America are faced with the dilemma of defaulting on interest payments and being categorised as uncreditworthy, or meeting their loan repayments at the cost of severe recession in their domestic economies. Latin America is now a net exporter of capital to the industrialised countries and some 40 per cent of its export earnings are swallowed up by the interest charges. These debt-burdened and impoverished countries are now all being subjected to a process of 'adjustment' which in effect means lowering the standard of living even further. Most of this adjustment effort falls on labour whose real wages are reduced still further to achieve external competitiveness, thereby making possible the spectacular trade surpluses which Brazil and Mexico achieved in 1984. This is particularly unfair since the benefits of debt accumulation accrued, not to the working class but to the upper middle class and the financial sectors which often aided by a military regime benefited from the import spree and speculation. It is the factory worker, the peasant and the low wage-earner who has now to suffer for the avarice and recklessness of a few individuals.

Three contributors discuss the history and the economic condition of Latin America within the context of the present crisis and offer strikingly similar policy prescriptions.

Osvaldo Sunkel traces the roots of Latin America's current dilemmas in the light of changes in the international economy between 1930 and 1983. Within this broad historical sweep, Sunkel shows how Latin America's development strategies have been shaped by the ebbs and flows of international finance. The liquidity crisis during the great depression of the 1930s resulted in a general tendency towards protectionism and state-controlled planning. With the revival of international trade, finance and investment in the mid-1960s outward-looking development strategies gained currency. The transnationalisation of investment, production and consumption patterns hastened the drift towards monetarism, increasing the external vulnerability of Latin American economies and accentuating the already considerable structural problems of development. The availability of international private finance in the mid-1970s provided illusions of rapid economic growth to cover the grim realities of uneven progress. Heavy spending at home and erratic borrowing abroad has placed Latin America in the unenviable position of having borrowed too much and developed too little. Sunkel sees no easy way out of this dilemma. Nothing short of radical structural change at both the international and the national levels can free Latin America from its debt bondage. What is needed is a serious reconsideration of past development policies and a concerted effort to redress the inequalities that have trailed in their wake.

Sunkel compares the national and global financial world to a minefield and underlines that there is as yet no evidence of a mine-clearing operation. He advocates the formulation of a strategy—both national and international—of much broader scope; a new international financial institutionalisation that promotes development and stability of the global economy.

Within this framework each country would have the option of negotiating its debt according to its particular circumstances.

Enrique Iglesias shares many of Sunkel's perspectives and provides further insights into the magnitude of the crisis that hit Latin America in 1982. He regrets the lack of theoretical models to explain the rapid structural transformations that are taking place in the developed and the developing economies. Uncertainties about future trends in the world economy and the different circumstances of each country in the region make it impossible to formulate even the most generalised solutions for Latin America as a whole.

Iglesias, however, sets about examining the overall measures that might assist in the recovery of Latin American economies. He doubts the practicability of radical measures in the midst of Latin America's worst crisis in nearly half a century and hopes to see the debt crisis resolved without the countries of the region having to abandon their responsibilities as members of the international economy. In a perfect world it might have been sufficient for Iglesias to warn the developed world yet again of the socio-economic and political disorders that are likely to accompany a net transfer of resources from the region. Recent events in Central America, pointing to an increasing convergence of American economic and strategic interests, suggest that Iglesias's reminders are unlikely to alter circumstances for the better. International banking interests are unwilling to lend with the enthusiasm of the petrodollar boom in the 1970s. This will make it difficult for Latin American countries to follow the classical prescription, endorsed by Iglesias, of broadening their domestic economies and amassing foreign exchange reserves to safeguard against future disorders in the international economy. So he recommends structural changes in macroeconomic policies and in the allocation of resources for new investments. By devising 'imaginative ways' to stretch their resource capacity, Iglesias believes Latin America can paint itself out of its corner. Painful adjustments will have to be made, and these obviously cannot be left to the whims of free market forces. There will have to be increased state intervention in order to reconcile economic efficiency with social objectives. To achieve a healthy internal balance, Iglesias recommends export promotion drives into regional and international markets, state support for schemes of cooperation and, above all, state initiatives in overcoming competition and protectionism in the international markets. All this is consistent with Iglesias's call for an even closer alliance between private interests and the state. Whether such an alliance can give due consideration to social needs is a question Iglesias thinks best not to raise for the time being.

Furtado exposes the inadequacies of the existing conceptual framework to explain the logic of the modern capitalist system. He shows how the transnationalisation process has created distortions in relations between national economies that cannot be corrected by presently available policy instruments. The nub of the problem, according to Furtado, has been the steady erosion of national autonomy in an increasingly interdependent world with a variety of power-centres incapable of acting together to either control or regulate the anarchic pursuits of transnational finance. He sees the debt crisis as an aspect of the rational way in which the decision-making system created by the transnationalisation of banks and enterprises has come to operate. The confusions generated by the absence of an institutional arrangement that corresponds to the relationships emerging between national systems are sending shock waves throughout the international economy. The effects are especially severe for the developing states. In varying degrees, they have become incapable of directing economic activity in order to meet the pressing needs of their respective societies. The erosion of state authority *vis-à-vis* transnational financial interests militates against any coherent regulation of international economic relations. There are ominous signs of a drift towards confrontation, both at the national as well the international level. Private financial lobbies in the developed world, the United States in particular, are now defining national interest without the constraints existing rules of international conduct impose upon sovereign states. Significantly, Furtado does not envisage curbing the activities of transnational finance altogether. This would be inconsistent with the need to bring about a transfer of capital to the developing world. He points to the rewards a mixture of semi-state controlled transnationalisation has bestowed upon Japan. By contrast, the unchecked expansion of American transnational enterprises was proven to be the single most important factor in plunging the world into the present crisis. Furtado favours the creation of an institutional framework, at the national or the international level, with sufficient political clout to subject transnational banks and enterprises to economic objectives defined by sovereign national states, acting severally or in a series of permutations. Such an organisation could stand as a buffer between the custodians of the present, less-than-just, world economic order and a variety of nation states struggling to assert their autonomy without buckling under internal pressures. Such an institution, if it can be established, would have to hammer out a realistic solution to the debt crisis. This would be a crucial first step in bringing about a restructuring of international economic relations to account for the development needs of the Third World.

The policy prescriptions proposed by Sunkel, Iglesias and Furtado underline the urgent need for concerted political action to rescue Latin America from its perilous dependency. So far the countries of the region have shown their inability to negotiate a common front, hinting at the enormous difficulties in squaring domestic interests with international imperatives. The inherent constraints of their social and political structures coupled with unashamedly extortionist tactics of the international banking community have worked to undermine the sovereignty of the state in Latin America. Latin America's ultimate choice if and when it is made, will be a matter of interest for the developing world at large. It will certainly be a vital factor in any future cooperation between countries of the South. The next four contributors provide some useful insights into the sort of thinking that is preceding the final decision.

Aldo Ferrer argues that the adjustment and stabilisation policies of the International Monetary Fund (IMF) are effectively prescribing the de-industrialisation of Latin America. These policies will only serve to strengthen the 'pre-industrial' bureaucratic structures, the principal stumbling-block to democratic forms of government. According to Ferrer, the only pragmatic way the Latin American countries can survive this erosion of their sovereignty is for them to live within their means. Development plans predicted on the availability of foreign capital are no longer feasible. Conditions in the world economy point to continued shortfalls in foreign exchange earnings. So Ferrer proposes that Latin America should learn to pay 'cash on the nail' for all its future imports. This, together with progressive tax reforms and the dismantling of expensive bureaucratic and military structures will pave the way for a sensible debt rescheduling arrangement. Orthodox adjustment strategies are, in Ferrer's opinion, the surest way to precipitate a Latin American default. Ferrer suggests that policies aimed at salvaging sovereignty and democracy in Latin America might also work to the advantage of the international banking community.

Juan Somavía strikes a cautionary note on the possible disjunction between sovereignty and democracy within Latin America. Political disputes among Latin American states have been a major obstacle in evolving a coordinated economic response against the developed world. Border disputes in Latin America have tended to strengthen military dictatorships which are generally more responsive to international pressures than to demands for restoring democratic processes. Somavia asserts that peaceful settlements of long-standing political conflicts are a necessary precondition to effective economic cooperation at the regional level. He lists a series of priorities which might prepare the ground for political cooperation amongst Latin American countries.

José Antonio Ocampo argues that the collapse of economic reciprocity in the region had less to do with political conflicts as such than with the sheer inadequacies of the existing system of payments. Once individual countries began to record substantial deficits in their overall balance of payments, there was a dramatic contraction in intra-regional trade. Adjustment policies tailored to help countries tide over their balance of payments difficulties discouraged them from participating in intra-regional trade. Advantages accruing from reciprocal trade were cancelled out by cut-backs in domestic production and the need to make good the loss of hard foreign currency. Ocampo considers the possibility of restoring a system of bilateral credits and multilateral compensation for deficit countries similar to the European Payments Union in the post-war era. Alternatively, he suggests that deficit countries be allowed to pay for their imports in their own currencies. But whether countries with regional trade surpluses will be interested in these policy prescriptions, much less to implement them, is yet another of Latin America's unanswered questions.

Despite regional variations, Latin America is precariously positioned in the international financial and trading networks. As the economic adjunct and strategic backwater of the United States, Latin America's development strategies have been susceptible to the prevailing climes in international markets. The bouts of lending and borrowing in the 1970s; the perplexing debt rescheduling negotiations and their result, agonising adjustment processes; the imposition of East-West rivalries on the already considerable social and political tensions in the region, are all indications of just how exposed Latin America is to the whims of the developed world. To make matters worse, the global pattern and composition of its external trade has made Latin America especially vulnerable to fluctuations in the world economy. Dragoslav Avramovic points to these special features and assesses the potential of internationally organised schemes designed to help in the financing of trade. The initiatives taken by the Economic Community of West African States, Citibank of New York, The Group of 77 and, most recently, the idea of a Third World bank are considered from a comparative perspective.

While some of these initiatives have yet to leave the drawing board, Latin America is an old hand at working out regional responses to changes in the international economy. Its experience in regional economic integration is a useful gauge against which to measure whether regional and sub-regional cooperation can blunt the edge of chronic imbalances in the world economy. Four contributors take stock of Latin America's attempts at regional and sub-regional economic integration. Gert Rosenthal focuses on Central America, by far the most successful of Latin America's experiments in regional integration. Despite the gap between rhetoric and reality, Rosenthal detects a promising trend. Reciprocal trade, the main element in economic interdependence, grew substantially between 1960 and 1975, and continued to flourish until 1980–1981. In Central America, intra-regional trade did complement extra-regional trade. It even provided compensation during the downward cycles in international trade. The slowing down of intra-regional trade after 1983 was a direct outcome of the overall deterioration in the balance-of-payments position. But it also had something to do with the emergence in Central America of governments with markedly divergent views on economic policy. Significantly, political disagreements have not proved to be an insurmountable obstacle to economic cooperation; indeed, economic interdependence has ensured that the integration process continues to display vitality. Rosenthal believes this trend can be reinforced in the future if due weight is given to what has been achieved in the past.

The Caribbean experiment at sub-regional economic integration has also had encouraging results. William G. Demas and Jasper Scotland review the performance of the Caribbean Community and Common Market (CARICOM). CARICOM did not merely emphasise trade liberalisation, it also sought to extend cooperation to the monetary, financial, political and cultural spheres. An elaborate set of institutions was established to administer various projects and programmes. There remained the problem of coordinating production activities. But Demas and Scotland believe that there is much to be learnt from the holistic approach and institution-building undertaken by the Caribbean countries. They advocate the creation of similar institutions to link the Caribbean sub-region to the wider Latin American region.

Yet it is precisely in the area of reconciling sub-regional interests with those of the dominant countries in Latin America that some of the thorniest problems arise. In 1969, the Andean countries, Colombia, Chile, Peru, Bolivia, Ecuador and Venezuela, signed the Cartagena Agreement. This was an attempt to forge a bargaining counter against the dominant countries in the Latin American Free Trade Association (LAFTA), namely Brazil, Argentina and Mexico. Germanico Salgado Penaherrera shows how regional cooperation tends to serve the interests of countries in a more advanced stage of industrialisation. Indeed, even with the countries of the Andean pact, a union of the underprivileged, there are conflicts of interest between those of middling economic status and the less developed, like Bolivia and Ecuador. These inequities—present even in the happiest of times—have been accentuated by the impact of the world recession on Latin America's balance-of-payments position. Penaherrera, a close observer of regional cooperation, is pessimistic about its efficacy in the immediate future. Internal disparities, together with shocks from the international markets have worked to deflate enthusiasm for schemes of regional integration. There have been efforts by the Andean countries to resuscitate the languishing programme of regional cooperation. Penaherrera has considerable reservations about over-ambitious recovery programmes, but argues in favour of salvaging the success stories of the original schemes.

Elvio Baldinelli feels that 'protectionism' and the debt crisis are compelling arguments for unity among countries of the region. Baldinelli suggests bilateralism in intra-regional trade and a multilateral stance in commerce with the industrialised countries and the Eastern bloc. He proposes closely regulated and balanced trading arrangements between countries of the region. Such arrangements would seek to eliminate the possibility of any outstanding trade deficits, the most awkward impediment to effective regional cooperation. In Baldinelli's view, bilateral agreements between countries of the developing world at large could provide a firmer basis for a common front against the developed countries. Some trends along these lines have recently emerged in Latin America, particularly in the southern cone of the continent.

As Luciano Tomassini illustrates, bilateralism is one among the many new forms of cooperation among countries in Latin America. He makes a sharp distinction between formal and informal methods of regional integration. The distinction is all the more important to make since Tomassini believes that the integration process itself is not in crisis. Its disintegration is one of the many consequences of development strategies adopted over the last decades. Tomassini maps the successive stages of economic development through which Latin America has passed. Each stage was marked by different forms of regional cooperation. Consequently, new relationships have replaced old ones, and cooperation outside the framework of formal integration is rapidly becoming a reality.

The last contribution to this volume surveys the role of the university in refining and spreading ideas of regional cooperation and integration. Ivan Lavados Montes shows how universities in Latin America have adapted themselves to the different stages of its development. In the last two decades there has been a remarkable growth in the infrastructure of higher education. Formal disciplines have been supplemented by programmes of research and study in accord with the development needs of the region. In addition, there has been greater emphasis on inter-university exchanges and of late, the foundation of a number of international universities and research institutes through public as well as private initiative.

Latin America's experience in regional cooperation provides lessons for planners of regional cooperation in all parts of the developing world. One lesson of immediate relevance is the need to promote debate outside the corridors of government agencies. In this respect, the international community of scholars has a significant part to play. By offering dispassionate and well-considered analyses they can bring clarity and coherence to both the theory and practice of regional cooperation. Such an effort is not only desirable, but necessary, in order to formulate a plausible and sound basis for cooperation among countries of the South.

The Third World Foundation is extremely grateful to our co-sponsors, the School of Economics, National University of Colombia, the Government of Colombia and in particular, His Excellency President Belisario Betancur for inaugurating and participating in the conference. President Betancur's vision of a new economic order and a new direction for the South is a continuing inspiration for those engaged in trying to improve the position of the developing countries. Osvaldo Sunkel was the moving spirit behind the conference. He was also very helpful in helping with its organisation and making it a success. I would like to thank him, Dr Ayesha Jalal and

Mr Robert Senior for their valuable assistance in preparing this volume for publication.

Altaf Gauhar
March 1985

I
Past, present and future of the international economic crisis

Osvaldo Sunkel

The current dilemma

The development policies of Latin America since World War II have been inspired by two main theoretical sources: post-Keynesian developmentism and neoliberal monetarism. The first is associated with Rául Prebisch and ECLA and the second with Milton Friedman and the Chicago School. Obviously, reality is always more complex and finely shaded than analytical distinctiòns, but the latter fulfil a useful function of conceptual clarification. The purpose here is to single out two theoretical conceptions that inspire different policies, and two historical periods, in which first one prevails and then the other, until they culminate in the current crisis, when once again they dispute the leading role.

Post-Keynesian developmentism places emphasis on the development of the material productive forces of industry, of agriculture, of the basic social capital and human resources infrastructure; externally, on regional integration and public international cooperation. The State and planning play a major role in the promotion of social and economic development and in international relations. This approach prevailed during the 1950s and 1960s with varying degrees of intensity and coherence in different countries.

Neoliberal monetarism, with its emphasis on the liberalisation of the money, goods and services and labour markets, on external openness in respect of trade and finance, and on the development of internal financial systems, and its promotion of private and market economic agents in preference to the State and to planning, began to establish itself in the 1960s and prevailed in many countries in the 1970s.

This transition—in some cases moderate, pragmatic, complex and intelligent, but not so much so in others—reached extremes of ideological radicalisation in a number of instances, particularly in the countries of the Southern Cone. Although these national differences were determined, to a great extent, by the historical experience and the economic, social and political structures of each country, the general trend towards a transition from development strategies that were more protectionist and State-controlled to others more open to the exterior and privatising was undoubtedly connected with the changing international scenario of the post-war decades. The great world depression of 1929–32 and World War II initially encouraged developmentist strategies. In contrast, the process of expansion of the international private financial system begun in the mid-1960s accentuated the influence of monetarism, culminating in the present international economic crisis. This crisis now confronts every country, more or less urgently with a crucial economic policy dilemma: either submission to an extremely severe recessive adjustment of a monetarist character, which transnational financial capitalism is trying to impose, or recovery and maintenance of a sufficient degree of freedom to implement reactivating policies in the framework of a strategy based on development of the national and regional productive and social forces.

The privatisation of the international financial system

In my opinion, there is a close relation between the degree of integration or disintegration of the international economy—and in particular of the international financial markets—and the degree of protectionism or openness of the national economies, their resource allocation criteria, their options between consumption and investment, the form taken by their power structures and the degree of State intervention, the form taken by their power structures and the degree of State intervention, all of which is reflected in conceptual and economic policy reformulations.

During the period of outward-looking development, which extended from the nineteenth century up to 1930, there was a close economic, commercial and financial integration at the international level which resulted in the predominance of sterling—a currency which enjoyed strong economic as well as military backing—and found expression in wide and increasing international flows of trade, credit, investment and even migration. This world set-up of the British Empire and its zones of influence, such as Latin America, was accompanied by national situations of little protection and very open economies, both at the centre and at the periphery. This led to a process of allocating resources in relation to comparative advantages. As the comparative advantages acquired by the centre were concentrated mainly in manufacturing industry, its export trade became specialised in manufactures, and as the countries of the periphery had not gained similar advantages, they specialised in sectors characterised by intensive use of natural resources and labour.

To this structural situation corresponded a specific organisation of political power: a dominant coalition was formed by the exporter sectors (manufacturers at the centre, raw materials producers at the periphery), the importer sectors (raw materials in the centre, manufactured goods at the periphery), the big businessmen and, above all, the financial sectors. Their interest in maximising international trade and finance resulted in relatively little State intervention in the economy, except for the purpose of creating the infrastructure required by the outward-looking growth model, or imposing the rules of the game. *Laissez-faire* policies predominated, and their rationalisation in ideological and theoretical terms— i.e., the classic liberal theory of market allocation of resources both at the national and at the international level (static theory of comparative advantages).

This stage of capitalistic development ended with the Great Depression of 1930, followed by a long interregnum preceding the US hegemony that arose after World War II. During this period some profound readjustments took place: international markets disintegrated; the international private financial market disappeared, as did direct private investment; and only a few modest trade flows remained. The generalised crisis in trade, finance and international private investment was manifested in all countries in serious imbalances on their international transactions and in a severe depression of economic activity. Most countries withdrew from the international system and isolated their economies by applying protectionist measures in the field of trade and exchange controls in that of finance.

It is important to stress that this protectionism occurred simultaneously in the centre and at the periphery. Import substitution was not a perverse invention of the peripheral countries or of Raúl Prebisch and ECLA, as some economists seem to believe: it was the recourse to which the central countries turned in order to meet the crisis. Each country protected and encouraged what it had formerly imported: the central countries essentially protected their agriculture, and thence arose a whole institutional apparatus of support and promotion of agriculture which is still—fifty years later—a very serious obstacle to international trade and the agricultural production of the Third World.

In our countries, for their part, the 1930s crisis led to generalised protection for manufacturing, and marked the beginning of a phase of deliberate development of import-substituting industry. A gap was thus created between the internal and the international price systems, reflected in a change in the relative prices of agricultural commodities and industrial goods. Consequently, an adjustment took place in the allocation of resources: at the periphery towards the development of manufacturing and at the centre towards agricultural development. This process did not happen automatically, but through decisive State action and a re-articulation, in both the centre and periphery of the hegemonic coalition of power within the ruling classes. This coalition dominated by exporter, importer, business and financial interests, was ousted—not without radical political conflicts—by a coalition based mainly on entrepreneurial sectors, middle-class groups and the organised working classes, a change that was reflected in the importance attached to production, employment and income distribution in overcoming the crisis.

These were the decades from the 1930s to the 1960s, which were characterised in many Latin American countries by governments that subscribed to active State intervention in support of industrial development; investment in infrastructure; some structural reforms; income redistribution through an increase in social expenditure; and public policies favouring the middle income and low income groups.[1] In the international field regional integration and cooperation were actively fostered, as was public technical and economic cooperation between developed and under-developed countries, though this did not preclude denunciation of the iniquities and injustices of the system of international economic relations.

With the appropriate reservations, the post-war picture of the industrialised countries—the US, the European countries, and Japan—is not so very different. There too the State assumed a leading role in respect of the reactivation and reconstruction of the economy; the technical development and modernisation of the productive forces; the correction of unfair income distribution by application of the concept of a welfare state; and the adoption of systematic full-employment policies. In Europe, moreover, very marked emphasis was placed on regional integration and cooperation.

The institutional modernisation of the State and the practice of planning figured in both developed and developing areas as guiding instruments that modified and complemented the market. The economic theories revolved around economic growth in the centre and development policies in Latin America, where the subject of planning acquired outstanding importance. Theoretical discussion was focused on criticism of traditional neoclassical and Keynesian (static) economic theory, in relation to the need for a growth theory (dynamic and post-Keynesian), structural change and development.

While this was occurring on the internal stage, the international economic system was also trying to recover from the 1930 *débâcle*. During the next decade, international trade toned up, but private investment, both direct and financial, had completely disappeared. Instead, some public institutions were set up, such as Eximbank in the US to facilitate export expansion. Faced with the disappearance of the international private financial system after the end of World War II, an international financial system of a public character was created under the Bretton Woods agreements, including, in particular the World Bank and the International Monetary Fund (IMF). To these organisations were added the regional development banks such as the Inter-American Development Bank (IDB), the public bilateral and multilateral financial aid institutions and the State agencies responsible for extending export credits. By the mid-1960s the establishment of a public international financial system had been completed.

During the 1950s and 1960s direct international private investment reappeared, now embodied in the transnational corporations, which at first were solely North American, and later European and Japanese as well. They took advantage of the national markets created in the peripheral countries under the aegis of protectionist measures and industrial development policies, jumping commercial barriers by establishing local subsidiaries.

This was the start of a process of transnationalisation of the structure of production, which subsequently extended to patterns of consumption, life styles and culture.[2] The close of the 1960s saw the first steps in the re-creation of an international private financial market, whose expansion during the following decade attained extraordinary dimensions. A new period of international economic integration—this time of a transnational character—now dawned, beginning with the recovery of trade and the transfer of patterns of consumption and life styles, continuing with the expansion of transnational private investment and patterns of technology and production, and culminating, especially after 1973, in the creation of a transnational financial market of a private character, controlled by

Table 1
Net size of the Euro-currency market, 1964–82

End of year[a]	Net size of narrowly defined Euro-currency market (billions of dollars)
1964	12
1965	13
1966	16
1967	21
1968	20
1969	44
1970	57
1971	71
1972	92
1973	132
1974	177
1975	205
1976	247
1977	300
1978	375
1979	475
1980	575
1981	661
1982	686

Source: Stephany Griffith-Jones, *International Finance and Latin America: Past and Future*, ALIDE (forthcoming), Table 7.
[a]Refers to December for the years 1964 to 1981, and to September for 1982.

a few big transnationalised banks, which gradually acquired great freedom of manoeuvre as they outgrew supervision by the national financial authorities.

It is of interest here to underline five central characteristics of this process. In the first place, the re-creation and accelerated expansion of this new international capital market, which had disappeared forty years before and which grew from US$12 billion in 1964 to almost US$700 billion in 1982 (see Table 1). Secondly, the privatisation of external financing: in 1961–5, 60 per cent of the inflow of external financial resources into Latin America was of public origin and 40 per cent came from private sources; in 1978 public financing had shrunk almost to nothing—7 per cent—and the share of private financing had risen to 93 per cent (see Table 2). Thirdly, the predominance of the banking system in this capital market: in 1961–5, out of the 40 per cent inflows of foreign private capital, 25 per cent was direct private investment and only 2 per cent bank financing, proportions which in 1978 were radically different; bank financing increased to 57 per cent and direct private investment dropped to 16 per cent. These two phenomena also signified that the large-scale expansion of credit was channelled essentially towards the petroleum-exporting and semi-industrialised countries, bypassing the poorer countries which do not represent an attractive market for the private banks.

Fourthly, the oligopolisation and subsequent monopolisation of the international capital market. The copious inflow of external financing into many countries and enterprises was organised by some thirty big transnational banks, which obtained a considerable proportion of the financing from hundreds of small and medium-sized banks through the system of syndicated loans. For the purpose of managing the crisis and obtaining monopoly rents from the renegotiation of debts, the oligopoly has turned into a monopoly formed by about seven or eight large North American banks which join forces for solidarity and self-protection in *ad hoc* committees.[3]

Fifthly, in consequence of all the foregoing circumstances, the total lack of public control and responsibility with respect to this process of expansion of the international financial oligopoly, features which are at the very heart of the present financial crisis, and are shared equally by the transnational banks, the governments of the industrial countries that are hosts to the banks in question, and the governments of the over-indebted countries.

Here the governments of the OPEC countries and of the Third World in general wasted a unique opportunity to convert the obsolete Bretton Woods institutions into an international public system genuinely representative of the interests of the community of nations, accountable to their governments, and directed towards promotion of the development of the Third World and preservation of the dynamism and stability of the international economy.

Just as Monsieur Jourdain spoke prose unawares, throughout the 1970s we have lived through the equivalent of a Marshall Plan, without referring to it or even noticing it. The recommendations of the Brandt Commission were in fact applied, but *avant la lettre*, in accordance with market criteria, and by the transnational banks, instead of by a public international mechanism which was under the control of the national States. The result was, on the one hand, a fundamental Keynesian contribution to the maintenance of some degree of expansion of the international economy during the 1970s, which enabled it partly to overcome its trend towards stagnation as from the end of the 1960s; and, on the other hand, a colossal waste of productive resources during that period, since they were allocated, in part at least, to financing Pharaonic and over-sized investment projects which were left incomplete or only partially in use; to a great increase in luxury consumption; to the production and purchase of armaments; and even to flight of capital, and corruption.

This chaotic situation contrasts with that of the public international financial system and, in general, with the whole of the international system of bilateral and multilateral cooperation and aid for development which prevailed in the 1950s and 1960s. That mechanism, despite all its deficiencies, implied certain social criteria as regards anti-cyclical stabilisation and resource allocation policies, which were superseded by private, bank and market criteria, and, in the last analysis, as far as can be seen, by sheer lack of judgment. Under the first system referred to the allocation of international public financial resources was subject to State mediation both in the donor and in the recipient country. Public resource allocation criteria were established which reflected long-term socio-political options, such as promoting industrial development, providing basic social capital, introducing structural reforms and modernising agriculture, saving foreign exchange and creating employment. These were criteria which the parliaments of the developed countries imposed upon their own States and their foreign aid and financing institutions, and on the basis of which the State of the underdeveloped country negotiated, in so far as it too reflected long-term national interests.

In their stead, market criteria correspond to the maximisation of profits in the minimum possible time, to inequitable income distribution, to the consumer preferences of high income groups and to the market strategies of the most powerful and dynamic national and transnational private groups. Here there is a difference of transcendental importance: governments and entrepreneurs have had great freedom to obtain and allocate vast quantities of external resources, but this increased freedom has not necessarily been to the advantage of the countries receiving that plentiful inflow of private capital. Apart from the much heavier financial cost it represents, which has become a terrible burden because of the high interest rates, the problem lies firstly in the fact that when the governments concerned are not firmly committed to a development policy, the readily available supply of short-term external private financing takes the place of long-term external and internal saving and is deflected to consumption, instead of helping to broaden and diversify production capacity; and secondly the market is not the most appropriate instrument for channelling resources towards the development of a diversified production system, accompanied by social justice, and sustainable over the long term.

In cases where the State continued to control the allocation of resources for development, in face of the abundance of external resources it often lost all sense of prudence and moderation and sank into a kind of financial fools' paradise, forgetting that real institutional and human capacity for rational utilisation of financial resources is limited, and that disproportionate short-term external borrowing is never a fit base for development strategy. In the petroleum-exporting countries, another great mirage took the form of confusing structural adjustments in petroleum prices with a sustained long-term trend on which to base grandiose investment projects and a reckless boosting of consumption. It would seem that all these issues, fully discussed in the literature of development, were likewise forgotten in the great financial conjuring act of the 1970s.

Transnational financial integration, the restoration of easy and ample access to the international private financial system and the possibility of large-scale borrowing exerted strong pressure in favour of the adoption of policies of trade and financial openness and liberalisation. When the political conflict between different coalitions is defined in these terms, the result is over-expansion of imports of consumer goods and of the commercial and financial services sectors, and a reallocation of resources to the sectors with natural comparative advantages—including, in some countries, activities with advantages acquired during the import substitution process. All this was accompanied by an attempt to consolidate the new hegemonic coalition: supported by international private financing, and under the leadership of the financial sector, exporters, importers and businessmen entered upon the scene with renewed vigour, seeking to take the place of the coalition formed by the industrial sectors, middle-income groups and working classes. There was a definite effort to reduce State intervention in order to leave the market—i.e., the main economic groups —to operate as freely as possible, an updating of *laissez-faire* policies and the whole market ideology of free exchange, static comparative advantages, private enterprise and individualism. All this of course with the energetic backing of the new transnational centres of financial power.

In a commentary written on the eve of the crisis the following questions were propounded in this connection: how long will the pendulum remain at the extreme of transnational financial integration on which the strategy of external openness is so decidedly based? How far can the already taut cord of private external borrowing be stretched, especially in view of trends towards stagnation and protectionism in the centres and their effects on peripheral exports? What limits are there to a strategy of economic growth with external openness essentially grounded on expansion of consumption of imports, of the financial and services sectors and of primary export activities? Has 1930 been forgotten? How can oil-importing countries keep up and even accentuate a development style which encourages imports in general, including imports of fuels, with real prices going up over the long term and with uncertain supplies? And, conversely, in the case of the petroleum-exporting countries, what would happen to such a strategy if fuel prices stopped rising? What will be the effects of this strategy on the diversification of the production system, on capital accumulation, on employment and on income distribution.[4]

Reactivation without a future

A recession in the central economies, less acute but more protracted than that of 1974–5, has sufficed to answer the questions posed. In Chile and Mexico, in Argentina and Brazil, in Uruguay and Ecuador, the shortcomings of both monetarism and developmentism have been exposed. Even in Colombia, a country which throughout the last decade pursued prudent policies, prompted by a healthy pragmatism, without succumbing to the allurements of the flag-wavers on either side, there is now visible evidence of the vulnerability and the structural and socio-political weaknesses which are characteristic of an underdeveloped and dependent economy, and which not even an admittedly reasonable mix of developmentist and monetarist policies has been able to overcome. In a burst of groundless optimism, many had believed these weaknesses to have been conquered or non-existent, on seeing that the Latin American economy continued to grow throughout the 1970s despite the relative stagnation of the economy of the centres and the petroleum crisis.

The structural problems of Latin America's development are well known. Although the growth rates of production, especially in the industrial sector, have been exceptionally high, urban and rural poverty is still present on a massive scale in shocking contrast to small islands of extreme wealth; unemployment, underemployment and marginality are widespread; social inequality and the concentration of income and wealth are enormous; and the degree of vulnerability, disequilibrium and external dependence continues to be high.

As regards the conjunctural situation, the figures are deplorable: a slump in production and real income for the first time in forty years; an appalling increase in unemployment, especially in the cities; gigantic external and internal debts; speeding-up of inflation; fiscal, monetary and external imbalances; growing social and political tensions and conflicts. Notwithstanding the heterogeneity of situations in the Latin American countries—large and small, more and less industrialised and urbanised, net importers and net exporters of petroleum—and the differences between them in respect of economic policy, the crisis affects them all with varying degrees of intensity.[5]

The generalised character of the crisis in Latin America has induced governments and those responsible for economic and financial policies, to regard it as of external origin (just as not many years ago they attributed the boom—brought about by virtue of exceptional external borrowing—to the wisdom of their internal policies). Blame is laid on the high interest rates that were engendered by the depressive monetarist policies introduced towards the end of the Carter Administration and were accentuated by the giant fiscal deficits built up under the Reagan régime, in combination with the rather original contribution of the 'supply siders'; on the world recession and the contraction of international trade; on the deterioration of the terms of trade; and on the drying-up of capital flows.

But this does not account for the fact that although the crisis is indeed generalised, it is no less true that its intensity and characteristics differ markedly from one country to another. For example, the steepest drops in production, income and employment have occurred in the countries of the Southern Cone and some others which have faithfully adhered to the monetarist prescriptions and the stabilisation programmes of the International Monetary Fund.[6] This being so, even though the crisis may have a common external origin, there can be no doubt that its internal effects have been attenuated or aggravated by the countries' own characteristics, their previous development strategies and their policies for dealing with external problems.

Nor does it explain another singularly significant fact. As has already been pointed out, notwithstanding the frequent comparison of this crisis with that of 1929–32, the two phenomena are not, up to now at least, very much alike. It is worthwhile recalling that during the earlier period the gross product of the main industrial countries plummeted by about 20 per cent between 1929 and 1932, while total world imports shrank to one-third. Unemployment swelled to enormous dimensions and nominal wages fell; but as prices declined by a similar proportion, real wages were maintained. Profits vanished into thin air and investment stopped dead. Money stocks were reduced, along with short-term interest rates. The national and international financial system underwent a severe crisis; many banks failed in the United States and Europe; and governments had to intervene or abandon the gold standard.[7] Between 1980 and 1983, on the other hand, although GDP and foreign trade witnessed a reduction in their rate of increase they did not significantly decrease in absolute terms. Unemployment, although high, does not approach the figures for the former period, and movements of prices and wages are very different, as are also the characteristics of the financial system.

What is more, in 1974 and 1975 a similar recession took place, without causing Latin America's economic policy the least headache. Why should it happen that now, in contrast with recent recessions and with the 1930 crisis, the centre has only to sneeze for Latin America to suffer a heart attack? Why, it may also be asked, is this upheaval so explosive in Latin America, while its effects on the other regions of the Third World are much less virulent? Why, on the other hand, does it seem to have got past the Iron Curtain, and had some impact on several countries in the socialist area?

To be able to answer these and other germane questions it is of fundamental importance to understand the nature of the crisis. In essence, two attitudes are taken towards it. One maintains that it is just a recession, somewhat more protracted than is usual, in which unfortunately several coincident negative factors have combined to produce particularly severe effects in Latin America, but that there are already signs of recovery in the United States; one must be patient and 'adjust' until its positive effects begin to make themselves felt, for then will come a new phase of expansion that will alleviate the acute problems of today.

Another very different view sees this as a deep-seated structural crisis, in which the recessive and financial problems, as well as the more manifest disequilibria, are only symptoms which may easily be confused with a transient recession, but behind which in reality lies a profound and immensely far-reaching long-term crisis, whose outcome cannot be forecast with any certainty. It is essential to take up a position *vis-à-vis* these alternatives. In the first case, the appropriate strategy is to ride out the storm and to go ahead with the traditional development strategies. In the second case, it is a matter of understanding that this is no passing storm, but the tempestuous close of an expansionist epoch or phase of capitalism, and that an attempt must be made to advance by new routes, learning from the lessons of the past, but not turning back, exploring new future options, and all this in a turbulent and difficult international context, very different from that prevailing in the first decade or two after the war. This is the alternative towards which the author of the present study inclines, for reasons that will be set forth more fully below.

Before attempting an interpretation of what I hold to be a deep-seated crisis of the post-war development style, which in my opinion calls for fundamental changes in the development strategies of Latin America and entails powerful regional and Third World cooperation, I must refer to the economic reactivation or recovery which is taking place in the United States, and on which many authorities in the national and international economic and financial world are pinning such high hopes.

It is important to form a clear judgment of this phenomenon, for if it is confidently felt to be the beginning of a recovery which will subsequently draw the industrialised world in its wake to a new phase of sustained and dynamic expansion, creating the right conditions for the Third World to enter upon a fresh spell of rapid growth, and therewith the requisites for lightening the heavy burden of external debt servicing, there might be some justification for short-term adjustment policies. If, on the other hand, the real outlook were not so flattering, the costs of persisting in adjustment policies and postponing radical changes in development strategy might be overwhelming.

In contradistinction to the optimistic declarations of the national and international economic and financial authorities, eager to create an atmosphere of confidence, a review of the specialised press, and of some recent reports by international institutions, reveals little reliance on the durability of a short-term, still less of a medium- and long-term, recovery, or on the possibility that the positive drive will be efficaciously transmitted to the Third World.

Particularly significant are the recent declarations of Mr Fritz Leutwiler, President of the Bank for International Settlements (BIS). This bank, together with the International Monetary Fund, is the nearest thing there is to a world central bank. Apart from the fact that its annual reports carry indisputable authority, in recent years the Bank has been in the eye of the financial storm, actively participating with the IMF in debt re-negotiations between the biggest borrower countries and the leading creditor banks.

In a recent address Mr Leutwiler warned that it would be dangerous to assume that the industrial world is 'about to enter an era of high and sustained growth', which is a prerequisite for any expansion of the developing countries' exports. 'Anaemic economic growth in Western countries would annihilate the hopes of less developed countries to expand their exports to any significant degree', which means that the debt problem is likely to drag on for a long time and there is no alternative but to ask the banks to continue helping countries to finance their debts. He added that 'one should start looking for alternative ways to reduce the debt burden of developing nations'. One possibility, he suggested, was for the countries in question to 'sell some of their national assets to their creditors. For those countries with large endowments of natural resources or profitable State-owned enterprises, this is certainly an option worth considering' (*Financial Times* (London) 5 December 1983, p 1).[8]

These gloomy pronouncements coincide with those of various recent commentators and reports.[9] First, it is acknowledged that the recovery of the US economy is very vigorous and that growth rates varying from 4.5 to 5.4 per cent might be reached in 1984 (forecasts by OECD and the National Institute of Economic and Social Research, United Kingdom, respectively). Many commentators note, however, that the rate of recovery will slacken by 1985 with the flagging of the initial drive generated by demand on the part of certain consumer expenditure sectors and by replenishment of inventories. They also think that the maintenance of high real interest rates, strengthened by enormous and persistent fiscal deficits and by the recovery itself, together with the weakness of other sectors of demand, part of which is filtered off towards imports favoured by an overvalued dollar, will hamper the recovery of investment, since there is a wide margin of idle capacity which is being taken up very slowly. In these circumstances, the initial impulse deriving from the expansion of consumer expenditure is not likely to result in an increase in investment, and unless this were to revive expansion could not be sustained.

Table 2
Latin America:[a] percentage structure of net inflow of external resources, 1961–68

Percentage structure	Annual averages			1976	1977
	1960–65	1966–70	1971–75		
I. Net public inflow	60.2	40.1	25.2	19.6	12.0
A. Multilateral	19.5	15.7	13.4	14.4	7.4
Development	16.6	17.1	11.6	6.6	8.4
Compensatory	2.9	−1.4	1.8	7.8	−1.0
B. Bilateral	40.7	24.4	11.8	5.2	4.6
From United States	36.9	23.6	6.8	2.6	1.7
Other countries[b]	3.8	0.8	5.0	2.6	2.9
II. Net private inflow[c]	39.8	59.9	74.8	80.4	88.0
A. Banks[d]	2.1	9.3	43.8	61.0	48.3
B. Suppliers	7.7	13.8	2.3	3.7	5.8
C. Bonds	5.0	2.5	2.5	3.3	14.8
D. Direct investment	25.2	33.3	26.2	12.4	20.1
III. Percentage total	100.1	100.1	100.0	100.0	100.0
Total actual level (thousands of dollars)	1,575.8	2,641.3	7,561.9	15,301.5	15,637.0

Source: Stephany Griffith-Jones, *International Finance ...*, *op. cit.*, Table 4.
[a] Includes the member countries of the Inter-American Development Bank and its subregional agencies.
[b] Includes the socialist countries and the OECD members except the United States.
[c] Includes credits for nationalisation.
[d] Includes financial institutions other than banks.

The vigorous US recovery would not seem, however, to be reproducible in the other OECD countries. In several of the smaller countries and in France and Italy, monetary and fiscal policies will continue to be restrictive in view of heavy fiscal deficits, rates of inflation that are still high, shaky external accounts and pressure on exchange rates, accentuated by the high US interest rates and the strength of the dollar. The conservative governments of the United Kingdom and the Federal Republic of Germany, too, have declared that they will go on pursuing their restrictive fiscal policies.

With a more monetarist approach, BIS reaches similar conclusions. It maintains that the progress already made in reducing inflation should itself foster recovery by setting afoot several processes: an increase in the real money supply, reduction of the real losses sustained by holders of financial assets, expansion of saving and the propensity to spend, capital gains, entrepreneurial confidence, a backlog of demand in respect of durable goods, housing, replenishment of inventories and even investment. It points out, however, that these processes are highly sensitive to the level of interest rates, especially in real terms. In this sense it would seem that the progress made is insufficient. Although normal interest rates have come down, they have done so by less than the decline in inflation, particularly in the long-term market. Consequently, the real interest rate remains at levels that are historically high, especially for a period of recession. A major cause is to be found in the present and predicted United States budget deficits. If this situation remains unremedied, the risk will persist that the recovery will be aborted.[10] Professor Martin S Feldstein, Chairman of the Council of Economic Advisers to the President of the United States, fluttered the dovecotes by asserting that 'it would be unwise to assume that growth alone will reduce the deficit to an acceptable level' (*International Herald Tribune*, 6 December 1983, p 13). He added that if Congress did not act soon to reduce the deficits, it ran the risk of plunging the US economy back into recession (*Ibid.*, 28 November 1983, p 10).

The above-mentioned institutions predict a growth rate of 3.3 per cent for the European economies in 1984, which seems decidedly hazardous in the light of the individual countries' situations, and in comparison with the 1.5 per cent forecast by the European Economic Community.

Forecasts suggest that unemployment will continue to increase in the ten EEC countries throughout the recovery, and even through the rosiest-coloured spectacles no significant effects on unemployment figures can be glimpsed ahead. Private economists who extend the analysis beyond 1984 do not think that the recovery will become more marked in 1985, but rather that there is likely to be a fresh setback in 1986.

Even if a significant recovery takes place, as the more encouraging forecasts suggest, it in no way guarantees immediate relief for the Third World countries. To that end, essential requisites are an expansion of demand for imported primary commodities and manufactures, willingness on the part of importers to increase their purchases and stocks, and an upward trend in the prices of the products in question in relation to exports from the industrial world (many of these tied to the overvalued dollar). In turn, it will be necessary, *inter alia*, for the expansion of spending in the centres to be channelled towards sectors directly or indirectly using inputs from the Third World; for reactivation prospects to be sustained and for interest rates to fall, so that importers may have medium-term incentives to step up their purchases and replace inventories; for unemployment to be reduced so as to attenuate protectionism; and for income and demand to be strengthened in the lower-income sectors.

The difference between the rates of economic recovery in the United States and in the European economies is also of importance for the Third World, since the members of the European Economic Community, whose growth will be less, absorb almost one-fourth of total world imports (excluding intra-Community trade) while the US accounted for only 15 per cent in 1980.

For all the foregoing reasons, the prospects of the recovery's being reflected over the short term in significant increases in demand and prices for the primary commodities, food products and manufactures exported by the underdeveloped countries look very doubtful, especially if the recovery, as everything seems to suggest, has little likelihood of being maintained.

What is more, the underdeveloped world, far from contributing to the recovery as it has done in the past, helps to limit it. The suspension of the flow of private external financing into these countries on account of their heavy external indebtedness, the insufficiency of official financing to stabilise the balance of payments, the reduction of external aid and the deterioration in the value of exports, besides substantial losses of reserves, have compelled many countries to adopt stricter austerity policies and to compress their imports severely, and this has strengthened deflationary pressures in the industrial countries.[11]

To the prospect of a relatively ephemeral recovery must be added another factor with potentially explosive short-term repercussions, which may help to prolong stagnation over the medium and long term: the highly delicate international financial situation.

A political and strategic factor at the international level, which is undoubtedly causing far greater concern to the United States and Europe than the economic and financial crisis, is the sensation of standing on the threshold of a direct or indirect armed confrontation between the super-powers, in the strategic fields of Europe, the Middle East, Central America and the Caribbean. Almost ludicrous though it may seem to speak of any of the economic consequences of a war of incalculable projections, two at least must be mentioned. On the one hand, the fear of an armed conflict encourages the purchase of dollars for security reasons, which weakens European balance-of-payments positions and supports the trend towards overvaluation of the dollar, enlarging the United States trade deficit and intensifying protectionist pressures. On the other hand, there is a prospect of further increases in US military budgets and of the maintenance of the inordinate fiscal deficit and the high interest rates. It is a remarkable paradox that Europe, which will be the first victim of a flare-up of hostilities, is helping to finance this policy.

A second factor is uncertainty with respect to the stability of the inter-national banking and financial system. William R Cline, a recognised specialist in this field, estimates that if Brazil were to declare a moratorium for a specific period half the profits of the nine leading United States banks would be wiped out, which would precipitate a run on the banks and would compel the Federal Reserve Bank to support them. Even if it did not entirely eliminate profits or seriously affect capital in most cases, it would undoubtedly be a severe blow to the economy. The incentives for debtors to 'walk away from their obligations' are increasing: in 1982 the interest paid by the non-petroleum-exporting developing countries (US$ 59.2 billion) exceeded net inflows of capital (US$57.4 billion). The same writer describes the situation as one of 'an underlying structural vulnerability in international lending' (*International Herald Tribune*, 28 November 1983, p 9). The defaulting crises of Mexico and Brazil, during their crucial phases, sharply reduced the value of the shares of the banks most deeply involved and obliged the US Treasury to mount rescue operations to avert the risk of a run on the banks and the failure of some of them. The President of BIS remarked, in the address quoted above, that while the financial world was much better prepared than a year ago to handle a possible default, this was still something that could not be ruled out. He was no doubt referring to the emergency renegotiation operations which had been organised and to the intolerable pressures to which the governments of the debtor countries have been subjected by the IMF, and which have caused the stability of more than one to totter.

The delicacy of the international political and financial situation has its internal repercussions in the creditor countries themselves. The authorities controlling the US banks currently record the largest number of financial institutions in danger of bankruptcy since the 1930s. The Federal Deposits Insurance Corporation (FDIC) considers that more than 600 banks are at risk of failure, and the authorities were expecting that number to increase before the end of 1983 (*International Herald Tribune*, 26–27 November 1983, p 11). Two recent reports, one from the Treasury Department and one from the House Ways and Means Committee, state that the two most important bank control institutions—the Office of the Comptroller of the Federal Bank and FDIC—are incapable of detecting potential bank crises and enforcing preventive and remedial measures. The National Bank of Switzerland is to request five new sets of informational data from the banks, including details on their external activities, this latter on account of the international financial crisis which has shown that effective supervision of the international banks is impossible if their external subsidiaries are not taken into account (*Ibid.*, 30 November 1983, p 13). And this in a country where there are no cases of banks overinvolved in loans to heavily indebted countries, a state of affairs which the Swiss bankers themselves attribute, of course, to the strict provisions regarding capital assets coefficients with which they have to comply (*Ibid.*, 29 November 1983, p 12).

The displacement of governments which were committed in the 1970s to the monetarist policy of external openness, and of their technical cadres linked with the transnational banks and responsible for the immense external debt and its consequences, will imply significant changes in these countries' bargaining position. Not unconnected with this concern is the attention devoted by the international press to the elections in Argentina and Venezuela, and the satisfaction expressed that in both cases ample democratic majorities were obtained. This, it was thought, would make it possible for the new presidents to impose severe austerity policies 'acceptable to the international banks' (*Financial Times* (London) 6 December 1983, p 18). Here the dilemma posed at the beginning of the present article appears in its crudest guise: it is hoped that these new presidents will govern in accordance with the interests of the international banks, which certainly do not coincide with the needs of the peoples who elected them.

The nerves of the world financial authorities are on edge and public opinion in the countries in question is by no means willing to see their tax payers helping to subsidise rash and irresponsible bankers while they themselves are subjected to austerity policies which reduce employment and social services. The same view is taken by the small and medium-sized banks, which put up much of the external financing of the big banks through syndicated loans, and which are now involved in the renegotiation processes being carried out by those that are the most deeply committed. The Michigan National Bank is suing Citibank in a legal battle which is being watched with the keenest attention by international banks throughout the world. Michigan National is challenging Citibank's decision to effect a rollover of its share in a loan to Pemex without its consent. This is the first case of its type in recent years, and its settlement could have important repercussions on the viability of many recent debt renegotiations (*Ibid.*, p 21).

In short, the national and international financial world gives the impression of a minefield into which the chief protagonists—banks, international financial institutions, governments—are venturing with more equipment in the way of experience and devices to detect and temporarily defuse the mines and to look after the wounded when they stumble against one. But as yet there are no signs of any real effort to mount a systematic cleaning-up operation. Attention is focused on the very short term. The banks and governments of the industrial countries and their chief agent —the IMF—want to lay the whole burden of the cost of adjustment on the debtor countries, subjecting them to intolerable economic, social and political demands.

The exhaustion of transnational growth

In my exploration of this field I shall seek the company of several authorities, seeing to it that they represent a broad ideological spectrum. According to Paul Samuelson, whose position is well in the centre of the doctrinal gamut, no one can confidently predict the future; but after careful consideration he thinks the last quarter of the twentieth century will show a rate of economic progress far below that attained in the third quarter.[12]

Within the Marxist tradition, one of its most outstanding representatives, Professor Ernest Mandel, by the early 1970s already saw in the 1974–75 recession one of the recurrent crises of the capitalist system, characterised since the mid-1960s by a decline in the profitability of enterprises in consequence of a twofold process of overaccumulation of capital and under-consumption. The boom phase of the lengthy cycle which the system is experiencing at present would seem to have come to an end in 1967, when a long recessive phase began.[13]

The third quotation, from a conservative standpoint, comes from the BIS document already cited on several occasions:

> The process of disinflation upon which the Western industrial world had embarked in the wake of the second oil crisis ... has been accompanied, at least until recently, by stagnation of output in the industrial world as a whole. It is probable that the wrong policy mix, i.e., the excessive burden borne by monetary policy in imposing global restraint, made the stagnation more protracted than it would otherwise have been. And it is certain that by exerting upward pressure on interest rates the policy mix has had a particularly inhibiting influence on capital formation, thus mortgaging future growth potential. But one should not forget that the Western industrial countries' growth problems did not begin three years ago, when they jointly undertook to resist the cost-push of the second oil shock. The first signs of a break in growth trends, at least as far as fixed capital investment is concerned, were evident in the late 1960s and early 1970s, well before the first oil shock. The deeper-seated causes of the break remain uncertain, but the more immediate ones are not: the rising share of labour in income distribution, the declining profitability of businesses, the expanding role of the public sector, sluggish capital formation and weakening productivity growth.
>
> Nor should one attribute the current level of unemployment exclusively to the demand-restraining policies of the last three years. Unemployment, particularly in Western Europe, was on an upward trend well before that, under the combined influence of slower growth, an expanding population and in some countries increases in the labour-force participation rates. Last but not least, the excessive rise in real wage costs and growing impediments to labour mobility gave a major incentive to labour-saving investment and innovations. It is against this background that the recent declines in real wages, beyond their direct contribution to slowing inflation, are a helpful element of adjustment.[14]

The exceptional post-war boom began to fade out by the end of the 1960s (see Table 3). In all the industrialised countries productivity increased from the mid-1950s to the mid-1960s. This trend was reversed in almost all cases in the second quinquennium of the 1960s, after which a slight recovery was shown in some countries in the early 1970s, to be followed in the rest of the decade by a slump. This decline in productivity towards the end of the 1960s was also reflected in such indicators as the profitability of enterprises, the decrease in the rate of capital formation

Table 3
The growth of labour productivity in selected OECD countries
1955–80
(Percentages)

Country	Total economy				
	Late 50s	Early 60s	Late 60s	Early 70s	Late 70s
United States	1.8	3.0	1.0	1.4	0.3
Canada	1.7	2.5	2.0	2.8	0.2
United Kingdom	2.2	3.1	2.8	3.1	1.1
Sweden	n.a.	4.5	3.1	2.0	0.4
Denmark	5.2	3.7	3.3	2.8	1.3
Norway	3.8	4.5	3.5	1.5	2.5
Finland	3.6	4.7	5.1	4.7	2.5
Netherlands	4.0	3.1	4.4	4.4	1.9
Belgium	2.5	5.2	3.9	4.4	2.4
Germany	4.6	4.9	4.6	4.1	3.2
Austria	5.0	4.6	6.4	5.2	2.8
France	4.3	5.0	4.5	4.7	2.9
Italy	4.6	5.0	6.2	4.2	1.7
Japan	8.4	12.5	8.6	6.3	3.0

Source: Herbert Giersch and Frank Wolter, 'Towards an explanation of the productivity slowdown: an acceleration-deceleration hypothesis', in *The Economic Journal* (93) March 1983, Table 1, p 36.

and the increase in unemployment. Most of the analyses of the period, which are based on trends in the gross product and in foreign trade, overlook that essential turning-point, since those indicators, after a reduction in the years 1970 and 1971, made a vigorous recovery in 1972 and 1973. Accordingly, many analysts of the crisis take the year 1973 as a major milestone, which in the present writer's opinion introduces a serious bias into the analysis, by attributing the end of the post-war era of expansion implicitly and often explicitly to the oil crisis. The fact that the process of stagnation had begun by the mid-1960s is thus lost sight of.[15]

In order to see this phenomenon in a clearer light, it should be fitted into a broader historical framework (see Table 4). This throws into relief something which economists had forgotten, or which, with their characteristic arrogance, they thought had been overcome by the progress and perfecting of economic policy: the irregular, cyclical nature of capitalist

Table 4
Growth characteristics of different phases, 1820–1979
(Arithmetic average of figures for the individual countries)

Phases		GDP	GDP per head of population	Tangible reproducible non-residential fixed capital stock	Volume of exports
			(Annual average compound growth rates)		
I	{ 1820–1870	2.2[a]	1.0[b]	...	4.0[a]
	{ 1870–1913	2.5	1.4	2.9	3.9
II	1913–1950	1.9	1.2	1.7	1.0
III	1950–1973	4.9	3.8	5.5	8.6
IV	1973–1979	2.5	2.0	4.4[c]	4.8

Source: Angus Maddison, *Phases of Capitalist Development*, Oxford: Oxford University Press, 1982, p 91.
[a]Average for 13 countries.
[b]Average for 10 countries.
[c]1973.

development, not only over the short and medium but also over the long term.

It can be seen that, from the beginning of the nineteenth century to our own time, capitalist development has passed through several protracted phases of expansion and stagnation of production, per capita income, productive fixed capital formation and exports (see Table 4). The first phase of expansion lasted almost a century, up to 1913; then supervened a long wave of recession between 1913 and 1950; next a new and very marked expansionist cycle followed, between 1950 and 1973; and later still, between 1973 and 1979, came the dawn of what would appear to be a new and long-drawn-out phase of recession. This last period really began several years before, and the last few years should also be added, making up a period of about fifteen years of relative stagnation. It is not surprising, therefore, that there should have been a revival of Kondratieff's theory of long waves or cycles.[16]

Does this last period really constitute the beginning of a lengthy phase of stagnation, or is it merely a matter of taking a deep breath, or heaving several profound sighs, before resuming the noteworthy rate of expansion characteristic of the period following World War II? To decide this point, it is necessary to examine the nature of that extraordinary phase of expansion and to see whether the conditions on which it was based still exist or have disappeared. To that end, I shall examine some aspects of the evolution of the primary factors of production (human, natural, capital and energy), of the state of the productive forces and their technological base, and of the national socio-political organisation and its international context.

As regards productive resources, it should be recalled that the labour force has increased significantly in the developed countries, as a result of the population explosion recorded in the US after World War II and the immigration into Europe, especially into West Germany, of the displaced population of the countries of Eastern Europe. Subsequently, this manpower contingent went on expanding in the North Atlantic economy in consequence of immigration from the European and US periphery, the 'Gästarbeiter' phenomenon in Europe, and the quotas of Mexican, Central American and Caribbean immigrants in the United States.

With respect to raw materials, investment in mineral, energy and agricultural resources was rapidly renewed after World War II in view of the prospects of expansion of US and, later on European and Japanese demand, both for the purposes of reconstruction of these economies and to supply the demand deriving from the Cold War and from hostilities such as those in Korea and other subsequent conflicts. A factor of importance in facilitating this investment was the gradual dismantling of the European colonial empires in Asia, Africa and the Caribbean, which opened up these countries to US, German and Japanese investment.

Where capital infrastructure was concerned, the United States economy had not succeeded in fully utilising its accumulated productive capacity until the last stage of World War II. And this tempo of activity did not recover until the end of the 1940s.

This incorporation of relatively idle factors of production into the economic process was possible thanks to an exceptional expansion of global demand. It was manifested mainly in the resumption of military expenditure on rearmament in consequence of the start of the Cold War as from 1948, the Point IV programme to support the development of the less developed countries, the Marshall Plan for the reconstruction of the European countries devastated by the war, the creation of the European Common Market, the introduction of a set of redistribution and full employment policies, as part of the conception of the welfare state, and the generalisation of the US life style and consumer patterns in the European countries and Japan at first, and later among the privileged sectors in the rest of the world.

The logistic support for the establishment of the political, military and economic hegemony of the US was, moreover, one of the chief sources of the extension of the great US oligopolistic corporations to the rest of the developed and underdeveloped world, or, in other words, one of the bases on which the transnational enterprise was able to expand at world level until in time it contributed to the generation of the transnational system.

The sustained expansion of demand and of internal and international markets, the utilisation of accumulated production capacity and the enlargement of scales of production in the big multinational corporations, the introduction of technological innovations deriving from World War II and from the nuclear and space race of the post-war decades, together with the mass adoption of US vanguard technology in the European and Japanese economies, made possible a striking increase in capital formation, radical changes in the structure of production, economies of scale, agglomeration and conglomeration, and improvements in productive efficiency, with a marked upswing in the productivity of labour. Behind all this a major contributing factor was the low price and gradually increasing cheapness of petroleum, the source of energy which came to be predominant in the post-war economy. This new energy base in process of expansion facilitated the increase in labour productivity by promoting the rapid and mass substitution of capital equipment for manpower. This was reflected, furthermore, in greater dynamism in those sectors of the economy that were most directly linked to the utilisation of so exceptionally versatile and cheap a source of energy: the automobile industry, the metal-working and electronics industries producing durable consumer goods, the petrochemical industry, and the artificialisation of agriculture (mechanisation, chemical inputs, artificial climate and conservation).

This combination of factors was favourable to a highly oligopolised economic structure, in which the dynamics of competition between the great transnational corporations was increasingly channelled into rapid innovations in technology and design, differentiation of output, and inordinate promotion of consumption and manipulation of the consumer, through publicity and sales techniques as well as the almost unlimited extension of consumer credits: all this based on a veritable revolution in communications.[17] The levels and patterns of consumption of individuals, families and society as a whole became their central social objectives and values, determining their social status within the national framework and in the international system. The demonstration effect came to be the lode star of social aspirations both among countries and among the social classes in a single country, and the development criterion and ideology of national growth and 'modernisation', taking this to mean the assimilation and reproduction of the behaviour patterns, values, consumption, technology, social and even institutional and political organisation characteristic of the industrialised countries and in particular of the United States.

In the case of Latin America this interpretation of development policy took formal shape in the Alliance for Progress. The idea, in essence, was to promote economic growth by means of major transport, communications and energy infrastructure projects, in order to facilitate industrial development, the modernisation of agriculture (including its institutional transformation through agrarian reform) and urbanisation, which, together with the expansion of general and higher education, were aimed at creating a large urban middle class; which by sharing the life style, consumer patterns and values of the developed world, would be the pillars of an economic development of capitalist character under a democratic political system, closely linked to the North Atlantic alliance.

As has been noted, the exceptional dynamism of this economic growth of the industrialised countries began to slacken at the end of the 1960s. The reasons are various. In the first place, during the period analysed, and especially in its early phases, there were certain initial conditions and factors and unique phenomena that were irreproducible, such as the existence of idle capacity in the United States economy, European reconstruction, the integration of Europe, industrial and agricultural modernisation, especially in Europe and Japan, and the liberalisation of international trade, all of which helped to stimulate expansion, but once their possibilities were exhausted disappeared from the scene.

Another group of factors served as driving forces up to a point, but in so far as their use was extended beyond certain limits they changed from positive to negative and began to turn into constraints on expansion. Cases in point were the increasing costs for the State of financing gigantic military set-ups and performing income redistribution and social welfare functions, and the rise in the real cost of labour deriving from full employment policies and the strengthening of the trade unions' bargaining power. These were at first factors making for the expansion of demand, but when certain levels were exceeded they resulted in a reduction of the profitability of enterprises and in inflationary pressures, either on account of the fiscal deficit or because of increased taxation.

The expansion of foreign investment through the transnational corporations also enjoyed an extremely dynamic and positive phase, but the time came when high real costs of labour, heavy taxation and environmental protection requirements meant that the profitability of the subsidiaries surpassed that of the parent firms. These latter began to transfer their operations en masse to other countries, developed, underdeveloped and even socialist, not only to broaden their markets, but, what was more, to re-export from them to their countries of origin, ousting traditional activities in the process of generating unemployment problems.[18]

Another phenomenon of this type is the rapid reconstruction, modernisation and exceptional dynamism of the European and Japanese economies, which at first contributed to the economic expansion of the industrialised centre, but which as time went by began to cause friction among the countries forming it with the intensification of competition among the European countries, between them and the US and between Japan and all the rest. Trade deficits were thus generated in the less competitive countries, which adopted restrictive and protectionist policies, thereby cramping not only their own expansion, but also that of the more dynamic countries, and indirectly that of the less developed countries and in the last analysis of the entire world economy.

A similar case was that of the developing countries which diversified and expanded their exports of non-traditional items and manufactures and began to gain a foothold in the markets of the industrial countries which provoked a protectionist reaction.

The increasing US trade deficit generated by these differential trends in productivity and international competition, and aggravated by military, external aid and foreign investment commitments and by such events as the hostilities in Vietnam, finally led to the relinquishment of the dollar/gold standard in August 1971. This marked the collapse of the system of international economic institutions established at Bretton Woods, with the dollar as a reserve currency, on the basis of the fact that at the end of World War II the United States possessed a gold reserve much larger than that of all the other countries put together. By virtue of the process described above, this situation underwent a radical change. In 1950 the Federal

Republic of Germany, Italy and Japan together possessed a reserve of US$1.4 billion which by 1970 had increased to almost US$24 billion; US reserves in the same period dropped from US$24 billion to US$14.5 billion, and went on rapidly falling.

As the vulnerability of the dollar became increasingly patent, a number of speculative manoeuvres against the existing parities were initiated, facilitated by the elimination of exchange controls in Europe and the rapid expansion of the Eurocurrencies market, in which it was easy to obtain credit for speculative purposes. The agreement reached in December 1971 on the management of exchange adjustments was annulled in 1973, inasmuch as fixed parities were no longer possible in face of the creation of an international financial market which facilitated speculation. Once again an expansionist process of trade and financial liberalisation took place, which in a world of fixed and foreseeable parities had facilitated international trade and investment during a given period, but which in face of growing real imbalances among the member countries and the re-creation and vast expansion of an uncontrollable transnational private financial market fell prey to speculative instability. The introduction of fluctuating exchange rates brought permanent instability into the system, and with it uncertainty and extreme caution in respect of productive invest-ment, especially of a long-term character.

The energy crisis might be regarded as an exogenous shock which had an impact on the situation at two key points of time: 1973–74 and 1979. But from a longer-term standpoint we have been formulating the hypothesis that this was one of those virtuous circles which become vicious circles in the course of time. Because of the United States' exceptional resource endowments and its relative shortage of manpower, it had tended ever since the last century to adopt capital-intensive technologies. The plentifulness of oil resources, and the price and other advantages of this fuel, encouraged its widespread use and dissemination in the automobile and petrochemical industries and in the manufacture of electrical house-hold appliances. Hence was engendered the development style described above, based, *inter alia*, on intensive utilisation of this source of energy, and, in general, of all the natural resources and environmental conditions which were exceptionally abundant in the US. With the transnationalisa-tion process this style was generalised throughout the world, whereby demand for petroleum expanded to an inordinate extent and became increasingly inelastic as it was to a greater or lesser extent incorporated in patterns of technology, of production, of consumption, of territorial organisation and of human settlements in all countries, including those lacking in oil.[19] Thus it was that the petroleum-exporting countries realised that specific geopolitical circumstances had been created which allowed them to form a cartel and fix prices at a much higher level.

Whatever the interpretation of this phenomenon, its effects on the international economy have been of the greatest importance. In the first place, it has caused a structural costs inflation effect on account of the restriction of supplies of a basic input; secondly, it has rendered obsolete a considerable proportion of the fixed capital structures whose operation depended upon petroleum, with the consequent capital losses; and in addition it has considerably enlarged the deficits on current account of the petroleum-importing countries. At the same time it contributed to the formation of the transnational banking system and the infusion of a formidable mass of liquidity of some US$2,000 billion into the international economic system during the past decade. This was a means of preventing an even worse recession, but it helped to generate very strong additional inflationary pressures, especially as a result of the 1979 oil crisis. Hence a new direction was given to economic policy: the economic growth and full employment targets adopted after World War II were abandoned, and every effort was concentrated on counteracting inflation and restoring basic systemic equilibria through a monetarist purge.[20]

Economic stagnation and growing unemployment, increasingly intensive inflationary pressures and the contradictions deriving from a succesion of short-term policies designed to 'warm up' and 'cool down' the economy time and again, were reflected in greater social tensions and subsequently led to the breakdown of the coalition between capital, the middle-income sectors and labour, which was the political cornerstone of the welfare state and of the Keynesian policies of full employment and expansion of consumption that characterised the prolonged post-war boom. What was possible in a period of expansion, when the struggle for redistribution was taking place in a situation in which everyone could gain, became impossible in a situation of stagnation, when the gains of some were obtained at the expense of the rest. It seems to me that this fundamental political fact—the disruption of a broad social and political consensus which extended from organised labour to the entrepreneurial sectors, and included the large middle-income strata of professionals, technicians and employees of public and private bureaucracy—is what lies behind the resurgence of a highly reactionary position on the political right wing and of a revolutionary one on the left.

The reactionary position has two major manifestations: the use of the monetarist model as a macroeconomic explanation, and, more essential still, the philosophico-ideological return to the classic traditions of Adam Smith's capitalism, that is, a radical revaluation of individualism. Society is not made up of social aggregates—classes, groups—but of individuals; everything can and must be interpreted in supply, demand and market terms, be it law, the State, society, family life or marriage: to everything can and must be applied the economic cost-benefit analysis. All this comes to consitute an ideology, a political programme, in which an attempt is made to dismantle the State apparatus as far as possible. The welfare state system is severely pruned because it interferes with each individual's decision as to what he must do with his income; State intervention in respect of investment is also restricted; and the weight carried by the State in terms of taxation and in particular of income tax is reduced, in order to demolish a system which deprives the individual of incentives.[21]

Other necessary steps are to destroy the trade union organisations in order to forestall artificial interference in the labour market; to strip the State of all enterprises and activities that can be privatised; and, of course, not only to apply the principle of *laissez-faire* in internal affairs, but also to promote total openness of the national economy to the world economy, so that the domestic price system is regulated by the international price system to ensure that static comparative advantages determine resource allocation.

In macroeconomic terms, the monetarist model consists essentially in liberalising the financial market to the greatest possible extent, elminating the fiscal deficit and strictly limiting monetary expansion so that the rate of interest may reach its 'true' real level, and may serve as the chief instrument for encouraging saving and allocating investment resources. As long as these monetarist policies were applied in industrial countries of secondary importance in the international system, and in under-developed countries, the world economy was not affected. But when this programme was implemented in the US economy, nominal and real interest rates shot up to extremely high levels, not only in that country but throughout the world, whereas they had been barely positive since the war. Thus the recession was exacerbated and prolonged, investment, particularly long-term investment, being restricted, and in many countries the problem of the external and internal debt reached boiling-point.

In the upshot, this attempt at an interpretation of the evolution of the international economy after the war would seem to suggest that the phase of dynamic expansion had come to an end by 1970, as a result of the disappearance, exhaustion and reversal of a number of long-term forces, which were in operation during the period in question and since then have not been replaced. During the 1970s the political and energy bases that supported the development style in question collapsed, and an economic policy directed towards growth and full employment was substituted for another centred on monetary and financial stability at both the national and the international level. Thus a period of serious instability, uncertainty and confusion was generated in both national and international economic policies, which have culminated in an acute and prolonged recession, superimposed upon the long-term structural crisis of the style.

A future without reactivation

It is very possible that this diagnosis may be mistaken. But I am in good company:

The 1980s and 1990s are likely to be decades of profound change: changes in the technological sphere, with massive introduction of computers and the increasing use of robots in the production system; changes in the energy field, where oil will be replaced by other sources of energy; changes in consumer tastes and their repercussions on consumption patterns; changes in the international environment, especially with the increasing competitiveness of newly industrialised countries; and, last but not least, changes in the financial and international monetary system brought about by the increasing disorder of recent years.

During most of the post-war period the ECE market economies have shown their adaptability to changing patterns of production and consumption; however, this was essentially achieved under conditions of relatively rapid economic growth. One of the main questions for the coming years is whether, in the present sluggish economic environment, these countries will be able to adapt their economies smoothly to the changes foreseen and whether, under the acute pressure of current problems—like very high unemployment rates—short-term policies may postpone or at least slow down the pace of the necessary structural changes....

A further general conclusion of the present study is that low economic growth and high development levels seem to increase the rigidities of the sectoral structures of production and employment. In the currently prevailing economic environment, these rigidities may imply a long transition period ... in making the necessary structural adaptations.[22]

An emininent specialist in technology remarks that:

The stock of inventions and innovations now at hand does not give the impression that they could furnish the needed impulse for rapid growth in the developed countries in the period ahead. The experience of the 1970s has underlined that the structural changes which had served to cushion the impact of deceleration also seem to have exhausted their resilience. Nor are the longer-term social aspects (management of enterprises in the economy, an easy to achieve balance between conflicting social interests, a better distribution of income and reduction of working hours) being handled so as to offer the much needed impulse.[23]

Maddison's excellent and comprehensive study concludes that the expansionist 'golden age' of the post-war decades came to an end in 1973, and that we are entering upon a new era which is structurally different from the period 1950–70. The following would appear to be the most deep-seated causes: changes in economic policy, where the commitment to maintain high and stable levels of demand has faded out and the dominant influence has become that of monetarism, which as a pre-Keynesian economic theory shows little concern for growth and full employment; the collapse of the Bretton Woods system and its replacement by a system of fluctuating exchange rates, which introduces instability and uncertainty into the international economic system; changes in the labour and merchandise markets and the creation of strong inflationary expectations as a determining factor in price-fixing and wages; the oil shocks; the end of a phase of rapid increase in productivity in the European countries and Japan, which have now made up the leeway with which they started after the war and are approaching a slowly expanding technological frontier, determined essentially by the United States economy; the exhaustion of the productivity increments attributable to structural transfers from agriculture to industry and to international specialisation; and, lastly, the establishment of restrictive policies which reduce productivity by stunting the growth of the stock of capital and undermining the efficiency of resource allocation.[24]

On the Latin American internal plane, the transnational development style which so dynamically asserted itself during the post-war decades, on the basis of unbridled promotion of imitative consumption, began to show serious shortcomings and disequilibria as early as the 1960s. It managed to keep going until 1980, however, thanks to international liquidity and the greater financial permissiveness which made it possible to step up the expansion of consumption, investment and exports by means of external and internal borrowing. The recent international recession has therefore had exceptionally serious repercussions on Latin America, bringing to light in addition the gravity of the structural problems which the development style had long been trailing in its wake, and which the financial boom had made it possible to cover up. They are essentially problems of external imbalance, dependence and vulnerability; of intensive concentration of the fruits of economic and social progress, in terms both of income and ownership and of their geographical complement; and of unemployment, underemployment and poverty and socio-political marginality in very large sectors of the population.

As regards the external structural framework, to the traditional problems of instability and the relative downward trend of commodity prices, exacerbated in a climate of sluggishness and great instability in the industrialised economy, are added strong protectionist pressures, especially in respect of certain traditional agricultural products and the new exports of manufactures which the Latin American countries have been taking such pains to develop in order to diversify their exports and obtain access to an international economy which is now closing its doors to them.

On the imports side, the period of expansion and prosperity in the international economic and financial system permitted the consolidation of a transnationalised segment of the national economies, characterised by life styles and consumption patterns that imply a capital- and oil-intensive structure of production and technology with a high and very dynamic external content. This has been a serious problem not only for the petroleum-importing but also for the petroleum-exporting economies. Severely cutting down imports in order to cope with the long-term maladjustment, in a situation of high petroleum prices and heavy external indebtedness, has implied a radical reduction of domestic consumption and investment, with pernicious effects on employment and levels of living among the low-income majorities. Meanwhile behaviour patterns, habits and expectations have been generated which are totally untenable, and which together with the corresponding aggravation of unemployment and poverty, will inevitably break out in the end in acute social and political tensions.

This is, moreover, the basic reason why the crisis has so drastically affected Latin America, and even some of the socialist countries, which have also been invaded by the transnationalisation process, with its sequel of increasing external imbalances and accelerated international private borrowing.[25] The rest of the Third World, relatively less infiltrated by the transnational phenomenon, for both economic and cultural reasons, has not experienced to a similar extent either its past dynamic impulse or its present crisis.

In view of the prospects of a gloomy future in the international economy —stagnation, instability, uncertainty and a financial crisis—and the increasing seriousness of the structural problems of the development style both in the industrial countries and in our own, there can be no doubt of the misguided inadequacy of an approach concentrating on overcoming short-term problems by means of adjustment to a temporary recession in the international economy. It is a matter of supreme urgency to reformulate long-term development strategies, together with short- and long-term measures conducive simultaneously to surmounting the difficulties of the recession and unemployment, and directing development towards a more dynamic, equitable and autonomous style, sustainable over the long term. Regional cooperation among the Latin American countries, and between these and the other Third World countries, should play a fundamental role in this new development strategy.

Development and re-activation: conditioning factors and options

To serve the debt or not to serve it, that is the question today. All the Latin American governments declare that they want to serve it, but many have been unable to do so and have left matters in suspense for spells of as long as six months. Nor have they been able to let this situation drag on for any greater length of time, finding themselves compelled to negotiate an agreement with the International Monetary Fund. The IMF is imposing monetarist policies of severe restriction of global demand, designed to generate balance-of-payments surpluses on current account, in exchange for which it facilitates the refinancing of the debt for annual periods, with contributions of its own and from the creditor banks. These agreements have managed to survive in some cases but in others have been unable to withstand internal socio-political pressures, so that this very short-term cycle starts all over again. Thus we have gone on for three years, waiting for Godot to bring a world reactivation that has not yet come, and probably never will.

This reveals a situation in which the costs of serving the debt and of not serving it are equally intolerable in terms of economic and social penury, and of political instability. The transnational banks and the developed countries are prepared to accept temporary moratoria and prefer short-term refinancing, a sign that they fear the consequences of a financial breakdown; but they do not dare to embark upon long-term refinancing or financing, a sign that they place no reliance on the resumption of dynamic international development or on the payment capacity of the debtor countries. Neither alternative would appear to offer a way out. They are only stopgap arrangements, with no prospect ahead but a gradual worsening of the existing situation.

It is essential to avoid catastrophic options, as well as the current deterioration. To that end, an international and national strategy of greater scope and breadth would need to be designed. It would be a question of establishing common basic principles for the creation of a new set of international public institutions to support development and the dynamisation and stability of the international economy. Within this framework, each country would be able to negotiate its debt or not, according to its own special circumstances, but in a context that favoured development rather than hampering it. However, the efforts in this direction that have been made year after year have met with no response in the leading industrialised countries.

Furthermore, it is absolutely indispensable that the industrial countries should start out again on the road of economic expansion and should re-open their economies to international trade on the basis of active industrial and agricultural readjustment policies and the maintenance of policies of full utilisation of production capacity. The Bank for International Settlements itself recognises that room for manoeuvre has been created which makes greater economic activity possible without the risk of unmanageable inflationary pressures, and that restrictive monetarist policies have been carried too far.[26] Nevertheless, the analysis presented in the foregoing sections reveals the serious structural and political obstacles to such an advance.

The exorbitant external debt accumulated by most of the Latin American countries is the responsibility of the transnational banks, of the governments of the industrial countries and of the governments and ruling classes of the debtor countries. The servicing of this debt is impossible on a basis of constricting the debtor economies and reducing them to a state of stagnation. That will inevitably lead to further defaulting. Moreover, it is morally unacceptable that the burden of the debt should be laid by monetarist policies, through unemployment and reductions of real wages, on present and future generations of workers who have had nothing to do with it. It is therefore indispensable that the cost of debt servicing should be shared by those responsible for the debt and those that have enjoyed its ephemeral benefits. At the international level, the transnational banks and the governments of the industrial countries must assume their quota of responsibility, facilitating debt servicing by extending maturities to periods of twenty or thirty years, establishing grace periods of at least five years and reducing real interest rates to their historical levels. In addition, these countries must provide new long-term credit at similar rates of interest so that reactivation can be achieved through new development strategies in the debtor economies. Nor are these objectives easy to attain, although implicit or sometimes explicit recognition is beginning to be accorded to the necessity of making some move in this direction.

At the internal level, the more heavily indebted the Latin American countries are, the more need they have to reformulate their development policies, directing them towards three fundamental objectives: employment, export expansion and diversification and the concentration of available resources on meeting the basic needs of the deprived masses. Only a reasonable and sustainable proportion of the foreign exchange obtained from export earnings should be allocated to debt servicing; the rest should be reserved for importing essential goods directly or indirectly for popular consumption and capital accumulation, the latter in its turn to be used exclusively to satisfy popular consumer requirements and accumulation itself. The restriction of non-essential consumer imports would be the contribution of the privileged sectors to the servicing of the external debt for which they were partly responsible.

The adoption of measures favouring an internal reactivation geared to the application of a new development strategy calls for a freedom of manoeuvre in economic policy which the agreements with IMF prevent. As was pointed out at the beginning of the present article, the crucial dilemma facing economic policy at the present time is the question of how to achieve a severe compression of imports which will allow a considerable surplus to be built up on current account for the purpose of serving the external debt. The monetarist prescription, one of the objectives of which is to maintain or obtain external openness, consists in restricting global expenditure on consumption and investment to the point at which demand for imports dwindles sufficiently for this objective to be attained, while it is assumed at the same time that in this way resources will be set free to increase exports. According to our analysis, this approach is mistaken and overburdensome in economic and social terms. Mistaken, because the mobility of the factors of production is low and the short-, medium- and long-term prospects of the international economy are discouraging, so that a rapid and considerable expansion of the volume and value of exports is very unlikely unless as the consequence of a deliberate medium-term policy at the national and international level. Over-costly, in terms of employment and popular consumption, because the import demand function can be modified by direct acts of intervention to restrict imports through taxes, tariff duties and exchange controls, discriminating between those that are essential and those that are of less critical importance, and thus ensuring a level of investment, production and essential consumption which will minimise the effect of the crisis on employment and the levels of living of the lower-income sectors. While this policy involves a change in relative prices and assuredly a rise in price levels, it does not necessarily imply uncontrollable inflation in so far as idle capacity exists, a tax policy is applied which strictly limits the income and expenditure of the most affluent sectors, and an income policy is adopted which prevents unjustified wage increases.

Economic policy also requires enough freedom of manoeuvre for short-term reactivating measures to form part of a long-term development strategy, oriented towards the objectives indicated above, and founded primarily on those natural, human and infrastructure resources with which these countries are fairly comfortably endowed, and which constitute the only sound and permanent basis for sustained development.

Obviously, the less the negative international context improves and the less support is given to proposals in respect of trade, finance and investment, the more austere these policies will have to be. It is urgently necessary to face up to the possibility that perhaps nothing of any significance may be obtained from the industrialised world or the international institutions and carefully to explore what this would mean in terms of development strategies designed to cope with such a situation.

The lessons taught by history must be learnt. A development of the productive forces which is directly channelled towards the satisfaction of the basic needs of the people and the elimination of dependence cannot be achieved through the massive incorporation of a transnational development style of the individualist-consumerist type, making highly intensive use of imported capital, energy and technology. This has not been possible either through the deliberate promotion of such 'modernisation' (post-Keynesian developmentism), or—much less still—through indiscriminate external openness and privatisation (monetarism), even in an exceptionally favourable international context. The transnational style simply cannot be generalised to the whole of society. In the best instance, the case of developmentism, it benefits a minority more or less sizeable according to the country concerned, but the broad masses linger on in hopeless poverty. In the case of monetarism, insecurity is far greater, development and diversification of the structure of production far less, and external vulnerability and dependence are overwhelming.

It must be recognised that true national and regional development will have to be based primordially on transformation of the resources and natural environment in which Latin America is relatively rich, incorporating the efforts of the entire population, together with the adoption of life styles and consumption patterns and of techniques and modes of organisation appropriate to this natural and human environment; with very prudent and efficient utilisation of the little capital available, especially its imported component; and all this with the explicit aim of producing current goods and services and accumulating the basic social capital required by the majority sectors of the population to improve their levels of living and of productivity. It must not be forgotten that in this respect Latin American has substantially improved its potentialities in recent decades.

Regional cooperation must play a role of the greatest importance in these new internal and international tasks: at the level of North-South negotiations, by persisting in the promotion of a reform of the international system such as that suggested above, and in this context, supporting the renegotiation of the external debt of countries so requiring on the terms indicated, but at the same time exploring the alternatives that might be adopted should this line of action fail. A second aspect of supreme significance is the revitalisation of the regional integration institutions, which will facilitate inter-Latin American trade, payments and investment, and to which end greater room for manoeuvre in the economic policy will also be needed. A further crucial aspect is support for all possible forms of integration and cooperation as between the Latin American region and the rest of the Third World. Lastly, it would be impossible to exaggerate the importance of economic and technical cooperation, in every respect, and particularly as regards exchange of experience and information on all topics pertinent to the new national and international development strategies suggested.

From the type of analysis set forth in this article it is obvious that the proposals put forward, both at the domestic and at the international and regional level, imply radical political changes. In the last analysis, it is necessary that the predominance of international trade and financial interests and their respective local transnational bases be replaced by broad national coalitions, representative of a majority of social sectors, which accord priority to the expansion of employment and economic activity and to income distribution, rather than to excessive concern for monetary and financial equilibrium. This happened in many countries after the 1930 crisis, and it may be that the crisis of today will do much to enforce a similar adjustment. But this is not a matter of history repeating itself. There are now new social sectors which did not exist in the past or which were ousted or bypassed by recent development policies. They include, among others, the vast marginal urban sectors and the rural pockets of extreme poverty, the new contingents of young people who have had access to education, the labour force resulting from the incorporation of women into the labour market, the important highly skilled middle strata, all of which would have to be well represented in the formulation and implementation of the new development strategy that is needed now to overcome the crisis.

This is the most important of the many issues that will have to be very seriously tackled as part of the effort to find new paths to development.

Notes

1. I am referring to the propositions, intentions and measures incorporated in development policy, not to what was actually achieved.
2. See O Sunkel and E Fuenzalida, 'Transnationalization and its national consequences', in José J Villamil (ed.), *Transnational Capitalism and National Development*, Hassocks, Sussex:

The Harvester Press (in association with the Institute of Development Studies, University of Sussex), 1979.

3. See R Devlin, 'Commercial bank financed from the North and economic development of the South: congruence and conflict', and 'Renegotiation of Latin America's debt: an analysis of the monopoly power of private banks', in *CEPAL Review*, No. 9, December 1979, and No. 20, August 1983, respectively.

4. See O Sunkel, 'Comentarios sobre E Bacha y C Díaz-Alejandro: Mercados financieros: una visión desde la semiperiferia', in R Ffrench-Davis (compiler), *Las relaciones financieras externas, su efecto en la economía latinoamericana*, Mexico: Fondo de Cultura Económica, Serie Lecturas No. 47, 1983, p 69. The foregoing pages are a revised version of this article.

5. For the most recent detailed description, see Enrique V Iglesias, 'Preliminary overview of the Latin American economy during 1983', in this same issue of the *Review*.

6. *Ibid.*, Table 2.

7. See Charles P Kindleberger, *The World in Recession 1929–1932*, London: Allen Lane, Penguin Press, 1973.

8. This is neither the time nor the place to discuss so disquieting a hint of mass transfer of the natural and public wealth of our countries as a means of attenuating external indebtedness, except for the purpose of drawing attention to the strategies which the international financial community may be exploring. Furthermore, it is logical to suppose that this process must already be taking place in the private sector, in which respect too we must keep our eyes open.

9. The next section is based mainly on the following documentation: Bank for International Settlements, *Fifty-third Annual Report*, Basle, June 1983; United Nations, *World Economic Survey 1983. Current trends and policies in the world economy*, New York, 1983; UNCTAD, *Trade and development report, 1983* (Part I. The current world economic crisis), September 1983; *Financial Times* (London) 'Financial Times Survey: Europe', 5 December 1983; Anatole Kalestsky, 'West Europe's economies: sink or swim together', *Financial Times* (London) 5 December 1983, p 16; *International Herald Tribune*, 'Euromarkets, a special report', Part I and Part II, 28 and 29 November 1983, pp 7–15 and 9–14, respectively.

10. Bank for International Settlements, *Fifty-third . . .*, *op. cit.*, p 31.

11. The current value of Latin American imports has shrunk by almost one half between 1981 and 1983: from US$90 billion to US$56 billion (see Enrique V Iglesias, 'Preliminary overview . . .', *op. cit.*, Table 1).

12. 'The world economy at century's end', *Japan Economic Journal*, 10 March 1983.

13. See *Late Capitalism*, London: New Left Books, 1975; *The Second Slump: a Marxist Analysis of Recession in the Seventies*, London: New Left Books, 1978.

14. See Bank for International Settlements, *op. cit.*, pp 3–4.

15. This phenomenon is well documented. See H Giersch and F Wolter, 'Towards an explanation of the productivity slowdown: an acceleration-deceleration hypothesis'; A Lindbeck, 'The recent slowdown of productivity growth'; and E F Denison, 'The interruption of productivity growth in the United States', all in *Economic Journal* (93), March 1983. See also D M Leipziger, 'Productivity in the United States and its international implications', *The World Economy* (3) (1) June 1980; T P Hill, *Profits and Rates of Return*, Paris, 1979; S Rosenberg and T E Weisskopv, 'A conflict theory approach to inflation in the postwar US economy', *American Economic Review* (71) (2) 1981; OECD, *Economic Outlook*, December 1978.

16. See, for example, Angus Maddison, *Phases of Capitalist Development*, Oxford and New York: Oxford University Press, 1982; W W Rostow, 'Kondratieff, Schumpeter and Kuznets: trend periods revisited', in *Journal of Economic History*, December 1975, and his book *The World Economy*, London: Macmillan, 1978. See also Mandel, *op. cit.*, and the special number of *Futures* (Vol. 13, No. 4, August 1981) on 'Technical innovation

and long waves in world economic development', edited by Christopher Freeman.

17. See F M Scherer, *Industrial Market Structure and Economic Performance*, Chicago: Rand McNally, 1971.

18. See F Fröbel, J Heinricks, O Kreye, *Die neue internationale Arbeitsteilung*, Reinbek bei Hamburg: Rowohlt, 1977.

19. The hypothesis set forth can be applied, with the appropriate reservations, to other non-renewable as well as to renewable natural resources, and particularly to certain ecosystems of critical significance for human survival in specific localities. This subject has been explored in recent years by the Joint ECLA/UNEP Development and Environment Unit in a number of studies: *Estilos de desarrollo y medio ambiente en la América Latina*, selection by O Sunkel and N Gligo, Serie Lecturas No. 36, Mexico, Fondo de Cultura Económica, 1980; O Sunkel, *La dimensión ambiental en los estilos de desarrollo de América Latina*, E/CEPAL/G.1143, Santiago, ECLA/UNEP, 1981; N Gligo, 'Estilos de desarrollo, modernización y medio ambiente en la agricultura latinoamericana', in *Estudios e Informes de la CEPAL* No. 4, E/CEPAL/G.1117, Santiago, ECLA/UNEP, 1981; 'Estilos de desarrollo de la industria manufacturera y medio ambiente en América Latina', in *Estudios e Informes de la CEPAL* No. 11, E/CEPAL/G.1196, Santiago, ECLA/UNEP, 1982; 'Informe del seminario regional sobre metropolización y medio ambiente', E/CEPAL/L.266, Santiago, 1982; 'Estilos de desarrollo, energía y medio ambiente: un estudio de caso exploratorio', in *Estudios e Informes de la CEPAL* No. 28, E/CEPAL/G.1254, Santiago, ECLA/UNEP, July 1983; *Expansión de la frontera agropecuaria y medio ambiente en América Latina*, CEPAL/CIFCA, Madrid, 1983; *Sobrevivencia campesina en ecosistemas de altura*, E/CEPAL/G.1267, Santiago, ECLA/UNEP (in the press).

20. Bank for International Settlements, *Fifty-third Annual ...*, *op. cit.*

21. A good summary, with neoliberal leanings, is to be found in H Lapage, *Mañana, el capitalismo*, Alianza Editorial, 1979. See also P Dews, 'The nouvelle philosophie and Foucault', in *Economy and Society*, (8) (2) May 1979, in relation to the critique of the welfare state.

22. United Nations Economic Commission for Europe, *Structural changes and analysis of labour productivity in the ECE market economies and some implications for future economic growth*, December 1982, pp 57-9.

23. See S J Patel, *Reflections on the economic crisis and the Third World* (mimeographed text).

24. See A Maddison, *Phases of ...*, *op. cit.* A similar list is to be found in W Arthur Lewis, 'The slowing down of the engine of growth', *The American Economic Review* (70) (4) September 1980, pp 558-9.

25. United Nations Economic Commission for Europe, *The impact of international economic relations on medium- and long-term trends and prospects*, December 1982, pp 16-25 and 34-7.

26. Bank for International Settlements, *op. cit.*, pp 7 and 31.

2
Crisis, development and options

Enrique V Iglesias

In recent years, the changes which have occurred at every level throughout the world, including Latin America, not only in the socio-economic field, but also in political relations, have shaken everyone. The structural shifts in the leading economic centres, the changing character of relations between the centre and the periphery and the transformation of economic and social relations throughout Latin America have built up and interwoven at a pace which is perhaps too fast for us to comprehend, or at any rate to slot into a neat framework of ideas. We have also seen the failure of populist movements, as well as the rise and fall of attempts to return to outmoded neo-liberal systems.

There has been a kind of flight from reality, the result of a lack of coherent theoretical models. This has been most apparent in the major industrial centres, which in the past were the birthplaces of the great intellectual doctrines which have dominated the international economic scene. The neo-Keynesian approach, which was the major influence on internal economic systems and which established the principles and method of organising the international economy, is now clearly in crisis, but there is no equivalent model which can be put in its place. A dangerous dichotomy has thus developed between, on the one hand, the tendencies towards an increasingly interdependent international economy and, on the other, the lack of mechanisms which could function on a global scale to bring about change and to control the crises which are becoming steadily more international in their scope.

This confused and disturbing panorama poses a major challenge to existing theories and economic policies, both in countries at the centre and on the periphery. It is a challenge that we are going to have to face up to during the years to come. We must begin by making a balanced evaluation of past experiences and of the possible opportunities, and limitations, created by the increasingly international and complex relations existing between the centre and periphery. At the same time, we must bear in mind the great diversity of conditions that are to be found in the present-day world, and the inherent weaknesses of any attempt to establish generalised economic models for Latin America at a time when it remains unclear what direction the world economy is going to take, or what structural changes will occur in its main centres. Below, I intend to look at some of the elements of these issues on which the work of the Economic Commission for Latin America (ECLA) concentrates today.

The crisis of the 1980s: its effects on Latin America

Latin America is now going through the most severe economic crisis it has suffered since the grim years of the Great Depression. Undoubtedly, internal factors have played their part, but we can also find causes in problems arising from the nature of the economic cycle of the industrialised nations. The most notable aspect of the crisis is that it has affected all the countries in the region, although admittedly there have been significant differences between them. The severity and length of the crisis are also a source of concern. In the three years from 1981 to 1983, falls in production —both overall and per capita—went hand-in-hand with reduced levels of investment, a spectacular reappearance of inflationary factors, an equally startling increase in unemployment and, naturally, a fall in real wages.

These unfavourable national developments were accompanied by serious international ones, the most obvious signs of which have been the crisis in the region's balance of payments, the fall in value of national currencies, the loss of reserves, and, most serious of all, the intolerable burden of servicing the region's external debt. In short, we are witnessing the biggest economic contraction to be seen in the past 50 years, bringing with it a massive destruction of the capital accumulated over many years and a six-year regression in terms of the social progress of the region: living standards in 1983 have fallen to the levels that they were in 1977.

The suddenness of the crisis has been even more painful because it interrupted a period of economic advance which had lasted several decades. Between 1950 and 1980, the GNP for the area as a whole grew at an average annual rate of 5.5 per cent, which meant that in 1980 the overall volume of economic activity was five times that recorded 30 years earlier. Industrial production experienced an even more rapid rate of growth, increasing more than sixfold in this period, as did the formation of capital, which led to a gradual but steady increase in the coefficient of investment from the middle of the 1960s.

The crisis had another effect: it spelt the collapse of economic strategies which gave excessive encouragement to foreign borrowing, strategies which relied ultimately on the extreme permissiveness of the major international finance centres and on the traditional wisdom—which was proved wrong on this occasion—that world inflation would 'dilute' the burden of indebtedness over a period of time. Thanks to abundant supplies of private capital, Latin American countries were able to maintain high levels of imports and satisfactory rates of economic growth during the 1970s. These rates of economic growth were in reality practically higher than those of the industrialised nations and allowed the region to emerge relatively unscathed from the international recession of 1974–75, which was caused in part by the adjustments in the world market to the new prices of energy raw materials.

The situation remained more or less under control until the end of the 1970s. The real problems only became clear at the start of the 1980s, when the full weight of widespread recession struck the North, bringing with it persistently high interest rates, both in nominal and real terms, and depressing the exchange rates of countries on the periphery. Thus a country's ability to maintain a relatively satisfactory rate of growth began to depend increasingly on its capacity to attract new and exceptionally high amounts of foreign funds.

The final link in the chain was provided by the financial depression of 1982–83. This saw a massive reduction in income generated by new capital, and brought, on top of the depressive tendencies created by the economic cycle in the major world centres, a severe contraction caused by the need to readjust the balance of payments following the withdrawal of private capital. This has been an extremely brief summary of the course which the present crisis has taken. In these circumstances, and given the above process, three kinds of questions naturally arise: a) How did this state of affairs come about? What are the characteristics of the Latin American crisis?; b) What perspectives are offered for the immediate future by the adjustments and reactivation taking place in the world's economic centres?; c) What implications does this perverse combination of long-standing structural problems, and problems which remain as a consequence of the recession in the 1980s, have for future models of development in the region?

To answer the first kind of question, it is necessary to look more closely at recent events. The long-standing structural problems which have been analysed so often in ECLA documents are also relevant. However, these problems do not reduce the influence in the present situation of contemporary internal policies and the pattern of the external cycle during the 1970s.

I have mentioned above that one of the basic causes of the present crisis was an economic policy which gave disproportionate encouragement to the abundant provision of financing from abroad. The Latin American countries were able to obtain this financing only because of the extraordinary financial permissiveness of the major international banks, whose assets had multiplied as a result of the liquidity produced by the petroleum surpluses. All these developments were watched with great complacency by the entire international economic system, both public and private, which gave the private banks the role of recycling these liquid funds, and allowed their uncontrolled multiplication in the Euromarkets.

Because of this situation, a large public and private debt built up in the region, which today amounts to almost $310 billion. By accumulating this debt, it became possible to increase national spending. In some cases—unfortunately the minority—the internal surplus was put into programmes of productive investment. In many cases, however, these were based on over-optimistic forecasts about the behaviour of the market, with the result that the investments remained more or less idle; this created a paradoxical situation of passive capital not being matched by productive assets. In other cases the accumulated debt only helped to support policies aimed at an indiscriminate opening up of the market, thus stimulating massive imports of consumer durables. Sometimes, by building up their foreign debt, countries were able to maintain high rates of exchange to back price control programmes, instead of developing strategies to reduce inflation. Incoherent macro-economic policies were also to be found which undermined confidence and brought a flight of capital, which, in turn, led to a loss of foreign reserves and an increase in indebtedness. Foreign borrowing was also used to cope with deficits in the balance of payments caused by the rise in oil prices, or to pay for major programmes of military spending.

In short, the funds obtained from abroad were used for a variety of purposes, which differed widely between countries. In discussing and evaluating foreign borrowing over recent years one cannot, therefore, make blanket judgments. One has to look at each country individually, or even the different stages of development within a single country.

The level of indebtedness began to cause concern at the end of the 1970s, when the region's total debt reached $200 billion. However, the fears which might have been aroused by an analysis of the figures were mitigated by the international economic situation and the region's performance in foreign trade. In fact, during the second half of the 1970s, the region's countries saw a considerable growth in their export capacity. In Mexico, for example, gross national product increased at an annual average rate of 6.4 per cent betweeen 1970 and 1979, while the annual growth in exports was 10.9 per cent. Comparable figures for Brazil in the same period show rates of growth of 6.7 per cent and 9.1 per cent respectively; and in Argentina a very modest rate of growth of gross national product over the period as a whole—2.6 per cent—was accompanied by a 10.7 per cent rate of expansion in exports. To those who warned about the rapid rise in indebtedness, the normal response was to point to both the growth in exports and to the financial and commercial trends in the world market.

The situation changed completely at the beginning of the 1980s. At the beginning of this decade the international outlook shifted spectacularly for the countries of the area and particularly for those with the biggest debts, because of the steady increase in interest rates and the sharp fall in foreign capital being invested in the region. As Table 1 shows, interest rates, which had been negative, or just positive throughout the previous decade, now rose violently in real terms. At the same time, net receipts of capital fell sharply.

Table 1
Real interest rates and net capital revenue
(in percentages and billions of US dollars, respectively)

	Interest rates	Capital revenues
1973	2.94	8.1
1974	0.11	11.6
1975	−2.21	14.5
1976	−0.22	18.3
1977	−0.50	17.3
1978	1.23	26.4
1979	0.66	29.0
1980	0.86	30.2
1981	6.11	37.9
1982	6.91	16.7
1983	6.71	3.2

Source: ECLA.

Furthermore, the exchange rates for the Latin American currencies also dropped dramatically (in 1981 the index reached minus 13; in 1982, minus 7; and in 1983, minus 7.2). If we turn to changes in nominal interest rates, which are decisive in resolving current account problems, the situation appears still more serious. The fatal combination of these factors caused the foreign debt of the region as a whole to rise to its present level of $310 billion. Countries were obliged to contract heavy debts simply so that they could keep up their debt service payments. The figures demonstrate the spectacular influence which economic developments abroad had in creating and aggravating the crisis, and they also indicate that from the start of the 1980s it has become virtually impossible to control the crisis, since its course depends fundamentally on external factors.

In 1982 and 1983 a new ingredient brought an acceleration of the crisis: this was the major contraction in financial activity produced by the private banking system. Having provided abundant funds, whose rate of growth was over 20 per cent per year by the end of the 1970s, funds have been cut drastically over the past three years (see Table 1). This reduction would have been even greater, had it not been for the action of the International Monetary Fund (IMF). ECLA called this phenomenon a 'financial depression'. It came on top of the economic contraction caused by the high interest rates and worsening rate of exchange for Latin American currencies which are products of the international economic situation. It is worth reflecting that if, during 1983, the exchange rate for Latin American currencies had been the same as in 1980, and if interest rates had been 40 per cent lower (which would actually have meant that they were still above the historical average), the region would have had $25 billion extra in its foreign account. This would have enabled it to cover its interest payments of about $34 billion far more painlessly, without the violent reductions in imports of the past two years. As a result of all this, Latin America has become a net exporter of wealth—a reversal of the historical pattern and in flagrant contradiction of the developing nations' role as importers of capital.

Since it came into existence, the ECLA has made the relationship between the centre and the periphery a key element in its analysis and explanation of underdevelopment in the region. In the 1950s, the slow growth of world trade, and the restrictions in international markets provided the conditions in which the region could opt for the development of its internal market and strategies for import substitution. In the 1960s and 1970s, the growth of the world market encouraged an unprecedented expansion of world trade, with annual averages rising to six or seven times their pre-World War II level. This international climate led to the introduction of expansionist policies and the diversification of exports, giving a new appearance to the structure of foreign trade in Latin America. During the 1970s, the permissiveness of outside financial institutions made possible strategies involving increased spending in areas with differing degrees of social and economic productivity. So far in this decade, the prolongation of an economic period characterised by very high interest rates has limited the ability of the Latin American economies to recover.

This kind of vulnerability to foreign influences makes plain the risks involved in development strategies based essentially on foreign borrowing. These risks grow markedly in a situation of international crisis which is quite remarkable for the post-World War II period. The vulnerability is still more serious and lasting in those cases where foreign funds were not channelled into investments which could have increased the capacity of the economies of the region to generate currency.

The inevitable adjustment, and the tensions created by extreme measures

After such a major collapse abroad, which has had a severe effect on the revenue of the region, the countries of Latin America were inevitably obliged to make adjustments in their economic policies, and these have exacted a high price in economic and social terms. Certainly, given an international economic situation of the kind described, it would be utopian to imagine that adjustments could be made painlessly. The question one must ask is whether the adjustment, as well as being necessary, has been equitable in terms of ensuring that responsibility is shared with others who have contributed to the crisis; and whether the time has not come to look at the mechanisms being employed, given the persistence of an uncontrollable situation generated by the international crisis.

As is well known, the adjustment process in every country was characterised by a massive deflation, designed to bring about a reduction in imports in order to produce the trade surplus necessary to service the country's foreign debt. There was a reduction in spending both on consumer goods and on investments; national currencies were heavily devalued to provoke radical changes in the structure of prices; and there was an erosion of international reserves. Inevitably, and as a corollary of the above, on top of traditional pressures on price levels there were further pressures caused by persistent and rising fiscal deficits. These, on the one hand, fuelled strongly inflationary tendencies and, on the other, led to heavy cuts in public investment, especially in the social services. It is no surprise therefore that this adjustment, as well as bringing the widespread destruction of fixed capital through the collapse of innumerable businesses, concentrated its negative effects on the mass of the people.

In implementing these policies of adjustment, the region used the orthodox mechanisms recommended by the IMF, which applied within the narrow limits of a difficult payments situation and an international financial community which was unwilling to authorise fresh funds. Given this context, the policies could not have been anything other than clearly recessive. Their implementation was encouraged by the hope—soon to prove unfounded—of a rapid improvement in the international situation, which would influence interest rates and the rate of exchange.

No one would suggest that this situation could be resolved without having to make painful and inevitable adjustments. However, the relationship between the situation in the region and external factors outside the control of individual countries, the delayed recovery of the international economy, and the extent of the accompanying social and economic costs, have brought growing criticism of the mechanisms of adjustment being employed. The highest political level at which these criticisms have been expressed was the recent Conference of Heads of State and their personal representatives, called by the President of Ecuador, Dr Osvaldo Hurtado, and held in Quito at the beginning of 1984.

The criticisms are essentially political, and have the following starting points: first there are doubts about the long-term viability of a generalised adjustment in which all the countries of the region are obliged at the same time to contract their imports and expand exports at a period when the industrialised nations are employing new and increasingly sophisticated measures to protect their markets. Even if the United States' policy of maintaining a deficit in foreign trade represents an important exception, the criticism is still valid with respect to the other countries with which the region has commercial relations.

Secondly, it is justifiably pointed out that while a number of groups clearly share responsibility for having created the crisis—the countries themselves, the international banks and the whole system of international economic relations—the cost of the adjustment is being borne almost exclusively by the debtor nations. In fact, not only have the international banks not borne any of the costs, but they have managed to increase their profits to grotesque levels by charging for their intervention. At the same time, they have been able to ensure that the IMF keeps an eye on developments in internal economic policy, to the end that the countries keep up their payments. The banks have also managed to get national governments to guarantee virtually all their assets in the region.

Thirdly, only a formal criticism is made of the financial depression created by the cutback in new loans for development, and of the transformation of the region into a net exporter of wealth, a situation which cannot continue if there is to be a minimal economic recovery. Although some recent cases indicate the possibility of a change in this situation, the general tendency is the continued unwillingness of the international banks to increase their commitments in Latin America.

This kind of adjustment has also brought criticisms of a theoretical nature which ECLA has examined in the past, and which it has repeated recently.[1] In essence, these criticisms have centred on the fact that ... 'internal and external disorders, although they are related, have usually been looked at in isolation. Moreover, the analysis of the problem (and the policy recommendations) tend to ignore the interdependence between countries. Although this may be a useful way of approaching the subject of the "small countries", or when there are not common problems of payments or trade, it may at times lead to partial or mistaken conclusions when the opposite is the case.'

Although the countries of the region have reacted very responsibly to the situation which has been created, taking measures which have not only corrected problems, but have also involved painful social, economic and even political consequences, there is some doubt as to how long the social systems of the countries will be able to continue these restrictive policies if there is no improvement in the international economic situation. This is why there have been warnings from various international financial and political centres about the internal crises which are being created and their possible consequences for the world financial markets. Paradoxically, the most radical and innovative proposals for different global formulae to solve the debt problem have been put forward by leaders in the industrial world, though increasingly by political leaders and the economic authorities of the Latin American region.

The central issue for the immediate future is to find new globally applicable mechanisms to enable countries to service their debts and to allow room for manoeuvre in the balance of payments. This would give rise to a higher level of imports and would thus start a process of recovery in the Latin American economy. All the solutions proposed favour a considerable reduction in the cost of financial intervention, the reprogramming of interest payments so that these do not amount to too high a proportion of income from exports—thus leaving a margin for the reactivation of the internal economy—and an extension of the period over which the debt is to be repaid. These proposals have already been discussed in other documents produced by ECLA. It is worth emphasising, however, that in the present circumstances the question of the financing of foreign debt has become the central point for the majority of Latin American countries in any policy for internal revival.

Along with the question of debt, the commercial issue has taken on a significance which cannot be ignored. If conditions are not created which will allow an increase in exports and improved access to world markets, it will be difficult to find a lasting and positive solution to the present crisis.

Short-term perspectives

Certainly, it is not easy to put forward a clear idea of the short-term perspectives for the international economy, nor therefore for the basic suppositions implicit in the mechanisms of adjustment being used today and which are supported by the international financial community and the IMF. In a recent article, Albert Bressand outlined the possibilities for the international economy like this:

We can envisage two broad scenarios for the coming years, depending on what relations exist between the 'real' world and the 'financial' world. The first, more optimistic scenario is one in which the real economy is able to grow more rapidly than the 'financial dead weight' with which it is burdened. If this happens, difficulties may remain for countries in special circumstances or for particular businesses, but, overall, the nightmare of debt will fade gradually away. Nothing more serious than a major rescheduling of the debt will be necessary.

The second scenario is, however, more likely, at least in the absence of concerted measures for economic recovery of the kind described earlier; policies for financial adjustments will meet at a global level, bringing deflation and increasing economic, social and political vulnerability, instead of reducing it. At some point the weight of accumulated debt may become so heavy that there will be no other course but to declare a moratorium on debt payments, and this could in fact be the only way of getting out of a mine-field.[2]

This is the terse summary of an authority on the subject, who presents the problem from the perspective of the developed countries. It unavoidably brings back memories of the financial problems of the 1930s.

Both these visions can be found in views held about the immediate future in Latin America. On the one hand, some analysts, mainly among the monetary authorities at present in control of the region's economies, believe that the reactivation of the North American economy will in turn bring a revival of the other industrial economies (the 'engine theory'). This will bring about a reactivation of the larger international economy on which the economies of the developing nations depend. With lower real interest rates and better prices for raw materials, it will become much easier to deal with the debt problem and there will be room to set in motion policies for internal economic revitalisation.

On the other hand, others question both the nature of the present recovery in the major economies, and its capacity to produce the expected positive effects in the periphery. First, they doubt the long-term viability of a recovery if interest rates remain at their present level, with the excessive strength of the North American currency caused by factors related to the level of interest rates, and with growth apparently being generated mainly by spending on consumer goods, rather than a dynamic pattern of investment. Secondly, they point out that in order for a recovery in the centres of world economy activity to have any real significance at the periphery, it must have a significant effect on interest and exchange rates, and new lines of finance to the region must be opened up.

Clearly, if we look at these three areas in relation to the economic revival in the United States in 1983, our conclusions cannot be over-optimistic. The expected lowering of real interest rates—a key factor in the whole process of investment in our countries—has not happened, nor has there been a strong reversal of the tendency for the rate of exchange of the Latin American currencies to fall. Neither has there been a positive response in terms of a new flow of private capital to the region, except to the extent that this has been provided to finance part of what is owed to the international banks in interest payments.

Obviously, the recovery of the economies of the industrialised countries is indispensable if there is to be a substantial improvement in the economic situation of Latin America. From this point of view, developments in the United States and some OECD countries are encouraging. On the other hand, it seems equally clear that given the extent of the recession in recent years in almost all the countries of the region, these countries will be unable to continue implementing such severe adjustment policies as they have in recent years. They have no alternative but to begin to grow. If sufficient support is not forthcoming from outside the region, it will be necessary to find urgently the support mechanisms which will allow the region to free a greater volume of resources to increase its imports.

Given this context, it will be necessary for both social and political reasons to put into practice some of the ideas mentioned earlier in relation to the administration and refinancing of the region's foreign debt. As developments in the regional economy in the past two years have shown, the possibility of positive support through a higher degree of import substitution should not be ruled out. But this measure has its limitations. From now on, an increased capacity to import will help to achieve much more dynamic conditions of growth than could be created by the administration of the payments problem in its present form, in terms of refinancing the debt and organising the commercial and financial resources of the region to that end.

Medium-term perspectives: the need for new approaches to, and policies for, economic development

The preceding points suggest that neither contingency economic policies, nor the noble objectives of development policies, nor even the instruments used to carry these out, can remain unchanged in the light of the lessons which will be left by the crisis of the 1980s. At the beginning of the decade it was generally held that concerted action to remove the different structural blockages which had revealed themselves in the course of the development of the region would lead to more dynamic rates of economic development, and this could create conditions for the gradual solution of social problems and would lay the foundations for sustained economic development. Today, with no dramatic changes in development policy in sight, which would be socially and politically acceptable, the approach in the Latin American countries should arguably be substantially different from that of the past. It would hardly be realistic to propose radical reforms, particularly in the middle of one of the worst recessions this century. Nevertheless, as in the 1930s, it would seem that basic factors have emerged which make possible a far-reaching revision of methods of development and basic economic policies. Undoubtedly, there will have to be changes, but it is important that these should have a certain rationale, and that advantage should be taken of past experience in order to minimise the social and political costs of these changes and to maximise their economic effectiveness.

In order to consider new policies and draw up possible options, we need to begin with a clear understanding our our starting point and also to be fully aware of the margins of action within which economic policy must be conducted. One of the most unfortunate effects of the developments of recent years has been to increase considerably the external vulnerability of the Latin American economies, and to reduce the region's governments' margin of action. These margins are clearly not the same for every country, nor do they start in equal conditions, especially if one considers, along with the economic variables, the relative importance of the different countries in the world economy, their standing in the financial markets and their position in the international political scene. There are conditioning factors at each country's 'starting point' which are related to its internal economic and social conditions, or arise from international developments and the country's own place in the international scene.

Some internal limitations

Inevitably, the first internal limitation is related to long-standing structural deficiencies, converted into the region's economic underdevelopment. The weakness of the productive structures, the slow rate of accumulation of capital, inefficient industrial development and the underdevelopment of agriculture all remain characteristic of the Latin American economic scene. The tendency for wealth to accumulate continues and, in recent years, has increased. The effect is that the majority of the people continue to be held back, and the countries' economies are not dynamic enough to generate employment. These are the factors which Dr Raúl Prebisch has characterised as being part of the general syndrome of peripheric and imitative capitalism prevalent in the region. These difficulties have not only not been resolved, but have tended to worsen because of the contraction of national income over the past years. They are basic structural problems with which any solution must start.

On top of these difficulties, the majority of countries also face the problem of growing inflationary pressures which have risen markedly in recent years and are clearly related to the problems of the present period. These inflationary pressures are difficult to deal with, even when it is a question of 'old inflation', and can be still harder to deal with for countries which are recently entering this syndrome and are facing all the inevitable social and political traumas that this brings. They are also difficult to deal with in periods of political transition. Recognition of these problems makes it even more vital to establish mechanisms for external cooperation which, by reducing problems in one field, would allow greater room for manoeuvre. This would reduce the potentially depressive effects of anti-inflationary policies, which would be superimposed on the recessive effects of the policies of external adjustment.

Within this category of internal limitations must be included the burden of foreign debt. Whatever the trends in interest or exchange rates, this burden remains a heavy one, and will continue to use up a large proportion of the wealth of the region. In today's circumstances, the majority of debtor countries will have to give between 5 per cent and 10 per cent of their national product to cover interest payments, which will certainly weigh heavily against the ability of the countries to invest, and is a 'mortgage' which will have to be taken into account in coming years.

External conditions

As has been the case throughout the economic history of the region, the scope for alternatives in internal policies will continue to be closely linked to the kinds of relationship that are established with the central world economies. To plan the development of these relationships in the future requires a view to be taken of future developments in trading and financial links. Without denying that a restoration of the creditworthiness of the countries in the region based on a rescheduling of debt and a restructuring of exports would create better conditions in which to attract foreign funds, it would be thoughtless optimism to base one's plans on a situation in which capital flows were at the same level as in the 1970s. It is more reasonable to think in terms of 'austerity' with respect to the availability of resources, and of marked selectivity in regard to sources of credit, both as to countries and in relation to the purpose for which the credit is to be used. This is the implication of recent policy decisions taken by the international banks. It would be more realistic therefore to think in terms of a much more restrained and limited financial context than that of the past.

The external atmosphere will be determined by the way in which international trade evolves. We have already pointed out that a lasting and definitive solution may come through the ability to obtain foreign currency by increasing exports and securing higher prices. It is therefore essential to look at the behaviour of the international market. Will markets open up, or will there be a worsening of protectionist tendencies? According to Bressand, '... the epoch in which free trade was regarded as a unifying principle may well have ended. By this I mean that a liberalisation of trade of the kind seen in the 1960s and 1970s would not solve the majority of trading problems which may arise in the 1980s. This is not to say that there will be no more free trade, or that free trade is not desirable as a normative principle. What is at issue is not the prescription but the diagnosis.'[3] Such statements are not, even as diagnostics, very encouraging for the periphery.

The Economist (London) has estimated that 40 per cent of world trade is affected by some form of intervention. In this situation, there must be concern about the possible consequences of any further increase in protectionism and an even greater loss of openness in world trade, given the desperate need for Latin American countries to increase their exports. For these reasons, it seems wise not to imagine that trading conditions will differ greatly from the present; on the contrary, it will be an important achievement if the present conditions remain unchanged, without any further deterioration. On the same grounds, it would seem unreasonable to suggest that world trade will grow at the same rate as in the 1960s and 1970s, when the rate of growth of this trade reached 8 per cent per annum. Instead, it may be more reasonable to imagine that the rate will be somewhere between this figure and that recorded for the first decades of this century, even the growth in trade was only 1 per cent per annum. This likely situation will affect both trading opportunities in Latin America and changes in the rate of exchange.

Finally, another question on which it is necessary to make some forecast is the effect which structural changes in production and consumption in the world's economic centres will have on international economic relations and on the comparative advantages which these centres have enjoyed in recent decades. In other words, technological changes which will involve the incorporation of advanced technologies into fields like biogenetics, the introduction of robots or microprocessors—to mention just some of the possibilities—will have a decisive effect on forms of production and will alter the international division of labour. This situation will, in various ways, affect the opportunities for the region to play a role on the international stage, and particularly its ability to compete as a producer of foodstuffs and in providing cheap labour. It should not be forgotten, when making forecasts about the future international panorama, that some experts consider that the world is going through a third industrial revolution, which must result in new relationships between the centres and the periphery. This will bring both dangers and opportunities, which need to be understood and prepared for, so that they can be taken into account in drawing up strategies and options for development. This issue needs to be studied urgently, to provide information on a field into which the region will necessarily have to venture.

Among the external factors which will continue to influence the possible ways in which the periphery can play its part in the international economy is the global hostility between East and West. Developments in this area have proved to be an important influence in North–South economic relations, and cannot therefore be ignored, however it may be to make predictions regarding them.

Some aspects of the new options in development policy

It would be vain to try to outline here a new economic pattern for the region. Many arguments encourage prudence. The most important is the well-known difference in the situation of the various countries of the region. We only need to compare the vast divergence between countries of continental significance, like Brazil, and the tiny states of the Caribbean to dissuade us from any attempts at generalisation. To this argument we may add an equally convincing one: the unknown elements in the policies of the major economic centres, which make it difficult to predict the possible changes in the relationships between these centres and the peripheral countries of Latin America. In recognising these limitations, we are not denying the importance of suggesting hypotheses and possible scenarios, in order to establish a body of 'undisputed points' on the basis of which a model for future development may be drawn up. These points will cover both the major objectives of development and the reform of instruments of economic policy. Without attempting to discuss these fully here, we will mention some matters of major importance in analysing them.

The objectives of a policy for economic development

It is relevant to emphasise three objectives which should be part of any future development programme: *a considerable increase in the rate of growth, greater overall economic efficiency and an increase in the equity and social efficiency of development policies.* These three objectives are obviously closely interrelated and are not always easy to make compatible, as experience has shown. In many cases a short-term increase in efficiency has contradicted the principles of justice. In other cases, it has been necessary to opt for either a higher rate of growth, or improvements in terms of social efficiency.

It is worth looking at the experience in different countries in the region over recent years. Those which put a premium on economic efficiency, whatever the cost, sacrificed social efficiency and created explosive conditions with inevitable political consequences which ultimately worked against many of the initial objectives. In other countries, exclusive concern with social objectives led to an excess of economic populism which in a short time was cancelled out by the general inefficiency of the productive system. Experience indicates therefore that the only valid options are those which do not give greater priority to any one of these objectives, but make advances in all of them by taking an overall view which is only possible with an integrated project for economic and social development.

In relation to the objective of growth, one may recall recent ECLA publications which have discussed possible scenarios for the future. Within a scenario which presumes the continuation of present conditions, analysis is made of the implications for the region of a rate of growth of about 3.5 per cent in the OECD countries until the end of the decade, accompanied by an annual growth of about 3 per cent in exports from the region, and real interest rates of around 6 per cent. Given these conditions—which would be an improvement on the present state of affairs—the region could achieve an average rate of growth of about 4 per cent over the rest of the decade. With this rate of growth, by 1990 Latin America would have the same levels of per capita income as in 1980. Thus we would have lost a whole decade of social and economic progress, and would see a consequent worsening of social conditions. This is demonstrated by the fact that, with this rate of growth, it would be possible to absorb only 90 per cent of those joining the labour force. These theoretical calculations point to the crucial need to embark on far more dynamic programmes and policies of development than those which have been put forward historically. These must be both qualitatively and quantiatively more dynamic, in order to provide better solutions to the social problems created by general poverty, the inability to satisfy basic social needs and existing levels of unemployment.

If we look more closely at the conditions which might make possible a more dynamic rate of growth, it immediately becomes clear that this depends to a great extent on a change in the basic terms of the region's foreign relations. This involves, in turn, a number of factors which are outside the control of the region. In other words, in order to plan for higher rates of growth, there must be more favourable terms for refinancing the regions' foreign debt—in relation to interest rates, the period allowed for payment and the availability of new funds to support the process of internal investment. Internally, it will also be necessary to prepare development projects, and highly selective investment programmes, in order to improve the social efficiency of economic growth.

In relation to the objective of efficiency, it should be emphasised that the coming stages of economic development in the region will be much more restricted in terms of the availability of foreign funding and the prospects offered by the international situation. This implies that regional development will have to rely to a greater degree on a process of internal accumulation and on the mobilisation of the region's own resources, instead of depending on an influx of foreign capital. In other words, as the documents issued by the ECLA Secretariat have suggested, the region 'will have to learn to do more using less'. This means, on the one hand, a substantial increase in internal saving and, on the other, increased efficiency in making use of available resources—in particular, the labour force and capital installations.

The aim of increasing efficiency has been given different connotations in writings on economics, and in the methods chosen to introduce efficiency as an explicit objective of economic policy. In recent years, the intention has been to achieve efficiency primarily through creating a free play of market forces by opening up the economy to foreign markets. Certainly, we can find examples where the competitivity of national production has been successfully increased by opening it up to the influences of the external market. However, it is also clear that it is not enough to use this mechanism alone, and that it can produce effects that are quite the opposite of what was expected, unless it is accompanied by coherent internal policies and sensible schemes for support which suit the stage of development reached in the particular country. In mixed economies the use of methods of increasing efficiency which may involve the introduction of the rules of the market-place must be matched by the participation of the state in global policies of support for the productive system and in ensuring coherence in the administration of the main macro-economic variables.

In the Latin American development process, tendencies towards inequality represent a chronic problem. In this respect, we need only recall the huge concentrations of people who live in conditions of critical poverty or severe unemployment, which, whether open or disguised, affects more than 25 per cent of the workforce of the region. These and other problems have been accentuated by the recession of the 1980s. Both in the short and long term, one of the objectives of the development should be to help resolve these problems, and this is in itself the basic aim of the development process.

In the short term, it is of crucial importance to give priority to programmes dealing with the most urgent needs, such as subsidies for basic consumer goods or job creation. In the medium and long term, emphasis must be put on the quality of investments, so that these not only create a more dynamic pace of economic growth, but also help to correct the serious social imbalances which exist within the development process. In all these spheres, the region has already gone beyond the stage of making a simple redistribution of nominal incomes, and it now has to create, using the existing structure and the mechanisms for the distribution of income, the conditions necessary for combining equity with efficiency, and thus develop a pattern of self-sustaining and equitable growth.

Some key mechanisms

As well as reformulating the objectives of development policy, it is also necessary to review some of its key mechanisms. Here we will look at only a few of these—those that seem most relevant in dealing with the challenges of a new kind of economic development, and which tackle the issues of what are the motors for economic growth, and what are the roles of the State and planning, and foreign relations?

What should be the motors of economic growth at this new stage of regional development? Approaches to this issue tend to fall under two headings, which are presented as antagonistic in political and intellectual debates: that which emphasises the internal market and that which opts for an opening up of the market and an expansion of exports. It is usual for these arguments to be supported by examples of the well-known economic achievements of South East Asia, without an adequate explanation of the key elements in the development policies followed by the countries concerned from the start of their export-based growth and throughout its consolidation. No mention is usually made of those countries' policies of strengthening their respective internal markets, of their active policies of redistribution of incomes or of the particular geographical and political context in which their economies are located. When discussion centres on the region as a whole, another weakness tends to emerge in the debate: the substantial differences between the countries in terms of their size, level of development and wealth of resources are not taken into account, although these are all inextricably involved in a definition of the relative contexts on which the discussion must be based. The debate therefore tends to be conducted at different levels of abstraction, which produces confusion and often means a loss of objectivity.

In the course of its history, Latin America has adopted different options which have acquired particular characteristics in the different countries of the region and at different periods of history. In the 1950s, facing demographic pressures and increasing urbanisation, and eager to incorporate technical advances into their productive processes, the majority of Latin American countries adopted a policy of industrialisation based on the use of the internal market as the principal motor of economic growth, given a situation of closed or heavily restricted international markets. At this stage it was impossible to escape the risks of inefficiency resulting from limited and scattered markets. At that point ECLA drew attention to the dangers of keeping the markets separate, and, as early as the middle of the 1950s, proposed the first attempts to expand the closed national development processes into sub-regional patterns of integration.

Later Dr Prebisch, by now working in UNCTAD, argued for an opening up of world markets to exports of manufactures from the countries on the periphery. In this way, responding to particular historical situations, industrialisation in Latin America developed through its early stages; it must be recognised that some of the policies adopted in this period demonstrated excessive protectionism and biases against exports and agriculture.

Later, with a more dynamic and open international market, more systematic and coherent policies were implemented which brought about an active promotion of exports. To a great extent this was the consequence of the earlier stages of industrialisation, which had developed experience and skill in business within the region. The expansion and diversification of exports of manufactured goods was stimulated, very successfully in some cases, thus adding the international markets to the internal market as a motor for development, and increasing demand. Although the import substitution policies of the time are today accused of having been excessively protectionist, it should be noted that over-promotion had social costs too. As Streeten puts it so well:[4] 'The inefficient use of resources may have different causes other than those directly or indirectly linked with a process of industrialisation based on a high level of protectionism. It is quite possible to find inefficient export policies, just as it is to find inefficient import substitution policies.'

When one analyses the depression and recession of recent years, their economic and social consequences, the burdens imposed by foreign debt and the uncertain international climate, one is forced to the conclusion that the region cannot afford to allow its pace of growth to rely solely on external stimuli, even less so when the difficulties of access to foreign markets are well known. In these circumstances, the motors for future growth—once the problem of the great distances between countries can be overcome—must favour the broadening of the internal market in all areas, in what could be seen as a return to a reliance on the internal dynamic. This change, however, clearly does not mean that the region should forget the lessons of the past, or allow inefficiency, which will in the end destroy the whole process. The broadening out of the market should be linked to an increasing, though highly selective, opening up of the market. This implies the wise use of import capacity, together with the vigorous encouragement of exports of all kinds. The two objectives—the broadening out and opening up of the market—will be present in different combinations in different countries and will establish complementary rather than conflicting spheres of action.

To broaden out the internal market means first of all to strengthen agricultural development in the region, which is still far from having exhausted all the geographical and technological resources which might enable it to take a leading position within the Third World as a producer and exporter of foodstuffs. It also means exploring the possibilities for industrial growth, both in terms of the production of consumer goods to meet the growing needs of the people and of expansion into hitherto undeveloped areas of industrial activity—in particular, the production of capital goods.

To progress in the external sphere clearly means first of all exploring the scope for regional complementarity and at the same time keeping an eye on the expansion of exports, of both traditional products and manufactures, to the rest of the world. The decisive factor in making the broadening internal markets compatible with a growing expansion into foreign markets will be the development of technological policies adapted to the new and dynamic phase of development.

Seen from an historical perspective, the debate about which of the possible options is the main engine of development seems more often than not to be too simplistic and to bear no relation to the experience of those countries which are today put forward as examples of alternative models. It is also often forgotten that the situation in a country at the start of a process affects both socially and even politically the way that changes are incorporated into the development of that process. Radical policies of structural change, such as those pursued in some of the liberal experiments of recent years, finally led to a massive destruction of capital installations, thereby eliminating so called 'obsolete' areas of activity, but without attracting enough support from the external market to encourage alternative activities. The result was a violent clash between economic objectives and the social and political reality which finally wiped out all the benefits which it was hoped the opening up of the market would bring. In other cases, however, development policies focusing predominantly on the internal market, without a parallel and dynamic process of opening up the economy, have also demonstrated serious inadequacies, creating inflationary pressures and ultimately a loss of the growth dynamic of the entire productive system.

The major task for the region in the future in relation to the motors of growth is to re-establish for each country the correct balance between the broadening of the internal market and the opening up of the economy to produce growing amounts of foreign exchange. To maintain this balance there will have to be structural changes in the allocation of investment and in macro-economic policy. To this end, there needs to be an intelligent programme of international aid which will find imaginative ways of cooperating with countries in the region over the difficult issue of re-allocating resources, increasing the capacity to accumulate and giving the whole productive system a greater degree of flexibility to enable it to cope with changing trends in the international economy.

One basic way of carrying out new development policies in our countries is through the modernisation of the State, which needs to assist more efficiently in achieving the aims of national plans in all fields, and should be able to mediate between the different complex and conflicting demands emerging from a society in crisis. This question of the State's role is not a new one, either in intellectual debate or political practice. In recent years the need to modernise the State has presented a major challenge—for capitalist countries as much as for those with planned economies. For the first, the issue arose with the crisis of the welfare state; for the latter, with the crisis of the bureaucratic State. Latin America's experience may have similar characteristics. The State in the region was not the result of a national vision of society, but rather arose from a number of smaller structures which led to a number of different functions being performed without any overall idea of the central objectives of this action, or the best way of achieving these. This was how the traditional role of the liberal State was extended. Its activities spread into the complex field of macro-economic policy and a growing participation in the day-to-day economy as an administrator and manager of national resources. In many cases, this resulted in a lack of efficiency and incoherent policies.

Critics with different ideological positions have argued consistently, especially more recently, that whatever the State does is by definition bad, and that it should therefore be relieved of some of its functions. It should retain only the traditional functions of the liberal State, and leave the rest to be determined automatically by market forces. However, the experience of recent years has shown clearly that not everything that the State does is bad, nor does all that is bad come from the State. Equally, it has also become clear that the market on its own cannot resolve the complex problems of modern society—particularly in relation to social demands—nor can it foresee or anticipate future developments: this is what Dr Prebisch has referred to as the market's lack of a 'social dimension' and a 'temporal dimension'.

Given the present difficult conditions, in which the whole economic system needs to be highly efficient in order to make development projects as socially effective as possible, it is important to review thoroughly both the aims of any action taken by the State and the most appropriate means of putting this into practice. In relation to the demands of the development process, this review should be concerned both with the conduct of macro-economic policy, and with the State's administration of the resources which it controls. The management of mixed economies must rely on the full and active use of macro-economic policies with as great a degree of coherence as possible. No development programme will be viable in the long term if it is not based on an overall view of the economy, and on such forecasts for the medium and long term as can be provided by a modern system of national planning. A coherent macro-economic policy and the planning of action within an overall and long-term view of the economy and society are two vital functions of a modern State.

On the same basis, State-owned companies, which over the years have been the major source of instability in the revenues of the governments of the region, should be made to run with maximum efficiency. Given that these companies represent a large proportion of national capital, it will not be possible to increase efficiency within the economy as a whole without ensuring increasingly effective management in this area of national capital.

To put into practice these proposals for the modernisation of the economies of Latin America will clearly not be an easy task. It will undeniably demand political decisions which will come into conflict with vested interests and social and other forces in society. To overcome the temptation to create a populist state, in order to establish one which is actively committed to social and economic goals—and to do this without detriment to the overall efficiency of the system—constitutes one of the major political tasks facing Latin America today. This new State will be in a better position to reconcile economic efficiency with social effectiveness. At the same time, it should be in a position to establish a system of awards and penalties which will encourage the other important participant in the economy—the private sector—to modernise its practices and thus help to achieve objectives of general value.

The crucial importance of the external sector in the further stages of development has already been made clear. There is, of course, nothing new in emphasising the relationship between internal development and the external sector. On the one hand, it is obvious that in order to deal with its payments problems, the region will have to increase its capacity to generate foreign exchange through trade. On the other hand, in the earlier part of this paper it was argued that even the extension of internal markets will depend on the ability to generate foreign exchange at a fast enough rate. It is therefore necessary to employ three mechanisms simultaneously and in concert: first, that of ensuring the greatest possible coherence between policies for promoting exports; secondly, the strengthening of the regional market; and, third, the expansion and diversification of international markets.

Recent events have enabled the region to gain experience of the employment of coherent policies for promoting exports. They have also created awareness of the extent to which these policies need to be supported by clear and sustained incentives, provided by adequate price systems and by the provision of help both for internal promotion and attempts to enter foreign markets. The export boom of the 1970s, which is certainly instructive in spite of the problems of over-promotion mentioned above, is evidence of the considerable potential that exists and, in some cases, of a great deal of idle capacity which should be put to work.

Other contributors to the seminar examine the crucial role of regional cooperation in dealing with the present crisis and providing a fulcrum for the future expansion of the regional economy. In the present circumstances, regional cooperation has particular importance. It would be utopian to think that it could provide the solution to all our problems; on the other hand, it would not be helpful to adopt negative and simplistic attitudes—insisting, without any grounds for saying so, that no progress has been made in this field. Instead, it is better to acknowledge the progress made and the experience which has been gained, without being complacent about the potential for regional cooperation which has yet to be exploited.

First, we need to assess the potential for cooperation, as well as shifts in the focus of trade from outside to within the region, which will allow better use to be made of productive capacity. But it is also necessary to increase channels for trade by putting forward practical proposals for regional cooperation which are suited to present conditions. In many cases past mistakes can be attributed to the setting of over-ambitious goals, the cost of which could not be calculated by the economic and political authorities, making it very difficult for them to put them into practice. Ultimately, and inevitably, this caused frustration.

Considerable progress has been made in this field, and recent reforms and positions reflected in proposals for integration and bilateral relations indicate a recognition of the need to take a pragmatic approach to the issue. These pragmatic approaches must be extended in every way possible, through bilateral and multilateral relations as well as in the public and private spheres. This clearly demands political definitions of the process and positive support at governmental level, in order that the necessary political stimulus can be provided for all possible forms of regional cooperation and complementarity.

At the same time, there must be continued efforts to extend regional activity into the international markets. Here increasing competition and protectionism demand a clear alliance between private interests and the State. It will be difficult to cope with the battles of the future unless there is a clear agreement and a community of interest, as indeed must be the case in every country of the world wherever it is situated. The opening up of markets will have to be achieved increasingly through acquiring new clients. In this respect, while acknowledging that the greatest potential is offered by the development of our own traditional markets, we should make the promotion of relations with other developing countries and regions a primary aim. This is a difficult task, since it is not easy to interfere with the North–South links which dominate the developing world's relations in trade and cooperation. Nevertheless, we must make these aims a part of our foreign policy, because they offer political as well as economic benefits.

Some last points

Clearly, this paper has not attempted to propose a fresh paradigm for the region, and still less to examine the many objectives and mechanisms which will be part of the next stage in its economic development. It has simply drawn attention to some important features which will require definition, and indicated those aspects which should be taken into consideration in drawing up new development policies.

There is one key factor which has had to be left on the margins of this analysis, but which it would be naive to omit altogether. It is the political dimension. There is no doubt that the mobilisation of social forces to carry through the next stages of the process of economic development needs to be based on defined political programmes. The unaltering and unalterable ethic involved in the building of open, pluralistic societies based on full participation is of fundamental importance at the present day. In fact, it is impossible to imagine that a way can be found of meeting all those social demands whose satisfaction has been postponed, as well as those which will be put forward in the future, without democratic processes involving full participation. It is only this which will enable broad agreement to be reached and the major objectives of development to be achieved.

There seems to be a growing awareness of this throughout the region. It will be the responsibility of the political leaders and their parties to make this vital contribution to the creation of a society which, in controlling its own destiny, will unite its members around a broad consensus, making possible, if not the end of all conflicts, at least a reduction of the social, economic and political costs which these involve.

Notes

1. C Massad and R Zahler, *The Adjustment Process*, first draft, ECLA, 1984.
2. Albert Bressand, 'Mastering the "World Economy"', *Foreign Affairs*.
3. Bressand, *op. cit.*
4. Paul Streeten, *Outward-looking Industrialisation and Trade Strategies* (North–South Round Table, 1982).

3
Crisis and Change in the World Economy

Celso Furtado

An undefined concept

After a period of exceptional growth, which was sustained for a quarter of a century, the capitalist economy has entered a phase of instability which has already lasted a decade.[1] Not quite the crises of the past—in present-day organised capitalism we no longer find the cumulative processes which led to economic breakdown, followed by depression—this instability reflects a complex process of structural adjustment which overflows from the economic sphere into those of politics and culture. For the first time we are faced with processes whose understanding requires the formulation of hypotheses about the behaviour of the 'world economy', even before that concept has yet been adequately defined. The models we have available are derived from the observation of economic systems whose operation presupposes the existence of effective political power at national or multi-national level. In addition, a few ideas have been put forward on the nature of the commercial and financial relations between these economic systems, which we call 'the international economy'. But what a 'world economy' might be is far from being clear.

An economic system is much more than a constellation of markets: it presupposes the existence of an institutional framework in which there operates a power structure capable of controlling and coordinating the activities we call 'economic'. Between 'consumer sovereignty' and authoritarian planning there are many criteria on which to base the orderly running of so-called economic activities. But for such management to be effective, and for an economic system to exist *a fortiori*, the individual and collective decisions of the final users of the social product to some extent must be coherent, both in synchronic and diachronic terms. And this can only be achieved in a politically organised society.

In the cyclical models derived from the evolution of capitalism, so-called crises can be explained within the logic of given national systems. External commercial and financial relations can play an important role in reinforcing or even initiating certain cumulative processes leading to the imbalances which give rise to breakdowns or sudden reversals in trend. Nonetheless, the dynamics involved can be explained, *a posteriori*, in terms of the logic of the system—that is, on the basis of endogenous causal processes.

But, faced with the unstable situation we have been living through over the past decade, analysis of the behaviour of the major national systems has proved inadequate, perhaps because our understanding of the logic governing these systems has failed to take into account the effects of the new relationships developing between national systems. The major obstacle would thus seem to be the inadequacy of the conceptual framework we have been using. There is growing evidence that the increasing complexity of relations between the most advanced capitalist economies has already produced a structure with a certain degree of autonomy, the embryo of a possible economic system of greater reach than those at present in existence. But this development has not been accompanied by an advance at the institutional level, which explains the inadequate way in which regulation—namely, coordination and control— are being exercised within the framework of the new structure. The resulting tensions can only be absorbed if there is an effective advance at the institutional level, or if there is an about-turn in the whole process, so as to restore autonomy of decision to the national power centres.

The experience of the European Economic Community is revealing of the contradictions which must be overcome by a scheme for integrating national economies if an effectively coherent new system is to be created. The common policy for prices of basic inputs—devised under the European Coal and Steel Community—and the complementary Common Agricultural Policy of guaranteed markets for agricultural products provided a sound basis for the creation of a regional economic system. But, as little progress was made towards the establishment of a power structure capable of defining common objectives on the political and social planes, the Community has a hard time surviving, under constant threat of having to revert to the status of a mere customs union confined to trade in manufactured final products. Given the lack of any policy for organising the economic sphere in terms of social and cultural objectives capable of expressing the aspirations of the various population groups of the countries involved, the free circulation of goods, persons and capital inexorably produces a geographical concentration of economic activity, accentuating disparities in the living standards of population groups and bringing about the depopulation of some areas and excessive concentration in others. The solution to problems of this nature calls, in one way or another, for the political will historically produced by the domination of one people over others or by the consensus achieved in response to an external threat. Since neither situation has arisen, the European Economic Community survives only because its members are afraid to face international competition on their own, at a time when such competition is based on increasingly costly technology. But, with the exhaustion of the original dynamism induced by the integration of national markets, the negative aspects—loss of effectiveness in the national decisionmaking systems and lack of adequate regional coordination—make themselves increasingly felt.

Unlike the EEC, which emerged from a project for the effective reduction of disparities in production costs between national economies through the harmonisation of commodity prices, the evolution of an embryonic world economic system took place in the absence of any policy whatever, and even against the tenor of the rules devised at Bretton Woods (1944) and Havana (1948), under the tutelage of the United States, for the purpose of regulating international economic relations.

The Bretton Woods rules

The international economic institutions created in the immediate post-war period in the economic sphere are formally part of the United Nations system, but, in reality, they operate under the strict tutelage of the US government. When they were established, the aim was to create conditions to encourage international trade and to ensure balance-of-payments stability. It was taken for granted that the United States, with its enormous technological advantage, the relative size of its capital goods industry and the vast gold reserves it had accumulated, would continue to be a major exporter of capital for an indefinite period. Capital transfers, however, would have to be subject to strict control if the experience of the inter-war years was to be avoided, a period which had been marked by destabilising movements of speculative capital. Central banks were to be responsible for supervising the capital account and the balance of payments of the various countries concerned, introducing whatever control measures they deemed necessary.

Both the Bretton Woods rules and the Havana Charter principles were

based on the idea that the international economic relations would continue
to be what they had been in the past—namely, relations between economic
systems still centred on their respective domestic markets, with governments assured of the capacity to exercise effective macroeconomic
regulation. Within this framework, external balance would be achieved
through the correct fixing of the exchange rate and the careful management of reserves requiring a relatively small immobilisation of resources.
The expansion of international trade which it was hoped would result from
the dismantling of tariff restrictions (the application of the liberalisation
rules of the Havana Charter) was not expected to introduce qualitative
changes into this framework. Recourse to the International Monetary Fund
would ensure that governments had the means to overcome occasional
crises in their external liquidity. Since capital movements were controlled,
balance-of-payments difficulties would be the result of an undue expansion
of imports and/or an unexpected fall in the relative prices or volume of
exports. The supplementary reserves, which constituted the IMF credit
'tranches', would enable governments to make the domestic adjustments
required to reduce import demand and/or to encourage exports.

What needs to be remembered about the particular vision of international relations that served as the basis for the institutionalisation effort
of the immediate post-war period is that policies for correcting external
imbalances were to be defined at national level, in terms of domestic objectives. In fact, there had been a period of more than half-a-century during
which dynamism was internally generated by the industrialised economies,
with the domestic markets of the major industrialised nations growing
faster than their external commercial relations.[2] In the face of destabilising
external pressures, the maintenance of internal stability at a level of activity
approaching full employment became an undisputed rule of good economic
policy.

The opening up of national economies

The opening up of national economies brought about significant changes
in the structure of external trade, whose traditional character, based on
the exchange of manufactured goods for raw materials and/or natural
products originating from different climates, was changing. This type of
exchange had, in fact, been eroded by technological advances, which
provided a growing supply of synthetic substitutes for natural products,

reducing their share in the value of final products. The new international trade took the form of exchanging manufactured goods for other manufactured goods, based on economies of scale and, above all, on the diversification of supply in sectors where technological advance was most rapid. The dynamism of this exchange permitted a more rapid utilisation and diffusion of technological innovation. External trade ceased to be mainly a means of expanding a country's resource base, with technological advances acting as a hindrance, to become a major factor in stimulating technological progress.

But this opening-up process did not follow the same pattern in every case. In Western Europe, as we have seen, it initially took the form of an integration of national markets; it was only at a later stage that it was extended to tariff reductions in respect of third parties. But there is a qualitative difference between these two stages: in the first, trade liberalisation is part of a wider scheme designed to change national economies, with a consequent reduction in their internal capacity for control and coordination; in the second, the external opening-up simply follows the selective tariff reduction model developed through negotiations under the General Agreement on Tariffs and Trade (GATT).

In the opposite camp we find Japan, which gave its external expansion a voluntaristic character by concentrating its efforts on lines of trade with the greatest scope for technological advance. The opening up of the Japanese market to imports competing with domestic production was carried out in an orderly and selective manner. As a result, the dramatic expansion of Japan's external trade did not compromise its internal capacity for macroeconomic regulation, as was the case in Western Europe.

But it was in the United States that opening up to the outside world brought about the most far-reaching structural changes. In that country, the transnationalisation of corporations assumed considerable importance, and transactions between parent companies and subsidiaries located abroad began to account for a growing share of external economic relations. Many factors led to the transnationalisation of enterprises in the post-war period,[3] but there is no doubt that in the case of the United States the process was strongly encouraged by the low relative cost of capital in the country's financial markets and the high profit rates prevailing in the countries undergoing post-war reconstruction. Since subsidiaries frequently reproduced—in whole or in part—the range of products of the parent company, it was to be expected that, given the lower costs of production abroad, there would be a net flow of exports to the American market. In its classic form, the export of capital had strengthened the balance of payments of the exporting country through the consequent inflow of interest payments and dividends. This was, in fact, compatible with a decline in the external trade coefficient. Transnationalisation forced an opening and could weaken the balance of payments. And it is here that we find the origin of the structural changes which were to produce the future current account deficit on the US balance of payments, rendering non-viable the project for a world economic order devised in the immediate post-war period.

A comparison between the economic performance of the Western European countries and that of Japan shows the importance of an independent capacity for macroeconomic regulation in international competition. However, it is the comparison between the United States and Japan that also clearly reveals the underlying causes of the structural tensions responsible for the instability of the past decade. Japan's commercial expansion was based on a government-devised strategy whose main thrust was to direct investment into sectors where competition was based mainly on technological innovation. In addition, the Japanese authorities adopted a foreign exchange rate policy which tended to strengthen the value of the yen, creating the conditions for a fall in the relative prices of imports. Exporting firms benefited at the cost level, in view of the relative importance of imported primary and intermediate products in the cost structure. But they were also forced to pass on part of the benefits of their increased productivity to foreign buyers.

More than any other economy in the history of industrial capitalism, that of the Japanese was organised to favour increases in productivity, particularly through technological advance, and to create new opportunities in international trade by lowering the relative prices of its exported products. Japan thus changed the historical pattern of behaviour of industrialised countries by not retaining, for the benefit of its own population, all the fruits of its internally generated technological progress.[4] This gave it the added advantage of being able to practise a policy of flexible export prices, adjusting its sales pressure to competitive forces. Thanks to the control thus exercised over its external trade, Japan was able to build up a solid balance-of-payments surplus, which provided the basis for the subsequent establishment of Japanese firms abroad. In the case of Japan, it was not a matter of enterprises transnationalising themselves on the basis of their own individual projects, but of the economic system itself subdividing and penetrating another system's territory.

In the case of the US, government action indirectly encouraged the opening-up process by providing credit facilities for the reconstruction of market economies devastated by the war, by encouraging the dismantling of old colonial structures and by promoting tariff reductions. But trans-nationalisation arose from the evolution of the enterprise itself and was carried out in terms of the enterprise's own objectives. It should be borne in mind that American enterprises had already acquired considerable experience of decentralised management in the vast economic area of the United States and Canada. They also had wide experience in operating commercial and financial networks in a plurinational framework. The advance in information and communication techniques in the post-war period facilitated the use of this wealth of experience on an even greater scale.

Transnational decentralisation also increases the room for manoeuvre available to an enterprise in the face of trade union pressure and the regula-tory power of the State. In this way, the forces chiefly opposing the power of the enterprise—the trade unions and the State—gradually lost ground, a situation which brought about significant changes in the evolution of industrial capitalism. This was to be the starting point for far-reaching structural changes which seem to indicate the emergence of an economic system of global scope, whose institutional framework is still to be defined.

The transnationalisation of the banks

The restructuring of an industrial enterprise in the plurinational sphere creates, initially, a flow of exports from the parent company to the subsidiaries. These are mainly capital goods and technical services. Since interest rates were lower in the United States and since there was greater elasticity in its supply of equipment and technology, this particular flow of exports assumed considerable importance. This was during the 'dollar shortage' period, when the United States was in a strong balance-of-payments position, with a persistent surplus. In fact, if the Bretton Woods rules had been applied, the dollar would have been revalued. But there was general agreement on the need to avoid this corrective measure, both on the part of the US government, which was determined to encourage exports in order to counteract recessionary pressures, and on the part of importers, whose debits were payable in dollars.

In the second stage of this restructuring, exports from the subsidiaries to the parent companies would have to increase, a development encouraged by the overvaluation of the dollar. This process, combined with the trade offensive launched by countries which had completed their industrial reconstruction, led to a dramatic change in the situation, with the United States moving into deficit, at first in its trade balance and later in the current account of its balance of payments. The contradiction thus established was the basis for future changes in international economic relations, with investments abroad being used to finance productive activities which competed with activities located in the country of origin of the investment capital. This explains why the unemployment level in the US during the 1950s and 1960s was far higher than in other industrialised countries. Even though it was a net exporter of capital, the United States found itself running a deficit on the current account of its balance of payments.

In practice, the solution found for this paradoxical situation was to hold part of the dollar earnings from exports to the United States abroad. These dollars increased the reserves held by central banks or went on circulating in the international money markets. This situation, which began to emerge in the early 1960s, was the starting point for the Euro-dollar market.

It is true that the circumvention of the Bretton Woods rules, which allowed the dollar to remain overvalued for a considerable length of time, led to the anomalous situation we have described. But behind this apparent paradox, what was really happening was that an important segment of the American banking system was itself becoming transnationalised. The enterprises busy organising themselves plurinationally were seeking to evade the control of the monetary authorities by holding offshore financial and monetary resources. Management of this massive international liquidity became a highly profitable business, and the enormous capacity of banks to gather and process information could be placed at the service of the process of the transnationalisation of enterprises.

How could the Bretton Woods provisions for the control of capital transfers by central banks be maintained in a world of private trans-nationalised banks? And, in the absence of such control, how could speculative movements of capital be avoided? These and similar questions which began to be raised reflected the anxieties being generated by all these structural changes. The availability of international liquidity confers considerable power, since the mere transfer of resources between agencies of the same bank located in different countries can threaten the stability of any currency. Moreover, by providing each other with lines of credit, the transnationalised banks are able to create liquidity, putting into practice at an international level the old saying that 'a loan creates a deposit'. There thus emerged a new decisionmaking force in the monetary and financial systems, which would necessarily limit the freedom of action of national governments.

Once the foreign subsidiaries of an enterprise have gained access to the international financial markets, it is no longer possible to subject the parent company to a nationally based credit policy—that is, a policy based on internally defined macroeconomic balances. If it suits the parent company to circumvent the constraints imposed by local credit policies, it can find ways of obtaining resources from its subsidiaries. The action of local authorities is thus limited to enterprises which are not trans-nationalised, and this acts as a strong incentive for them, too, to move in that direction.

There is no doubt that the transnationalisation process reflects a long-standing trend in the advanced capitalist economies to grow by extending the concentration of economic power to productive resources belonging to other economies. Switzerland has been presented as the extreme case of an economy whose enterprises operate mainly outside the national territory, controlling vast resources abroad. However, a closer look at what has been happening in recent decades makes it clear that the structural changes brought about in the US economy by the transnationalisation of a large number of enterprises are of a nature that calls for a redefinition of that economy, too, since it no longer fits into the existing concept of a national economic system. Those changes are imposing new forms of external relations, including relations with other advanced industrial economies, which cannot be compared with traditional forms of inter-dependence or international economic domination. We are witnessing the emergence of a new configuration in the spatial organisation of economic activities, which is tending to produce an international economic order that seems to be incompatible with the existing distribution of political power.

The behaviour of the American economy

After the war the American economy began to operate on a system of low interest rates which seemed to be a necessary requirement for the main-tenance of a high level of employment. As we have seen, however, low interest rates led enterprises, which were in the process of becoming trans-nationalised, to finance themselves in the home country. This provoked an exorbitant growth in liquidity in terms of dollars held abroad, threaten-ing their convertibility into gold. In seeking a way out of this uncomfortable situation, the US authorities soon realised that their room for manoeuvre was extremely limited. The introduction of an interest equalisation tax in 1963, designed to discourage the raising of financial resources on the American market by enterprises investing abroad, was a decisive test. But, in fact, the process of transnationalisation had advanced so far that enter-prises and banks were easily able to find a way round this obstacle by holding a greater share of their liquid resources abroad. If US interest rates were low, capital left the country for application abroad; if capital outflows were taxed, the inflow of financial resources was reduced, adding up to the same thing in the end. There could no longer be any doubt that the counterpart of the increased freedom of movement of the transnation-alised enterprises was the curtailment of the capacity of the national authorities to control the economy.

Confronted with the constraints created by the transnationalisation process, the US authorities faced the dilemma of choosing between a policy of high interest rates—which would mean aggravating the already chronic unemployment—or the indefinite accumulation of dollar balances abroad, which could only lead to a crisis of the dollar, with unforseeable con-sequences for the international financial system. US foreign policy con-siderations, particularly the Vietnam war, exerted pressures favouring the second option, which led to the dismantling of the Bretton Woods system. But, by the end of the 1970s, there was an about-turn and the first option was returned to. The extraordinary increase in dollar liquidity outside the United States in the second half of the 1960s had already led, in 1971, to the suspension of the convertibility of the dollar into gold at the prevailing rate. But the real problem was, in fact, the overvaluation of the dollar relative to the currencies of other countries exporting manufactured goods which competed with those of the United States in both the home and foreign markets. Devaluation was carried out in stages: in 1973, a system of floating exchange rates was adopted, with the central banks intervening in order to prevent too sharp a fall in the dollar. In the following five years the dollar lost a substantial part of its external purchasing power.

The process of absorbing the surplus international dollar liquidity was facilitated by the dramatic rise in petroleum prices in the second half of 1973 and by the overall increase in prices which took place on the international markets between 1973 and 1974.[5] Simultaneously, there emerged for the first time a group of countries—the members of Organisation of Petroleum Exporting Countries (OPEC)—with a large positive surplus on the current account of their balance of payments but unable to invest these resources internationally. The 'recycling' of these dollars by private international banks contributed considerably to strengthening their autonomy, opening up new channels for the transnationalisation process, in which a growing number of European and Japanese firms were beginning to participate.[6]

The handling of these so-called 'petro-dollars' clearly illustrates the nature of the decisionmaking system which emerged from the process of transnationalisation of enterprises and banks. The sudden change in the terms of trade in favour of the petroleum exporting countries should have led to a short-term reduction in international trade and/or the accumulation of financial assets held by the countries in surplus. As no one was interested in prolonging the first solution, the real problem was to devise credit instruments capable of defending the interests of creditors without creating disturbances in the international financial system. The solution to this serious problem was entrusted to the transnationalised private banks, which hastened to offer highly attractive securities in the form of Euro-dollar Certificates of Deposit redeemable in six months. This allowed interest rates to be re-adjusted within the short term of deposit. But the same resources were then placed for much longer periods, with provision for a six-monthly adjustment of the interest rates. The use of the roll-over technique gave borrowers the illusion that they had access to resources for long-term investment, when there was no guarantee whatever regarding the cost of the money being lent.

What was really being done was to create a smokescreen, to disguise the fact that banks were using funds obtained from short-term deposits to take medium- and long-term loans. Ordinary commercial banking operations were given the false appearance of special credit arrangements.

The high risks implied justified fat commission charges, which made the whole business more profitable, attracting hundreds of banking establishments with no international experience whatsoever. Moreover, since interbanking operations give rise to an autonomous process of liquidity creation, once the system of easy credit had been established indebtedness could continue even though the petro-dollar pool had been reduced and the rise in real interest rates made it inevitable that many debtors would become insolvent. As rescheduling the principal and funding part of the earned interest opens the door to high-risk commission charges, most banks took the easy line of inflating the accounting rate of their profits at the expense of the quality of their assets.

The uncontrolled indebtedness of a large number of countries, particularly in the Third World, is merely one aspect of the irrational way in which the decisionmaking system created by the transnationalisation of enterprises and banks has come to operate. The existence of a considerable volume of uncontrolled liquidity put an end to the system of fixed exchange rates adjustable at the discretion of national governments. But it also made it extremely difficult to operate a system of floating rates. The instability of the latter has made exchange transactions a major banking activity—and a highly profitable one, in that the greater the opportunities for speculation against the major international currencies, the bigger the returns. Once the necessary environment for speculation has been provided —the floating exchange rate system—financial intermediaries take it upon themselves to find pretexts for speculation. Specialists in discovering 'warning signs' that a currency is about to weaken come to be consulted as oracles. Some idea of the size of this currency speculation business can be gained from the fact that the value of exchange transactions in 1977 was US$ 50 trillion, accounting for forty-four times the value of world exports in that year.[7]

The instability prevailing in the international sphere cannot be explained unless we take into account the behaviour of the American economy, which is itself conditioned by the process of transnationalisation. Since the end of the 1950s it has been operating on a high level of military expenditure, which, in 1973, accounted for 5.6 per cent of GNP. A high level of military spending in peacetime is a new phenomenon for which democratic societies are historically unprepared. By reducing the resources available for civilian purposes, such expenditure has the same effect as a capital amortisation fund which reflects the cost of capital reproduction.

If this cost increases, there will be a reduction in net productivity—that is, in the income available for consumption and investment per unit of capital invested. *Mutatis mutandis*, if there is a slackening in the growth of the economy's average productivity, military expenditure will become a heavier burden on civilian society. Under this hypothesis, the level of military expenditure can only be maintained if there is a rise in the rate of savings or if the tax burden is increased. In fact, the growth rate of the productivity of labour in the US was lower by half if we compare the decade following 1973 with the decade ending in that year.[8] Also, while there was an increase in military expenditure (accounting for 6.6 per cent of GNP in 1983) the rate of savings fell from 9.5 to 6.7 per cent of GNP between 1973 and 1983.[9] The absence of any fiscal reform to permit private and public spending plans for the nation as a whole to be brought into line with national incomes has created imbalances in the economy which are reflected both in fiscal and balance-of-payments deficits.

In 1982, the fiscal deficit represented 68 per cent of military expenditure and almost 100 per cent of private savings. In 1983, the imbalance was accentuated, since military spending grew at double the rate of private savings and was financed totally from the fiscal deficit. If we were dealing with a national economic system like that of the other major industrialised market economy nations, the financing of the deficit would call for a squeeze on private spending and/or drastic cuts in other items of public expenditure along the lines of the measures taken to finance World War II. But, thanks to the transnationalisation process, the US government has other options at its disposal, and can transfer to the international sphere the adjustments it fails to make at home.

The basic problem thus lies in the behaviour of the American economy. Here, a number of features stand out. The rigidity of the public sector has continued to grow, with the increase in the share of military expenditure a major contributory factor. At the same time, the incompressibility of public expenditure and the decline in productivity growth have generated inflationary pressures, with the level of real wages falling during the last decade. Meanwhile, the transnationalisation process and the low rate of domestic investment have given rise to a high level of chronic unemployment, which is now being classified as 'structural'. As a result of the transnationalisation process, the traditional policy of low rates of real interest, an instrument designed to encourage economic activity, has ceased to be viable, also leading to inflationary pressures. And the battle against inflation has taken the form of strongly recessionary policies, based on curtailment of the money supply.

In accordance with the classic behaviour pattern of market economies, the cuts in private investment and spending should have led to a fall in interest rates, but here another factor intervened. This was a huge fiscal deficit, which was being aggravated by the recession and whose financing took the form of a large-scale tapping of the capital market. The limited supply of domestic credit, combined with the pressure being exerted on the credit market by the government, led to a sharp rise in interest rates, bringing considerable transfers of capital to the American financial markets. The consequent rise in the value of the dollar created an increased demand for imports and reduced their cost, thus helping to cushion the inflationary pressures at work in the country.

In sum, the attempts being made to absorb inflationary pressures in the United States have not only led to a massive transfer of real resources to that country, but have also created a recessionary world outlook against which the other industrialised countries can do little or nothing. This is why the economic recovery under way in America, stimulated by tax cuts and by the sharp increases in military spending since the end of 1982, has little positive effect abroad. The resumption of private investment has intensified the capital drain on the Euro-dollar market, weakening the currencies of other countries, which defend themselves by stepping up their restrictive measures. On the other hand, the rise in the value of the dollar has reduced the competitive capacity of the American economy and has thus imposed limits on the expansionist process within the United States itself.

The international banking system, which benefits from the instability of the exchange rate, is constantly on the look-out for signs of weakness in a major currency, so that it can embark on a process of destabilising the currency concerned. But any attempt by a government to take corrective measures designed to offset the recessionary pressures coming from abroad will immediately lead to a loss of reserves, with the threat of destabilisation of the exchange rate. Unlike the US, other countries are not in a position to continue financing a large budget deficit by resorting to the international financial market without seriously compromising the stability of their own currencies. By deliberately creating conditions to bring about a rise in real rates of interest, the US authorities are placing a heavy burden on countries with debts payable in dollars. The extra charge can represent a significant proportion of domestic savings and considerably reduces the capacity to import. The four-fold increase in real interest rates between 1979 and 1982[10] has forced many Third World countries to assign a substantial share of their export earnings to the payment of interest charges to American banks. In this way, countries with low income levels, and with a large part of their population living in conditions of absolute misery, have become net exporters of real resources to the United States. The transnationalisation process appears to have introduced distortions into relations between national economies which cannot be corrected by means of the policy instruments at present available to national governments and international agencies.

An overall view, such as that outlined here, of the multiple forms that this distortion takes would indicate that the recurring periods of recession during the past decade had their origin in a growing erosion of the means of regulation and control available to the dominant economic systems. There can be little doubt that the present erratic evolution of international economic trends bears little resemblance to the classical crisis models in which there are simultaneous contractions in investment, factor prices and unemployment. The problem today lies less in the cyclical nature of certain processes in the market economies than in the difficulty of harmonising decisions taken by the governments of major national economies, given the new forms of interdependence and dependence that have arisen and the emergence of a sphere of transnational activities beyond the reach of existing systems of coordination and control.

If it is evident that there has been an erosion of the means of action available to governments, it is equally evident that the institutional framework for activities conducted on the transnational plane is totally inadequate. The Bretton Woods rules were devised in terms of an international reality which was already in the process of disappearing, and were applied at the convenience of the government exercising tutelary power. Hence the transnationalisation process was able to proceed outside any institutional framework capable of regulating its advance. In a world of floating exchange rates and the free circulation of capital lent at interest rates subject to short-term adjustment, the manipulation of information on a global scale has become an unparalleled instrument for wielding economic power. That power is being exercised by banks and enterprises whose sole aim is to increase their own sphere of action. Controlling small countries, which are transformed into platforms for international action, transnational agents are often beneficiaries of instability in the economies of the major countries. Against such agents, governments are mostly powerless and prefer simply to adopt placatory positions.

Challenges and options

The impasse which is creating intermittent recession can only be overcome if the traditional means of regulating international economic relations are restored or if new means of action are introduced for this purpose. What is needed, in fact, is to match the new forms of interdependence with internal balances guaranteed by authorities invested with political power, whether these be national or international. If national decision centres reduce their field of action and if international authorities fail to fill the gap, there will be growing disorder in international economic relations. A decline in these relations and/or in productive activities will be inevitable. The aim is not so much to curb transnationalisation as to subject it to economic policy objectives formulated at national or international level. The transnationalisation process was in large part a result of technological progress, particularly in the field of communications and information. The power it generated interfered not only in international relations, making them more complex and uneven, but also in the domestic control of national economies. It is at the latter level that action is required, and adequate means must be found to restore autonomy of decisionmaking at national level or at the level of groups of countries which agree to act in concept. The problem is most urgent in the case of monetary and financial systems which are the main centres of instability.

The first step required for the repair of the international economy is to solve the problem of the excessive indebtedness of so many Third World countries. Without this, it will be difficult for international trade to recover its impetus. To condemn poor countries to devote a substantial part of their savings and external payments capacity to the servicing of external debts inflated by an arbitrary rise in interest rates is not only irrational but a profound injustice. Yet two measures would be sufficient to restore normality to a large sector of the international economy—a return to normal rates of real interest and the setting of maximum percentages for the value of exports which can be used by debtor countries for servicing their external debt. The restructuring of assets held by creditor banks is a problem for the attention of the central banks of the countries involved.

In the absence of measures such as these, the prolonged downward movement in the economic activity of debtor countries, and the risk of default,
will continue to be a negative factor in international economic relations.

The second point requiring immediate consideration is the creation of
channels for transferring capital in favour of Third World countries. In
order to link such transfers to self-liquidating projects, and to encourage
the orderly development of international trade, they should be regulated
by specialised institutions run with the effective participation of the governments of both creditor and debtor nations. Nothing can have been more
damaging to the international economic order than the financing of long-
term investments on the basis of short-term deposits held by banks with
no experience whatever in specialised credit arrangements. A necessary
condition for the achievement of stability in the international economic
order is that capital transfers be subject to some form of control. This
requires joint action by national and international authorities. The idea of
a private international banking system holding no compulsory reserves,
subject to no supervisory control system and with no access to rediscount-
ing lines is incompatible with the orderly functioning of international
economic relations. Countries with a structural tendency to run surpluses
on their balance of payments should be made to comply with a framework
of rules, which would enable them to reconcile defence of their own
domestic interests with the orderly absorption of surpluses by countries
in deficit. To transfer the full weight of adjustment to the latter, in the style
of the IMF, is both irrational and unfair.

Creation of liquidity always implies appropriation of resources by the
agents responsible. If such appropriation takes place on the international
plane, it should be in accordance with rules agreed upon by the international community within the framework of a policy of cooperation
designed to favour the least privileged, or at least to assist in redressing
the balance in relations between countries. In the present situation, the
creation of international liquidity favours countries issuing reserve
currencies, particularly the United States, and the transnationalised banks.
Thanks to the privileges they enjoy, the latter are induced to over-expand
credit, which encourages destabilising speculation in currencies and
creates waves of inflationary pressure.

Strict control over the creation of international liquidity requires the
introduction of a reserve currency devised by international authorities.
Until this objective is achieved, private transnationalised banks should be

subject to some form of control designed to limit their field of action to financing short-term self-liquidating business transactions or commercial operations backed by government institutions.

But the coherence of the international economy depends above all on the internal equilibrium of national economies. The biggest mistake made when transnationalisation was in full swing was to think that the international economy had an inherent rationality, which would govern the economic activities of individual countries.[11] The assumption was that transnationalisation was simply the formative stage of a new economic system of global dimension, the logic of which would inexorably come to prevail over national economies. To oppose such a process was to try to restrain 'progress'. A mitigated form of this doctrine is implicit in the current belief that the international competitiveness of a productive activity is the final test of its economic rationality. The central aim of economic policy becomes a question of maximising external trade rather than the level of economic activity. What is ignored is the fact that productivity increases generated by coherent investment, social discipline and outlays on research and development are what produce effective performance in external markets, and not vice-versa.

How can we fail to realise that the only detectable rationality in the international economy is grounded on national interest? Indeed, the only *raison d'être* for international relations is that the sum of the advantages enjoyed by the participants is positive. It is up to each country to weigh up the advantages and disadvantages of the various types of external economic relations which it maintains. If there is to be a plurinational whole with a voice of its own, there must be plurinational decisionmaking bodies capable of defining the common interests of the countries making up the whole.

The problem deserves special attention in the case of the Third World countries. Historically, their entry into international trade created forms of external dependence which are often reflected internally in serious social imbalances. Thus, their external relations are a factor in domestic control. Transnationalisation brought new dimensions to the pattern of dependency. And the more relatively backward the economy, the further removed will be the logic of its development from that governing the transnationalisation process. This problem is at the heart of the debate on the need to bring about a change in the so-called 'international economic order'—that is, the rules governing relations between national economic systems. Thus, in the Third World countries even more than in the industrially advanced nations, the restructuring of external relations required in order to overcome the present crisis involves an effective recovery of the capacity to define the objectives of development itself.

There is no doubt that we will find the greatest challenges of the present time on the international plane, where there has been an intense proliferation of economic activity without any corresponding advance in the institutional framework. And it is in periods when institutions have been eroded and prove inadequate that human creativity is faced with its most difficult tasks. Until these are tackled, we shall continue to live in uncertainty, under constant threat of slipping into increasingly irrational forms of international confrontation.

Notes

1. In the period between 1950 and 1973 the capitalist market economies grew at an annual rate of nearly 5 per cent, more than doubling the average rate of growth of the previous century. In 1974 and 1975 there was zero growth; from 1976 to 1979 the rate was 4 per cent and from 1980 to 1981 it was 1.1 per cent. See the various data published by the International Monetary Fund in *World Economic Outlook*.
2. During the first half of the present century world trade in manufactured products grew less than manufacturing production. *Cf.* A Maizels, *Industrial Growth and World Trade* (London, 1963) pp 139–40 and 388. In the preceding half century we find the inverse trend. See A G Kenwood and A L Lougheed, *The Growth of the International Economy 1820–1960* (London, 1971) p 90.
3. *CF.* C Furtado, 'O capitalismo pós-nacional' in *Prefácio à Nova Economia Politica* (Rio de Janeiro, 1976).
4. The historical tendency for a deterioration in the terms of trade of countries exporting primary products was attributed by Prebisch to this form of behaviour by the industrialised countries, in his seminal study on the imbalances in international trade published in 1949.
5. The value of world exports rose from US$574 billion to US$836 billion between 1973 and 1974, while the physical volume of exports increased by only 3 per cent. See *Le Commerce International*, GATT, various issues.
6. Cf. *Multinational Corporations in World Development*, UN, 1973 and 1978.
7. Data given by Michael Moffitt in *The World's Money* (New York, 1983) p 136.
8. Cf. A Lindbeck, 'The recent slowdown of productivity growth' in *The Economic Journal*, March 1983.
9. On this point see the interesting article by Alain Cotta, 'Le poids croissant des dépenses militaires dans l'économie mondiale' in *Le Monde* (Paris), 17 May 1983.
10. See *Etude sur l'Economie Mondiale*, 1983, United Nations, p 8.
11. For a criticism of the 'global monetarism' of Professor Milton Friedman, which implies the postulation of a rationality proper to international markets, see C Furtado, 'Transnacionalizacaó e Monetarismo' in *Pensamento Iberoamericano*, No. 1, Madrid, January–June 1982.

4
Self-reliance for self-determination: the challenge of Latin American foreign debt

Aldo Ferrer

Latin America's relations with the International Monetary Fund (IMF) and the international financial community today raise problems which are fundamentally different from those of the past. The main differences are to be found in the matter of the origin of, and responsibility for, balance-of-payments deficits, the policies of the developed countries and the present-day vulnerability of the international financial system.

Origin of the balance-of-payments deficits

During the 1950s and 1960s periodic exchange deficits arose, as export earnings proved inadequate to pay for required imports. The repetition of this disequilibrium between domestic economic activity and external purchasing capacity gave rise to the so-called 'stop-go' growth model. That is, the external restraint called for periodic action to reduce economic activity and imports, in order to restore the equilibrium in international payments. In these circumstances, the Latin American countries would resort to the IMF in order to secure the temporary financing that would facilitate adjustment. They then committed themselves to a period of restrictive fiscal and monetary policies, and to the devaluation of their national currencies, in order to change relative prices in favour of export activities, as well as checking inflation.

The Latin American structuralist school of thought developed precisely in response to such policies, which ignored the deep roots of external disequilibrium and inflation. On the whole, however, the adjustments strategies did succeed in restoring equilibrium in international payments, though at a substantial social cost. The borrowing arrangements with the IMF entailed short-term commitments at the expiration of which the governments regained control of their economic policies, whatever their merits might be. Consequently, the Latin American countries did not lose control of their development strategies for indefinite periods of time.

Today the situation is quite different. The international payments disequilibrium does not originate in a disparity between domestic economic activity and foreign trade. It is induced by the huge external debt of the major Latin American countries. It is not a short-term phenomenon and, consequently, the problem cannot be solved through temporary adjustment programmes. The Latin American countries must adopt an entirely new approach to their overall development strategies and international position, if they are to cope with a disequilibrium which looks set to be of long duration.

Responsibility for the crisis

In the past, one would probably have accepted the IMF's view that such countries had to pay the price of the adjustment process because ultimately the disequilibrium was the result of faults in their own domestic economic policies. Under the conditions of the time, it is true that the countries may have got into debt because of unwise balance-of-payments policies. A case in point is Argentina, whose debt to private international banks increased sevenfold between 1975 and 1982, while overall production remained unchanged. But the problem does not end there. During the 1970s, the international banks were eager to invest their surplus funds and found excellent clients among the major countries of Latin America. The debts incurred by Argentina, Brazil, Mexico, Venezuela and other countries in the region largely reflect the aggressive policies of the international banks. Latin America accounts for over 50 per cent of aggregate bank loans to the developing world. Without imposing any conditions whatsoever, the banks financed such irresponsible and destructive economic policies as those followed by Argentina and Chile. It is the private international banks which are largely responsible for the financial crisis now afflicting the world's debtor countries and the world economy.

The policies of the developed countries

The third difference in the world economic situation today compared with the past lies in the behaviour of world trade and the international financial system. Until the early 1970s, there was sustained trade expansion, and protectionism in the industrialised countries was on the wane. Moreover, as a result of the financial policy followed at that time by the United States, interest rates were low and often negative in real terms. The purchasing power of exports grew and the cost of credit was either moderate or negative in real terms. Under such conditions, orthodox programmes had a permissive external framework which permitted rapid restoration of equilibrium.

This position has undergone a radical change over the past few years. The industrialised countries are following policies which inhibit the exporting capacity of debtor countries. Protectionism in the United States and the European Economic Community (EEC)—coupled with the export subsidies being granted by these countries in respect of commodities competing with Latin American products (cereals, meat, etc)—has brought about a deterioration of the terms of trade and a reduction of export volumes. This reduces the Latin American countries' capacity to meet their debt service payments. Furthermore, the fiscal and monetary policies of the US have substantially raised real interest rates.

The concurrence of these developments has made it impossible for most Latin American countries to pay their external debts—in other words, they have been plunged into international insolvency. This situation is similar to that created by reparations imposed on Germany by the Treaty of Versailles after World War I. The policies followed by the victors prevented Germany from generating the balance-of-payments surplus needed to pay the reparations. This led to the collapse of the mark in 1923 and to tensions that culminated in the emergence of Nazism.

Vulnerability of the international financial system

The fourth main difference in the economic problems of the present lies in the fact that, during the 1950s and 1960s, Latin American payments difficulties were purely a domestic problem. Today, they have assumed international proportions. Latin America's debt is double the combined equity of the major banks of the United States. In contrast to the situation in the 1950s and 1960s, the IMF does not now have adequate resources to meet the emergency. The external debt of the developing world, excluding oil-producing countries, amounts to US$600 billion, and interest paid to US$60 billion. On the other hand, the IMF's total resources are less than US$100 billion. The role of the IMF is restricted mainly to advising the private banks, whose policy now consists in collecting the interest that is due, increasing their fees and commissions, and spreading and reducing their net credit flows to Latin America.

Thus, in spite of the severity of the adjustment programmes that have been adopted, debtor countries continue to be subjected to unceasing pressure and demands from their creditors, who appear to be unaware that suspension of payments by one or more principal debtors in Latin America would cause several major banks to go into liquidation. So far, there is no last-resort lending agency capable of fending off such a risk. At the same time, the banks in the United States and other industrialised countries have only a weak political position and there is little inclination to save them from the consequences of their unwise conduct.

These four differences illustrate the unreasonableness of the present attitude of the IMF and the international financial community towards the external indebtedness of Latin America. The whole burden of adjustment is expected to be carried exclusively by debtor countries which are responsible for only part of the problem. Argentina or Brazil may be able to pay for their own mistakes, but not for those of the United States and the creditor banks. Yet neither recent experiences nor the obvious risks have helped to improve the operating practices of banks. Since the start of the crisis in the early 1980s, they have been fleecing their debtors by making additional charges in their debt refinancing arrangements which are considered, even in responsible circles in the United States and Europe, to be scandalous extortion. The argument of risk used to justify this attitude of creditors is untenable. The risk exists already and it is not now a question of negotiation of new loans. Furthermore, increased costs reduce the paying capacity of debtor countries even more.

Debt and sovereignty

The external debt of Latin American countries poses major problems for their economic activity, employment and the standard of living. It is also a challenge to the sovereignty of the debtor countries—that is, to the right of the peoples in those countries to decide their own destinies. The present arrangements between the debtor countries on the one hand and the IMF and the creditor banks on the other are different in nature from those of the past. The latter were temporary commitments to remedy temporary balance-of-payments disequilibria. Today, the arrangements involve commitments of indefinite duration, because the magnitude of the indebtedness forces debtor countries to resort to debt refinancing and to long-term commitments in regard to their economic policies.

Interest payments alone today represent an extraordinarily high proportion of available resources and of external paying capacity. The debtor countries are compelled to keep down domestic demand for both consumer and capital goods in order to release the necessary funds. In Argentina, interest represents about 8 per cent of GDP. Since the appropriate funds have to be transferred abroad, there must be a balancing entry in the balance of payments amounting to 60 per cent of the value of exports The figures for the other major debtors in Latin America are comparable. The necessary shrinkage of economic activity and of the standard of living is enormous.

For this adjustment to be possible without inflationary pressures, the government must levy taxes and depress both the real wages of workers and corporate profits. Private expenditure on consumer and capital goods has to be reduced in order to generate the necessary surplus between domestic production and demand. As this is politically and socially difficult to achieve, governments then turn to large-scale deficit financing, which leads to substantial monetary expansion. Thus, the necessary reduction in wages and profits is accomplished through inflation. The recent increase of inflation should be interpreted as a manifestation of the adjustment intended to permit payment of debt at a time when workers and corporations are reluctant to accept further deterioration of their real incomes.

Under such conditions, the only way to revive the economy and relieve the external pressure is to increase exports. But this is very difficult at present in view of the trends prevailing in world markets. Moreover, the contraction of industrial production brought about by a shrinkage of the domestic market reduces the potential for industrial exports. Thus, the debtor countries are gradually reduced to the simple role of producers and exporters of foodstuffs and raw materials. Consequently, the current orthodox adjustment strategy leads to a shrinkage of the economy, de-industrialisation and further increases in prices.

The external debt thus acquires a deep political significance. At the international level, it reveals the hegemonic aim of the world's power centres to reduce Latin America to a peripheral and dependent position. At the national level, it leads to consolidation of those groups belonging to preindustrial and bureaucratic structures which are closely connected with financial speculation. The North-South conflict and political tensions within debtor countries have been exacerbated by the external debt.

These political consequences run counter to the prevailing trends both in our own countries and the rest of the world. During the past few decades, Latin American development has been inadequate and socially unjust. But one cannot overlook the growth of the region's economic potential. Industrialisation, the manufacture of capital goods, technological progress, the improved quality of human resources, the growth and diversification of exports and the expansion of domestic markets have enlarged the frontiers of Latin American development and enhanced the region's ability to achieve self-financing through domestic saving. Poverty and injustice are still rampant, but the economic potential is much greater than it was at the end of World War II.

In the international sphere, in turn, there is a proliferation of centres of power. It is true that the monetary system continues to exhibit the overwhelming supremacy of the dollar with the concomitant dependence on US fiscal and monetary policies. But, how long can this situation last in view of the well-recognised growth of centres of real economic power outside the United States? The superpowers have even lost the capacity to discipline their own areas of influence. The recent experiences of the United States in Central America and of the Soviet Union in Afghanistan and Poland reveal the limitations of the Great Powers, as well as the costs of continuing to exercise the traditional mechanisms of domination.

Finally, the current insolvency of the Latin American countries imperils the stability of international banking. A reciprocal vulnerability affects both debtors and creditors. The Latin American economies cannot be subordinated indefinitely to external adjustment schemes that will destroy the wealth accumulated and the progress achieved over the past few decades. These countries will neither liquidate themselves nor submit indefinitely to policies of impoverishment that will ultimately lead to chaos—and the formal suspension of their debt service payments. These orthodox policies are also a burden on the industrialised countries. The United States sends 40 per cent of its exports to developing countries, and the rest of the world shows a comparable percentage. Adjustment on orthodox lines of the economies of the debtor countries depresses world trade, as well as economic activity and employment in the world's industrialised centres themselves.

Self-reliance for self-determination

The international insolvency in which our countries find themselves therefore confronts us with this crucial issue: are we, or are we not, sovereign countries able to decide our own destiny? The answer does not lie in isolationism or aspirations of self-sufficiency, but in regaining control of our economies so that our development and international standing are in keeping with our potential, and the need to preserve freedom and democracy where it exists and to implant it where it does not.

How then should we conduct ourselves at this critical juncture? The simple prescription is that we must live within our means. This implies that, while the crisis lasts, we should rely on our own resources to solve it, restarting the growth process and recovering international viability.

This issue of sovereignty arose long before the moratorium imposed by Mexico triggered off an international financial crisis in August 1982. With or without external debt, the development models prevailing in Latin America have touched bottom. Even before the present financial crisis, policies based on external indebtedness had lost viability. It is impossible to continue accumulation and growth models based on income concentration and on the extreme poverty of important segments of Latin American populations.

At the same time, the trends prevailing in the world economy since the early 1970s demonstrate the impracticability of growth strategies founded on the integration of Latin American economies into the world market. Under the conditions now existing in the greater part of Latin America, the only possible answers to underdevelopment and dependence are national integration, development of the domestic market, promotion of new trade channels and a new international stance, and regional co-operation.

The level of external debt highlights the economic problems of the Latin American countries, but it is not the main cause of these problems. International insolvency, however, reduces the possibility of implementing independent policies designed to achieve the basic objectives of individual countries. Financial vulnerability has reduced the freedom of action of governments to such an extent that to speak of 'economic policy' is linguistic licence. It will not be possible to restate the strategy for development and social change without regaining that freedom of action which is essential to manage national economic policies. Without this, the governments of debtor countries will continue to be reduced to the position of administrators of their external debt in the name of, and on behalf of, the international banks.

A settlement of the international payments problem and financial reorganisation are, consequently, indispensable. But, what settlement and what reorganisation? This question has two possible answers. One consists in using the orthodox strategy, the consequences of which we are now witnessing. The other, lies in a restatement of development strategy starting from, first, a profound financial reform that will eliminate the current budgetary and monetary disequilibria and, second, programmes for the use of available foreign exchange in conformity with priorities aimed at economic recovery and an affordable schedule of repayment of the external debt.

At this critical juncture, assertion of the right to sovereignty requires self-financing through one's own resources. Latin America's potential and its present capacity to make external payments are sufficient for a resumption of the growth process, as well as to cope with the most pressing social problems and to recover international viability. This observation holds good for most of the region.

The current experience of the major Latin American countries is comparable to the situation of the European economies in the post-1945 period, which was characterised by heavy indebtedness, huge budgetary gaps, strong inflationary pressures and a severe imbalance in international payments. Under these conditions, it is necessary to introduce profound financial reforms in order to restore equilibrium in the public sector, check monetary expansion and settle external claims. The causes of disequilibrium differ from country to country, but a number of common features may be identified in the different national realities.

An exaggerated growth of bureaucratic structures and overdevelopment of the State are to be found everywhere. There have thus emerged new sources of power and privilege which have little to do with development, social change, and the assertion of sovereignty. It is essential to put an end to the feudalism of some government enterprises and bureaucratic centres, which distort the use of resources. In many countries—as in Argentina—the armed forces use resources beyond the actual needs of internal security and national defence. Military expenses and arms imports have become a major factor in the wastage of resources and in creating imbalance in external payments and the federal budget. The role of the State as an essential tool for development and consolidation of sovereignty has to be restored. To this end, it is essential to dismantle the structures of bureaucratic privilege.

In the second place, most countries in Latin America need to introduce radical fiscal reforms in order to achieve a level of self-financing in the public sector, with the tax burden based on efficiency and standards of social equity, and public expenditure channelled towards basic social needs. The current disequilibria are reflected in an exaggerated expansion of money supply and in strong inflationary pressures. Internal privileges associated with underdeveloped structures are, of course, very difficult to remove. It is easier to protest against the injustices of the international economic order than to introduce a tax reform.

The third determinant of the budgetary gap is associated with public external debt service payments. In Argentina, in the 1970–74 period, these payments accounted for 12 per cent of the aggregate sales of government enterprises (energy, oil, communications, etc). Today, this proportion exceeds 50 per cent. It is not possible to restore equilibrium in the federal budget without rescheduling the greater part of accrued interest and the whole of the instalments of external debt principal. The equilibrium of the federal budget and the release of external purchasing power largely depend on a limitation of debt service payments to the real paying capacity of our countries. On average, Latin American countries are probably unable to devote more than 10 per cent of the value of their exports to the payment of interest on foreign debt.

At this juncture, foreign exchange has again become the critical—and scarcest—resource. Subject to a strict system of priorities for external expenditure, the exports of most of our countries allow both payment for the imports needed to use installed productive capacity and also capital formation. The current disequilibrium is financial, not commercial. Hence the need to 'live on a cash basis'—that is, to pay for imports out of current export earnings. Starting from this decision to operate within one's own means and to pay cash for imports, a new bargaining position *vis-à-vis* foreign creditors should then be set up.

In contrast to orthodox adjustment, a national strategy does not imply a generalised contraction of production and employment and the standard of living. The adjustment addresses budgetary, monetary and balance-of-payments disequilibria by eliminating privileges, redistributing income, rescheduling external debt payments and dissolving unproductive bureaucratic structures. Once budgetary and monetary equilibrium has been restored and external purchasing power released, it will be possible to expand employment and the standard of living. The cost of adjustment should not be borne by the low-income segments of the population, since they have already been hard hit by the recession and traditional underdevelopment problems. Moreover, the democratisation process now under way and the growing pressures for freedom reduce the political viability of orthodox strategies based on deindustrialisation and impoverishment.

Latin America has no choice but to defend unconditionally its national sovereignty and the right of our peoples to freedom and well-being. Our external debt should be negotiated starting from these premises. This is only possible if we put our house in order—that is, if we restore budgetary and monetary equilibrium and work out strict programmes for the use of available foreign exchange. Under such conditions, it will be possible to find compromise formulae that will permit debt rescheduling and the removal of the present serious threat to the private international banks. It is common knowledge that it will be possible to pay our debts only through the new credit flows, as has always been the case in the past. What we are discussing here is the conditions under which the credit flows will be resumed—conditions that will permit the restoration of the international solvency of the debtor countries and save the creditor banks from bankruptcy. These conditions do not involve any impairment of our national sovereignty or of the right of our countries to democracy and freedom.

In short, the external debts of Argentina, Brazil and Mexico will not be negotiated in New York or London, but in Buenos Aires, Brasilia and Mexico City. If our countries are able, by virtue of their own national decisions, to restore the budgetary and monetary equilibrium and to live within their means, the debt problem will be resolved. In the absence of a solution, financial disorder and social tension will reach unbearable limits. And the quickest way to default and to repudiation of the external debt is insistence on orthodox adjustment strategies.

5
Political cooperation, border disputes and democracy

Juan Somavía

Latin America and the Caribbean have been prolific in promoting schemes of regional economic cooperation. These range from bilateral treaties on trade and payments to agreements on integration, and are an area in which the region can claim rich experience. This activity has again today a major role to play in relation to national development strategies, as was indicated in the recent Declaration of Quito and its plan of action.[1]

The same cannot be said for political agreements. This issue has been the subject of little thought and still less action. Since the countries of Latin America gained their independence, the area's political history has been characterised by mutual indifference and conflict rather than by collaboration. But today, as we stand at the threshold of the 21st century, it is ever-more essential to give priority to ways of extending political cooperation.

During past decades, the attitude in Latin America has been that economic integration would lead inevitably to cooperation in the political sphere. But experience shows the inadequacy of this approach. Instead, we should be asking whether the reverse is not the case—i.e. that increased political cooperation would not perhaps be an important means of accelerating economic collaboration. Although so little has been done in the area of political cooperation, there is no reason to suppose that progress cannot be made. Indeed, there are two important precedents for regional cooperation in Latin American history—the fight for independence and the shared feelings of rejection against foreign intervention.

The precedents

The emergence of the republics of Spanish America was characterised by solidarity on a continental scale in the face of colonial domination. The creation of armies that liberated one country after another from foreign rule is evidence of the depth of American consciousness at this period and of a general awareness of unity as the basis of our strength as nations.

Yet the vision of Bolivar did not find its realisation in any of the new republics, and the continental feeling which had been aroused against the colonial power was rapidly transformed into a petty nationalism in a variety of forms. Divisive jealousy, struggles for power and petty betrayals were rampant, and made even Bolivar say that he had 'ploughed in the sea'. The main effect of this disunity was an eruption of wars and conflicts which hardened into the numerous border disputes which still divide us today and represent one of the major obstacles to cooperation.

At the same time, the ideals of unity, solidarity and a common destiny have left their mark, and are indelibly stamped on the cultural traditions of the continent. It would be difficult to find any significant opposition to regional cooperation. On the contrary, it is an ideal which is a prevailing theme of political discussion.

But, in practical terms, cooperation cannot thrive solely on rhetoric recalling our similarities and common history. There must also be a realistic recognition of the national and regional differences which exist in Latin America. In creating a Latin American consciousness, we must start from these 'cultural, racial, economic, social and political variations'. Only by recognising existing differences can we ensure that the fullest possible cooperation is achieved.[2]

Latin America has paid a high price for its experience of political independence. First British, and later North American, intervention absorbed us into their spheres of interest, so that they could exploit our wealth and culture all the more easily. In different periods, we have endured the full ferocity of the great powers in defending their spheres of interest. We learnt about imperialism from our own experience long before we read about it in books. Yet the present East–West divide is the same story told all over again: it is the superpowers' desire for hegemony in Latin America simply expressing itself in a new context.

This is something else that stimulates feelings of Latin American nationalism: deep in our regional consciousness is a fundamental, almost instinctive, attitude—we do not like to be told what to do and we demand the right to run our own affairs. A sense of regional dignity has evolved over the years, mingling cultures, races and ideologies, which encourages us to defend ourselves and work together when faced with hostility from outside. Both the legacy of Bolivar, and contemporary attempts to bring Latin America under foreign hegemony, encourage us to think in terms of regional political cooperation.

Priorities

What are the priority areas for regional political cooperation? Among others, there are:

1) Greater involvement by Latin America in preserving world peace through, for example, the creation of national and regional peace movements;

2) identification of the principles, mechanisms and governmental and non-governmental spheres in which we can promote democracy in the region;

3) the gradual solution of all border disputes;

4) bilateral and multilateral negotiations on reducing arms spending;

5) development of a Latin American doctrine of regional security, which distinguishes between internal order and security against external attack, and, at the same time, allows the region to distance itself from the tendency to define relations in terms of the East–West divide;

6) development of a Latin American doctrine of non-alignment;

7) the elevation of respect for basic human rights to a fundamental principle in relations between Latin American nations;

8) development of a Latin American doctrine of ideological pluralism;

9) nuclear disarmament in Latin America;

10) the establishment of a Latin American centre for military and strategic studies, which will look into the whole range of factors involved in defining the role of the armed forces in strengthening democracy in the region;

11) the study of the possibility of giving a Latin American parliament power to take decisions on matters relating to political cooperation, and to consider the feasibility of having national representatives chosen by direct elections;

12) the strengthening and encouragement of relations between non-governmental organisations, particularly between political parties, union organisations, social movements and human rights bodies;

13) the promotion of agreements at government and non-governmental level aimed at increasing the flow of information through independent channels within the region; and,

14) the setting up of permanent mechanisms of political coordination

and decision-making, and the development of the capacity of the Latin American Economic System (SELA) to take political action.

Past experience

Each of these areas for consideration and action will take time to put into practice. However, in many of them, initiatives have already been taken, or are being developed. The most significant example has undoubtedly been the efforts of the Contadora Group to ensure that it is the Latin American countries themselves that resolve conflicts in Central America, and that these settlements come by negotiation. This demonstrates the concern of people in the region to prevent its internal problems being put into an East–West framework. Along the same lines, the foreign ministers of the Andean Pact countries recognised the Sandinista National Liberation Front as one of the key participants (a belligerent party) in the struggle against Somoza. This opened the way for official diplomatic recognition and established a new perspective, suggesting that tyrannies are not governments which legitimately represent their people.

In a different sphere, we find the common position of Latin American countries towards the United States during the Nixon Administration, which was expressed in the consensus of the Vina del Mar Agreement, the support shown in Latin America for Panama's struggle to reestablish its national sovereignty over the Panama Canal, and the increasing identification of people in different parts of Latin America with the aspiration for independence emerging in Puerto Rico. And we should add the backing which Argentina received from many different sources during the Malvinas War.

Then there is the Tlatelolco Treaty, whose aim is to bring about nuclear disarmament, and which, even if it has not won unanimous agreement, has established a regional framework for discussion on the issue. We should also remember Mexico's continuing efforts to promote disarmament at an international level—efforts which were distinguished by the award of the Nobel Peace Prize to Alfonso Garcia Robles, former foreign minister of Mexico.

As far as theory is concerned, it has recently been suggested that Latin America should designate itself a 'Peace Zone', in which discussions on regional security would be based on the following principles:

a) A clear distinction between problems related to the external security of countries in the region and the United States on the one hand, and problems of internal order within Latin American countries on the other;

b) A more precise definition of problems of external security, distinguishing international security problems from those of regional security, and identifying the possible interconnections between the two; and,

c) To complement the strategic-military concept of security with an awareness of economic factors which affect Latin American security, taking this in its broadest sense.[3]

Finally, there is the recent rapid development of relations between non-governmental social organisations at a Latin American level. These include political, business, union, religious, cultural and academic links, relations between youth and women's organisations, alternative information networks and various social movements.

All this indicates the existence of areas of cooperation in Latin America which need to be looked at in political terms, and it suggests that there has been sufficient experience of cooperation, even if it has been somewhat disorganised, to justify looking more closely at the issue. But it is important to move from a short-term approach, where action is taken in an ad hoc way to deal with problems as they arise, towards a vision which encompasses the whole. One of the principal issues today is the relationship between regional political cooperation and the strengthening of democracy. What can democratic governments and organisations in different countries do to give reciprocal support to processes of democratisation?

This question implies taking on regional and collective responsibility for the restoration of democracy and its stability over time, as well as the emergence of a concept of democracy which demands a democratisation of power structures as well as respect for individual and political rights. This in turn requires a recognition that democrats have the right to promote democracy. Social movements, political parties, academics and governments need to give urgent attention to these principles and to the mechanisms which will allow the development of a system of regional political cooperation between democratic organisations which share this aim.

Let us look in a little more detail at what we see as the main priorities for regional political cooperation—the preservation of peace, through the gradual solution of border and other disputes which exist in the area, and the playing of a greater part by Latin America in the strengthening of world peace.

Border disputes and democracy

The political power of the armed forces
We believe that the restoration and consolidation of stable democracies in Latin America will be based on the achievement of three interrelated objectives—the urgent introduction of internal changes which will ensure national integration in the political, economic, social and cultural spheres; an end to the use of an East–West perspective in explaining social and political change in the region; and a redefinition of the role of the armed forces, given South America's experience of authoritarian regimes in recent decades, and particularly the political role they have played.

Here we will deal only with this final objective, but its attainment is directly linked to the other two. We believe that any realistic political strategy must start from an urgent consideration of the major political tragedy in Latin America today—the steady increase in social polarisation in the region. The enormous difference between the standard of living of a small sector of well-off people and the misery of the vast majority is unacceptable in both social and human terms.

Statistics which ten years ago seemed tragic have become even worse since then. Our present inertia can only lead to violence and civil confrontation. Unless there is immediate and radical change, Latin America will be caught between the military power of the armed forces exercised to protect the privileged and violent uprisings by the people who oppose them.

The majority of the people in the region want a rapid but orderly transition to a new social order where they have greater solidarity and justice. This can only be achieved through effective national integration which gives equal opportunities to all to participate in politics, to have a share in the wealth produced by the economy, to be able to progress within the social system and to take their part in cultural development. If these changes are to be effective, they will inevitably affect the interests of the powerful, whose reaction will be to beat on the barrack doors to bring out the armed forces to defend their privileges. Because this has already happened in the past does not mean that it will not happen again. If no changes are made, the armed forces will continue to be a conservative political force which acts against the interests of the people.

Equally, we cannot afford to forget that since the formulation of the Monroe Doctrine, and the later reinforcement of this doctrine in the Yalta agreements, our region has been within the United States' sphere of influence. Right up to the present, every internal change which has benefited the majority of the people has been interpreted by the North American 'establishment' as basically inspired by the Soviet Union and Marxist ideology, or at least as acting in their interests. This interpretation is blind to the internal factors which lie behind social conflict in the region, and it inevitably encourages efforts to block and, in different ways, reverse the process of change. This approach also leads to a definition of the armed forces' role as that of 'having to prevent' change in the interests of freedom and democracy. If we do not stop using this East–West approach to explain social and political developments in the region, the armed forces will continue to be called on to play a conservative political role.

But if it is true that for significant groups within, and outside, a particular country the armed forces represent an instrument to be used in the last resort to prevent structural change, this is because they are a power in their own right, because society legitimises their professional activities within each country. The political power of the armed forces is based to a considerable extent on recognition by citizens, that it is they who protect the nation's territorial integrity.[4] It is acknowledged that within Latin America many disputes over the extent of national sovereignty remain unresolved, and that these could lead to armed conflict.

Given these conditions, the armed forces are able to insist that the country maintains a high level of arms spending in preparation for possible conflict. Naturally, this means that the political power of the armed forces and their latent ability to intervene in the political process through the use of force is maintained or increased. Furthermore, these arms purchases account for a significant proportion of national expenditure at the expense of other much more urgent social needs.

Can this vicious circle be broken and spending reoriented towards socially more productive investment, in order to reduce the political power of the armed forces and limit their ability to obstruct the democratic process? I believe that it is possible, but only within the context of regional political cooperation between social groups and democratic governments.

Given the situation which exists in Latin America today and the national differences between countries, it is obvious that the armed forces will continue to play a role in national politics, leaving democratic governments weakened to different degrees. It is extremely difficult for a democratic government acting in isolation to sustain a unilateral policy involving a significant reduction in military expenditure.

Giving greater weight to world peace

Can this be done at a regional level? Our starting point must be reassessment of the concept of peace as it is understood both at a world level and in national terms. Traditionally, Latin America has not been active in promoting peace and disarmament, except in the case of Mexico, which we mentioned earlier. This has been true at government, as much as at non-governmental, level. It has been treated as an issue which does not concern us—beyond making formal statements—and the principal role of the superpowers, and the special concern of the European countries, has been taken for granted.

We believe that this is a mistake, and that this tendency must be reversed. It is in the interests of the entire Latin American region to work actively to create the conditions for world peace and to reduce tensions between the superpowers. An easing of international relations will allow greater national and regional autonomy. An increase in tensions will give greater significance to the military might of the superpowers and their local allies; this in turn results in greater weight being given to the East–West approach in explaining political developments in Latin America.

Latin America should argue forcefully in favour of the position that neither of the superpowers, nor any of the countries who have their own atomic weapons, have any right to start a nuclear holocaust. This stand implies that Soviet and North American nuclear arsenals pose an equal threat. It must be social pressure throughout the world that makes peace inevitable. We have to keep the finger off the nuclear button, not by building up superfluous supplies of arms, but by bringing massive political pressure to bear.

The wishes of the people

This reassessment of the importance of world peace as a strategic objective for Latin America is the starting point for initiatives aimed at resolving border disputes. First of all, we need to identify two factors of significance in disputes over sovereignty. In some cases, the central issue in the dispute is one of access to, or rights over, material resources (rivers, the sea and mineral resources, for example); here the resolution of the dispute brings different degrees of material benefit for the parties involved. It is therefore understandable that each side will try to get the other to recognise what it sees as its own rights, and to ensure that the practical results of the final agreement are as favourable as possible. In other cases, the material advantage involved is less, or even non-existent—except for the sake of the legal argument between the two sides—and the resolution of the dispute in favour of one or other of the parties will not bring significant material gains.

This distinction shows how important it is to be objective about the motives behind the dispute, and to avoid subjective or emotional arguments, in order that people may have a clear understanding of the real interests at stake. It is very likely that if a survey were carried out in the region today, we would find that—except in a few cases—the issue is one on which public opinion in the countries concerned expresses itself with great feeling, but with little knowledge of the facts. Such issues are normally dealt with solely by civilian or military specialists, who are given full authority to protect national rights. This approach has made it very easy for governments and the armed forces to arouse nationalist sentiments among the people in support of the position taken by the country.

This situation—which has recurred throughout modern history—tends to produce an automatic increase in national chauvinism. National chauvinism on both sides makes it harder to find a negotiated settlement, and means that it takes longer to reach the necessary agreements. As long as the conflict remains unresolved, the role of the armed forces within the country is reinforced, and its argument for higher levels of military spending is strengthened.

This brings us to the question: is this what the people of the region want? Is this pattern the result of a choice made by the people, or of traditional inertia? We believe both these factors play their part, but that the problem is essentially the product of long-standing attitudes which no one has seriously questioned. This is not apparent today, because the definition of what really is the national interest in the resolution of conflicts over sovereignty has not been put forward in the terms outlined above.

This leads us to the conclusion that Latin America is trapped in a nineteenth century style of dealing with its conflicts. One needs political vision and imagination to look at them with the mentality of the twenty-first century. Of all the challenges that we face, this is certainly one of the most complex and delicate. However, if we want to guarantee the necessary conditions for the survival and strengthening of democracy in the region, we must confront this issue head on, and have at our disposal the means to resolve it. This is the responsibility of all democratic groups and all democratically elected governments, whatever their ideologies.

The starting point in determining what action should be taken must be the wishes of the people. We must create ways of finding out democratically what the people want. But the people's opinion will only be meaningful if adequate information has been available and there has been open discussion of the material interests at stake and the effects on military spending of finding a negotiated settlement to any specific border dispute. Looking at it from the other side, there should be discussion of the implications of entering an armed conflict in defence of national principles, with all that this will mean in terms of destruction and the loss of material resources and human life. To put it in political terms, there must be access to the information needed to allow the nation to decide between two options: to persist in rigid attitudes, which mean that the possibility of military conflict on the borders remains latent, and which reinforce the political power of the armed forces; or to adopt flexible attitudes which allow negotiated solutions to be found which are mutually acceptable and which help to bring a reduction in military spending and to redefine the role of the armed forces when border conflicts no longer exist.

This discussion of the problem takes it as self-evident that the choice which is made will affect not only the foreign relations of the country, but will also have enormous impact on the balance of political power within the country. In brief, this perspective considers that in dealing with conflicts over sovereignty, the implications for the internal political scene need to be emphasised as much as, or more than, the purely territorial aspects.

This argument is based on the following perception of what might be the popular opinion in the region if people were called upon to express their views on this question, being given adequate information and details of the implications of an armed conflict:

a) The majority of citizens would have no wish to participate in a conflict to determine the limits of sovereignty, and still less to participate in a battle between the superpowers;

b) the majority of citizens would prefer the diversion of a significant proportion of military spending into social and productive uses, as long as there were a political agreement to ensure that there would be no aggression from abroad;

c) the majority of citizens would not wish the armed forces to exercise power in internal politics; and,

d) the majority of citizens would prefer stable democratic governments to military regimes.

If the above comes near to reflecting true popular feeling in the region, then it is necessary to make this opinion public. This is beginning to happen through a number of channels. For example, a declaration signed recently at the border-crossing of El Cristo by young Chileans and Argentinians, who represent a broad spectrum of political opinion within both countries, states that: 'On the assumption that foreign aggression would create the necessary internal unity to revitalise governments which have been rejected by the majority of their peoples, the Latin American dictatorships have kept their people in permanent tension, threatening them with the possibility of wars with neighbouring countries. This has been the situation in Chile and Argentina in recent years.' The statement also declares: 'The promotion of military conflicts between sister nations is a means of strengthening the grip of dictatorships and blocking the restoration of democratic systems as in the case with Chile and other countries in the Southern Cone.'

The central part of the document backs up this declaration by saying: 'We conclude this meeting with an agreement of principle between young Chileans and Argentinians, that we will not participate in a war between our two countries,' and it adds that 'the mood in our two countries, and in particular of the young people in our countries, is profoundly in favour of peace; only democracy, which is the expression of true popular sovereignty, provides the conditions in which to build peace.' This could not be expressed more clearly. The document was signed on 28 January 1984. It is an example of what we see as the true popular feeling of Latin America.

Lines of action

On the basis of this situation, a series of measures need to be adopted in civil society, among which it is necessary:

1) To publish as widely as possible information about the implications of unresolved border disputes and the possibility of armed conflict;

2) to make the desire for peace with neighbouring countries and an easing of international tensions part of the everyday political platforms in each country;

3) to encourage general discussion and public debate on the threats to world peace and to peace in the region, and the relationship this bears to national spending on arms and the role of the armed forces in a democracy;

4) to organise peace movements at a national and regional level, designating a 'Latin American Peace Day', which could be the anniversary of the birth of Bolivar;

5) to identify, according to the conditions in each country, the most appropriate means through which the people's unwillingness to participate in armed conflict with neighbouring states can be expressed; and

6) to put pressure on governments to make them adopt the 'commitment to peace on the borders' which is mentioned below, and to encourage non-governmental organisations to support this initiative.

Whatever initiatives may be taken by ordinary citizens, decisions on these issues rest ultimately with governments. So it is the advances made at that level which will be decisive. However, we must be aware of the problems involved in taking active and vigorous action in this sphere. Our traditional inertia still weighs heavily. We must proceed with caution in order to be sure of our advance. It is more important that governments take action of the right kind than that they take action very quickly. The main emphasis should be on the responsibility of democratically elected governments to make sure that border disputes are settled through peaceful means and not aggression. The concern should be to preserve peace and ease tension.

We have the opportunity therefore of initiating a period of 'peaceful transition' towards a situation in which all unresolved conflicts in the region will have been settled. Obviously, this is not going to take place smoothly, and the resolution of some conflicts will depend, in different ways, on how other conflicts are resolved. But in the long run, it could lead to a general détente and a breaking up of the existing status quo, bringing radical changes in the overall political situation in Latin America and greatly increasing the chances of survival for democracy. This is why the concept of a transition is important, as is the political commitment to peace which it involves.

The transition to lasting peace could begin with a *'regional commitment to peace on the borders'*. This would be a multilateral commitment, and would express a determination to give political priority at regional level to settling unresolved border disputes. It would include an agreement not to employ threats or use force against other countries in Latin America and the Caribbean.

In this context, a number of complementary measures could be considered for application at a bilateral or multilateral level. Some of these are:

1) To set time limits in which to settle outstanding border disputes;
2) to seek—where it seems mutually acceptable—arbitration, mediation, offers of help, or other forms of involvement by third parties to facilitate bilateral understanding;
3) to take action to reduce arms spending on the basis of non-aggression pacts—a Tlatelolco agreement for regional disarmament;
4) to identify possible ways of introducing international guarantees of the inviolability of frontiers, with a commitment not to use force;
5) to reassess the existing patterns of arms purchases and the training of military personnel;
6) to develop an active policy of informing the public and creating awareness about the factors involved in border disputes;
7) to evaluate the contemporary justification for the TIAR in the context of the development of a regional doctrine of security and non-alignment;
8) to ensure that countries outside Latin America do not interfere in the settlement of regional border disputes; and,
9) to redefine the national role of the armed forces under democratic governments where there are no border disputes.

By listing all the measures which could be taken at government and non-governmental level it is possible to see the scope and significance which this issue could assume within our societies. We believe that we should move with caution in this direction. We have to establish clear objectives, even if it takes some time to achieve them. If we believe that it is necessary to promote regional political cooperation in order to strengthen democracy, this must be based on a clear understanding of the boundaries within which we can begin to resolve existing border disputes. This is what young people in Latin America, in the symbolic action of the young Chileans and Argentinians, are asking of democratic forces and governments. Do not let us ignore this call for the future.

Notes

1. Among other organisations, it is worth mentioning here ECLA, LAFTA, the Central American Common Market, Caricom, the Andean Pact, ALADI, and SELA (the Latin American Economic System).
2. These ideas have been dealt with in greater detail by Juan Enrique Vega, in an internal paper produced by ILET.
3. These ideas have been explored in greater detail by Carlos Portales in his article, 'Security and US–Latin American relations' *Conor Sur* 2 (4) November–December 1983. They were initially put forward in a document entitled *'Democracy and Foreign Policy'* by Gustavo Lagos, Heraldo Munoz, Carlos Portales and Augusto Varas, Chilean Association of Peace Studies (ACHIP), May 1983.
4. The political power is also explained by the fact that in many countries they contribute to national geographical integration. Furthermore, they are seen as expressing 'national' values.

6

Financial aspects of intra-regional trade in Latin America

José Antonio Ocampo

One of the most striking aspects of the current economic crisis in Latin America has been the collapse of intra-regional trade. Until very recently, reciprocal trade was regarded not only as the most visible sign of economic integration, but it was also seen as an important basis for a common defence policy in an eventual international crisis. Thus far, however, all such hopes have been frustrated. I hope to show that what lies at the root of this is a structural imbalance in intra-regional trade which emerged well before the present crisis, and a system of payments which fosters policies that restrict reciprocal trade. Thus it will become evident that a lasting solution will be possible only to the extent that these problems are overcome.

The rise and fall of intra-regional trade

Latin American intra-regional trade first flourished in the 1960s. Although part of this growth was associated with the regional integration schemes which were then under way, it was also part of a more general search for trade opportunities which had been overlooked both under export-led growth and in the more inward-looking models of development. This process was especially noticeable in the Central American Common Market, where intra-regional imports grew at an annual rate of 26.2 per cent in 1961–70, compared with 10.7 per cent for total imports from non-member countries. In the case of the Latin American Free Trade Association (LAFTA), the corresponding rates were 9.6 per cent and 5.5 per cent.[1]

By 1970 regional trade within the Latin American Integration Association (LAIA) already made up 11.6 per cent of total trade (excluding fuels) and 12.4 per cent for all developing countries of Latin America. Furthermore, manufactured goods accounted for 46.9 per cent of total intra-regional trade (excluding fuels) in LAIA and 53.6 per cent for the developing countries of the continent (see Table 1).

In the 1970s, the high rate of growth was sustained, based on the rapid expansion of the international economy until 1973 and the increased

Table 1

Growth of trade among developing countries of America

(Million dollars f.o.b.)

	(1) Intra-regional trade		(2) Intra-regional trade, excluding fuels.[a]		(3) Intra-regional trade of manufactured goods.[b]		(4) Intra-regional trade as a percentage of total trade, excluding fuels	
	Total	LAIA	Total	LAIA	Total	LAIA	Total	LAIA
1970	3,028	1,274	1,635	1,114	876	522	12.4%	11.6%
1973	5,013	2,340	2,938	1,971	1,777	1,110	13.5	11.8
1974	9,689	4,006	4,584	3,156	2,969	1,940	15.5	14.5
1975	9,616	4,024	5,089	3,268	3,018	1,950	17.2	16.3
1976	10,681	4,693	5,569	3,661	3,571	2,209	16.2	15.1
1977	11,685	5,778	6,651	4,582	4,255	2,824	16.3	15.5
1978	12,470	5,911	7,575	5,098	4,876	3,256	16.6	15.4
1979	18,350	8,916	10,184	7,741	6,628	4,911	18.5	18.8
1980	22,536	10,944	11,931	8,830	8,229	6,097	18.9	18.4
1981	26,501	11,107						

[a]SITC 3.
[b]SITC 5–8.

Source: United Nations, *Yearbook of International Trade Statistics*.

demand from the region's oil-producing countries, coupled with the boom in the international financial markets in the years following. Thus, excluding fuels, intra-regional trade grew at an annual rate of 22 per cent and 23 per cent for the developing countries of America and LAIA respectively, and by 1980 it came to account for 18.9 per cent and 18.4 per cent of the total trade of the two. Furthermore, the relative importance of manufactured goods was even more pronounced, reaching 69 per cent of this trade by 1980.

This network of reciprocal trade has crumbled during the recent crisis. The first to show signs of weakening was Central American trade, which in 1981 fell by 17 per cent and in 1982 had contracted 32 per cent compared with its peak 1980 level.[2] By 1982, however, the crisis began to affect LAIA trade. Although this had already experienced a small fall of 0.8 per cent in 1981, if oil products are excluded, its rapid decline began in the following year, reaching 17 per cent for total trade and 23 per cent excluding fuels.[3]

The slowdown of Andean trade lagged behind that of the Central American Common Market and LAIA as a whole, owing to the delay produced by Venezuela's adjustment policies and continuing high levels of imports in Colombia. Nevertheless, this trade had suffered a drop of 5.8 per cent in 1981, excluding fuels, and a further fall of 1.4 per cent in 1982. However, the real collapse came in 1983, when there was a drop of nearly 50 per cent.[4] Furthermore, depressive tendencies have continued throughout the Central American area and in LAIA, and the contraction of the Andean Group has dragged down the exports of other LAIA countries. Thus, it is no exaggeration to say that in 1983 intra-regional trade in Latin America was only half of what it was at its peak in 1980–81.

At the root of this dramatic contraction of trade lies the balance-of-payments policies which were pursued by all countries and which reserved for national production a larger proportion of aggregate domestic demand. The impact of these policies on intra-regional trade has done nothing to correct the balance-of-payments disequilibrium of the region as a whole. On the contrary, they have proved to be quite counter-productive, to the extent that the decline of non-traditional exports in the region has fed, in some countries, pessimism about these exports. The contraction of trade has also been ineffective from the point of view of a balance-of-payments adjustment, in that it has centred on those segments of intra-regional exchange which were in bilateral or multilateral equilibrium in the years preceding the crisis.

Table 2

Intra-regional trade of the main developing countries of America, 1979–1981
(Annual figures in million dollars; exports f.o.b.)

Exports from ＼ To	Bolivia	Colombia	Ecuador	Peru	Venezuela	Andean Group	Argentina	Brazil	Chile	Mexico	Paraguay	Uruguay	Rest of LAIA	Costa Rica	El Salvador	Guatemala	Honduras	Nicaragua	CACM	Dominican R.	Jamaica	Panama	Others	TOTAL
Bolivia	—	7.5	1.1	29.4	4.0	42.0	246.1	30.8	30.6	1.9	—	0.5	309.9	—	—	—	—	—	—	—	—	—	—	351.9
Columbia	2.8	—	65.8	29.4	322.8	420.8	55.5	6.5	40.6	17.3	0.5	1.2	121.6	3.5	0.7	—	1.3	0.1	22.3	5.6	2.0	52.2	46.6	671.1
Ecuador	0.6	72.0	—	10.5	43.0	126.1	36.7	35.4	47.1	17.0	—	0.8	137.1	5.4	1.8	1.1	—	0.4	2.4	—	2.0	88.4	455.2	944.1
Peru	65.2	72.5	67.4	—	56.1	261.2	43.8	95.4	146.6	64.3	0.2	5.4	328.1	2.1	96.3	108.7	0.5	80.7	9.2	22.0	165.0	66.0	63.0	669.8
Venezuela	—	250.0	15.3	23.0	—	288.3	55.3	613.3	234.7	28.3	0.2	2.5	539.7	2.0	—	—	58.0	—	412.7	229.6	165.0	149.7	4165.0	6420.0
Andean Group	68.6	402.0	149.6	92.3	425.9	**1138.4**	437.4	781.4	508.7	128.8	1.2	13.6	**1683.1**	116.8	102.4	116.8	63.6	83.4	446.6	229.6	167.1	356.3	4729.8	**9056.9**
Argentina	126.5	47.5	16.8	92.9	109.1	392.8	—	748.6	188.7	180.9	180.0	297.3	1773.4	17.6	9.6	1.1	3.4	3.9	47.3	3.8	1.6	40.3	24.3	1922.0
Brazil	187.3	168.3	51.3	153.0	278.7	838.6	896.7	—	172.7	468.3	394.3	297.3	1475.0	62.7	35.0	17.6	15.7	36.1	62.7	16.7	6.3	7.3	94.4	3595.3
Chile	23.3	69.9	21.5	53.6	73.9	242.2	249.2	485.0	—	66.3	6.7	9.8	716.7	9.0	10.7	9.0	19.3	65.7	266.6	9.0	—	15.6	6.7	985.3
Mexico	0.7	47.0	46.7	23.0	75.3	194.7	39.0	66.3	66.3	—	1.0	8.0	517.7	56.3	49.0	266.6	13.2	48.0	384.8	73.3	31.7	56.3	80.3	1196.3
Paraguay	0.6	0.2	—	0.2	0.2	1.2	64.6	394.3	1.0	3.0	—	11.0	129.6	0.4	—	0.1	—	—	0.4	—	—	2.5	0.8	132.0
Uruguay	1.8	3.1	0.8	5.4	2.5	13.6	113.7	175.4	20.3	4.5	13.2	—	327.1	—	0.1	0.1	0.3	—	0.4	—	0.3	—	0.4	342.1
Rest of LAIA	342.2	336.0	137.1	328.1	539.7	**1683.1**	1363.2	1773.4	716.7	517.7	129.6	327.1	**5707.7**	73.1	75.1	384.8	75.1	211.4	1012.8	73.3	75.8	69.2	206.9	**8173.0**
Costa Rica	1.0	3.5	5.4	2.1	2.0	13.5	1.4	—	1.7	6.5	—	0.1	12.2	—	47.3	65.4	28.7	82.8	224.2	3.8	1.6	40.3	8.7	304.3
El Salvador	0.5	0.7	1.8	—	0.2	2.1	0.1	—	0.2	0.5	0.1	—	0.9	162.6	—	65.4	53.5	36.1	255.4	0.5	0.1	7.3	2.3	268.7
Guatemala	0.5	—	1.1	—	1.4	3.9	0.2	—	0.3	0.8	0.1	—	34.8	192.7	30.6	—	53.5	65.7	384.8	6.1	0.7	15.6	2.8	448.7
Honduras	0.5	1.3	—	0.2	4.2	5.5	0.2	—	—	0.8	—	—	1.7	12.5	16.7	30.6	—	26.8	73.3	0.1	1.2	3.5	16.7	104.7
Nicaragua	—	0.1	—	—	0.5	0.8	0.1	—	—	2.5	—	—	2.9	32.7	12.5	16.7	13.2	—	75.1	0.1	—	2.5	0.7	82.1
Central American Common Market	1.5	5.6	8.3	2.1	8.3	**25.8**	2.0	4.3	2.2	43.8	0.1	0.1	**52.5**	177.6	45.7?	252.6?	95.9	211.4	1012.8	13.4	3.7	69.2	31.2	**1208.6**
Dominican Republic	—	1.7	—	0.1	68.3	70.0	—	0.2	0.5	0.8	—	0.1	0.8	0.5	0.1	0.1	0.4	—	1.0	—	2.0	0.5	22.3	96.6
Jamaica	—	0.3	—	0.1	22.5	22.9	0.2	1.9	0.5	0.8	0.5	0.8	4.2	0.2	0.3	0.3	0.2	—	0.7	2.1	—	2.4	76.6	108.9
Panama	—	3.2	1.9	0.2	5.7	11.4	0.2	0.1	0.5	1.3	0.1	0.2	2.4	17.1	4.4	3.9	3.3	7.6	36.3	2.2	0.1	—	21.2	73.5
TOTAL	412.7	748.8	296.9	422.8	1070.4	**2951.6**	1803.0	2561.3	1250.7	889.5	599.1	653.1	**7756.3**	376.3	405.2	493.8	202.1	367.3	1844.7	323.1	212.8	540.7	5087.9	**18717.5**

Source: IMF. *Direction of Trade.* 1983, based on export statistics from the different countries.

Table 3
Intra-regional trade among the LAIA countries excluding fuels, 1980–1981
(Annual figures in million dollars: exports f.o.b.)

Exports From: \ To:	Bolivia	Colombia	Ecuador	Peru	Venezuela	Andean Group	Argentina	Brazil	Chile	Mexico	Paraguay	Uruguay	Rest of LAIA	Costa Rica	El Salvador	Guatemala	Honduras	Nicaragua	CACM	Panama	Cuba	Haiti	Dominican R.	Total Region	Total World
Bolivia	—	3.8	1.2	29.4	4.7	39.1	22.7	22.1	19.9	1.9	0.6	0.3	66.9	5.0	1.4	5.3	5.5	3.0	20.3	0.1	—	—	0.3	126.6	643.1
Colombia	2.9	—	71.5	37.1	305.5	417.0	59.4	5.5	46.3	16.1	0.3	1.5	129.4	1.6	0.3	0.5	0.3	0.5	2.4	60.3	—	—	5.8	618.5	3,370.3
Ecuador	0.6	86.6	—	9.6	47.1	143.9	30.9	3.8	23.8	14.6	0.4	0.8	74.2	4.6	0.4	0.3	—	2.0	8.4	1.1	—	—	—	221.8	891.3
Peru	52.9	40.7	52.8	—	46.3	192.7	30.3	69.0	55.6	78.2	—	5.8	239.3	—	—	—	—	—	—	74.2	—	—	—	538.0	2,557.2
Venezuela	0.6	45.8	12.0	17.7	—	76.1	8.4	25.9	1.8	27.1	—	0.1	63.3	5.8	4.0	—	—	—	14.9	1.0	—	—	3.5	158.9	1,141.5
Andean Group	57.0	176.9	137.6	93.7	403.6	868.8	151.9	126.2	147.4	137.9	1.3	8.6	573.4	17.2	8.3	9.0	6.0	5.5	46.1	136.6	—	—	9.7	1,663.8	8,603.3
Argentina	128.5	44.6	16.8	99.2	83.2	372.3	—	568.0	202.2	195.5	155.8	142.9	1,264.4	5.3	1.1	3.4	3.6	4.8	18.3	8.5	71.5	1.3	1.1	1,736.2	8,141.9
Brazil	214.5	168.0	59.4	207.0	317.7	966.6	913.4	—	543.4	550.9	396.4	313.9	2,718.0	16.4	2.6	13.1	14.4	19.1	65.8	30.7	27.8	—	19.6	3,806.1	20,643.3
Chile	22.8	73.6	17.9	69.4	73.7	257.4	237.0	361.7	—	69.6	7.4	22.5	698.2	2.9	0.8	1.6	0.9	—	6.4	7.1	0.1	5.2	7.9	977.1	4,299.2
Mexico	0.5	44.0	31.8	27.7	63.4	167.4	38.4	153.7	32.9	—	0.9	6.9	232.8	35.8	10.2	42.3	14.1	17.7	119.8	20.4	18.7	0.3	8.7	570.3	4,865.8
Paraguay	0.8	0.1	—	0.3	0.3	1.5	71.3	47.0	10.9	3.2	—	9.6	142.0	—	—	—	—	—	—	—	—	—	—	144.9	288.6
Uruguay	1.9	3.4	0.9	7.7	0.3	14.2	127.4	180.9	26.7	5.6	13.7	—	354.3	—	—	—	—	—	—	1.2	—	—	0.1	371.5	1,137.5
Total LAIA	428.0	510.8	264.4	505.0	944.3	2,652.6	1,539.5	1,437.6	963.4	962.8	575.6	504.6	5,983.4	77.7	23.0	69.7	39.4	47.1	256.8	204.9	118.0	7.2	47.2	9,270.0	47,979.8

Source: IBD-INTAL: Estadísticas de exportación de los países de la ALADI, 1980–1982, based on export statistics from the different countries.

However, the fact that the contraction of trade had either no effect, or a negative one, on the regional balance of payments, did not mean that some countries did not benefit from the policies adopted. Indeed, this seems to be a feature of the adjustment processes which have been witnessed in Latin America in recent years. The contraction of trade within the region could almost be regarded, in the terminology of balance-of-payments theory, as a Latin American version of 'beggar-my-neighbour'.

The dramatic impact on intra-regional trade of the adjustment policies that were adopted is reflected in the trade imbalances which were typical of the boom. The web of Latin American trade (Tables 2 and 3) shows, in the first place, the strong surplus position, obviously excluding fuels, of Brazil with respect to each of the LAIA countries. Also noteworthy are the strong surpluses of Colombia with respect to Venezuela and of Argentina with respect to Bolivia, Mexico and, to a lesser extent, Paraguay, Peru and Venezuela. Apart from its substantial deficit position with respect to Brazil and Colombia, and its deficit with Argentina, Venezuela also has a significant negative balance with Chile. Finally, looking at non-LAIA trade and excluding disequilibria associated with fuel imports, we should mention Nicaragua's deficit within the Central American Common Market, Guatemala's and Costa Rica's positive balance within that market, Mexico's surplus with Central America, and Colombia's and Peru's surpluses with Panama.

The main source of disequilibrium was Brazil's surplus position. As will be seen later, the Brazilian surplus in 1981 made up almost the whole of non-compensated LAIA trade. In some sense, intra-regional trade was operating as a mechanism through which Brazil partially solved its serious oil imbalance. Under such circumstances, the system worked only as long as a favourable foreign exchange position was maintained in Latin America as a whole, but led to a rapid collapse when deficit countries were forced to correct their general balance-of-payments disequilibria. In terms of intra-regional exports, Brazil has been the most affected, with sales to the region falling by US$1.381 million in 1982, equivalent to 69 per cent of the total contraction of trade within LAIA. Although the fall in Brazilian exports has been in most cases a direct effect of the adjustment policies adopted by other countries in the region, some indirect effects have also been important. One is the impact of the Venezuelan crisis on Colombian exports, which created an intra-regional deficit in a country which had traditionally been in equilibrium, leading it to reduce imports from Latin America, especially Brazil, with which it had maintained substantial deficits in previous years.

The form that the contraction of intra-Latin American trade has taken has thus been a reflection of disequilibria present in the years preceding the crisis. As we will try to show, no lasting reform of the payments mechanisms will be possible without a resolution of these imbalances.

The LAIA payments agreement

The LAIA system of reciprocal credits and multilateral compensation is the cornerstone of the intra-regional payments mechanism. According to this agreement, central banks give each other bilateral lines of credit to finance temporary trade deficits which may arise in either direction. The aim is to avoid situations in which bilateral deficits give way to foreign exchange transfers between central banks prior to the multilateral compensation of balances. Nevertheless, whenever a bilateral balance exceeds the credit line, the corresponding deficit must be cancelled in advance. Every four months there is a clearing of accounts through the agent bank (the Banco de Reserva del Perú), and debtors in the compensation arrangement must make a transfer to the Federal Reserve Bank of New York payable to the agent bank, which then cancels the surplus position of the creditors.

The former instruments are complemented by the Santo Domingo Agreement, which allows the concession of short-term credit to countries experiencing increases in their deficits or falls in their intra-regional surpluses, provided that they also face an overall balance-of-payments deficit and a shortage of international reserves. It should be noted that the Central American Common Market has parallel mechanisms with similar characteristics. In addition, the Andean Group has a common reserve fund which acts, however, independently of subregional exchange flows. Given the relative weight of the LAIA payments agreement, I will focus on the functioning of this scheme.

Since the reciprocal credit lines and the multilateral compensation of balances are mechanisms which lessen the need for actual foreign exchange transfers, they thus reduce the costs of intra-regional trade. Furthermore, they constitute a method of optimising the use of foreign exchange reserves in the region, by reducing the demand for reserves associated with such trade. Finally, the Santo Domingo Agreement acts as a multilateral credit instrument for some countries, beyond what is established under the compensation system.

Up until 1981, the payments system worked satisfactorily, gradually increasing its coverage of intra-regional trade and eliminating between 70 per cent and 80 per cent of foreign exchange transfers (see Tables 1 and 4). However, by 1979, the inadequacy of the available credit lines was becoming apparent, leading to an increasing proportion of advanced transfers. Furthermore, this inadequacy has forced some central banks into operations outside the agreement, in order to avoid exceeding their relevant credit lines. Nonetheless, the most serious difficulties were experienced only in 1982, when several countries exercised their right to withdraw part or all of their debtor balances from multilateral compensation, thus significantly reducing the system's coverage. In effect, total transactions fell by 30 per cent in 1982 in contrast to the 17 per cent decline in intra-regional trade.

Table 4
Growth of the LAIA payments agreement
(Million dollars)

	(1) Value of Compensation	(2) Anticipated Transfers	(3) Total foreign exchange transfers	(4) Total transactions *a*	(3) As a % of (4)
1966	31.4		31.4	106.4	29.5
1967	93.8		93.8	332.8	28.2
1968	129.5		129.5	376.6	34.4
1969	81.0		81.0	479.2	16.9
1970	94.5	15.0	109.6	560.5	19.6
1971	111.9	24.0	136.0	708.1	19.2
1972	179.9	8.7	188.6	984.4	19.2
1973	271.1	9.4	280.5	1,403.1	20.0
1974	309.6	77.8	387.4	2,288.3	16.9
1975	608.8	51.7	660.4	2,396.3	27.6
1976	546.9	105.4	652.2	2,925.5	22.3
1977	717.2	170.1	887.3	3,936.0	22.5
1978	1,079.2	55.7	1,134.9	4,459.0	25.5
1979	1,329.6	300.0	1,629.6	6,420.7	25.4
1980	1,338.6	681.9	2,020.6	8,663.1	23.3
1981	1,684.7	868.9	2,553.6	9,331.4	27.4
1982	1,293.6	632.9	1,926.6	6,553.0	29.4

a Not all exchanges are compensated through this mechanism.
Source: IDB-INTAL, *El proceso de integración en América Latina,* 1982, p 61.

These difficulties have been associated with the impossibility of financing the debtor balances of the largest countries within the framework of the Santo Domingo Agreement, thereby inducing them to withdraw from multilateral compensation in order to obtain a forced extension of bilateral credits. Furthermore, given the characteristics of this Agreement, especially with respect to maturities, it has been impossible to solve the problems of even the smallest countries, in particular, Bolivia, thus making it necessary to design an ad hoc mechanism to handle the situation.[5]

The payments system has tailed completely in the face of the collapse of intra-regional trade. Moreover, the contraction of trade is intimately linked with the current payments system. In effect, an essential feature of this system is the need to cover multilateral deficits in hard currencies. But once deficit countries have been forced to correct their overall balance-of-payments disequilibria, it is not possible to justify a preference for Latin American imports; in fact, there are good reasons for discriminating against them, since they are more competitive with domestic production and less 'essential' from the national point of view. Furthermore, even if it were deemed desirable to maintain these imports, no mechanism exists to finance a resulting intra-regional trade deficit without jeopardising the overall balance-of-payments position of the importing country.

Finally, it has to be said that, in the present crisis conditions, the payments system has been a major stimulus for bilateralism. In practice, the system is a mixture of bilateral (the reciprocal credits) and multilateral instruments (the compensation and the Santo Domingo Agreement). Nevertheless, as we have seen, no effective mechanisms exist for multilateral financing of deficit balances and, as we will see later on, neither is there a significant degree of multilateralism in LAIA's trade. Under these circumstances, the tendency towards bilateralism, which is implicit in the practice of direct import controls, has finally prevailed.

Theoretical problems of the payments system

Under present circumstances, the main justification that is put forward for intra-regional trade is its contribution to the generation of foreign exchange. In this regard, the classic arguments have centred on the possibility of greatly extended import substitution, based on the economies of scale and specialisation which a large market affords.[6] However, one should not lose sight of the role which intra-regional trade can play in the generation of new exports to the rest of the world, be it by virtue of the greater efficiency associated with international specialisation, the improvement in productive processes which stems from greater competition, or the learning process which derives from using the region as a platform for launching new export sectors. In Europe, these arguments, especially those relating to the virtues of competition in export development, played a bigger role in post-war debates than those relating to import substitution.[7] Nevertheless, it is important to bear in mind the possible bias which preferential trade mechanisms could generate against the region's exports to the rest of the world. These could diminish the beneficial effect of intra-regional trade on the generation of net foreign exchange.

The collapse of trade in 1982 and 1983 has made it evident that the danger of losing hard currencies weighs more heavily in the present situation than the advantages of reciprocal trade. Understandably, it would be irrational for deficit countries to incur the double cost of sacrificing foreign exchange and economic activity by simultaneously covering their deficits in hard currency and accepting imports from the region to the detriment of domestic production. But the current system is not a panacea for the surplus countries either, since the adjustment process in the deficit countries means that these, too, are deprived of foreign exchange and the economic activity associated with the export sectors. For this reason, the recovery of intra-regional trade is possible only on the basis of changes which greatly reduce payments in hard currencies.

In the past, this problem has received attention in both Latin America and internationally, but the restoration of orthodox thinking and economic practice on the one hand, and the fluidity of world capital markets on the other, relegated it to a secondary position in the 1970s. The best-known view of this problem was developed by Keynes in his proposals for an International Clearing Union.[8] These proposals were based on a diagnosis of the dangers facing the international economy under a payments system which placed the entire burden of external adjustment on deficit countries. At the global level, this system has an inherently deflationary bias, since it forces the deficit countries to adopt contractionary policies, while surplus countries are not obliged to adopt expansionary measures. With respect to international trade, this asymmetry of the international monetary system entails a double danger: on the one hand, there is a tendency to reduce world trade, if the adjustment policies of the deficit countries affect their imports more quickly than their sales to the rest of the world; and, on the other, there is a stimulus for restrictive trade practices and bilateralism, which reduce the benefits of international specialisation.

Confronted with the need to reconstruct international trade in the postwar era and to break the yoke of bilateralism which was a remnant of the Great Depression and World War II, European discussion in the late 1940s centred on the need for a payments system in Europe which would make credit to deficit countries almost automatic. The outcome of these debates was the creation of the European Payments Union (EPU), which became one of the basic instruments for the promotion of European trade and for a return to the convertibility of currencies and to multilateralism. The system had three essential characteristics:

a) The channelling of all intra-regional surpluses and deficits through a multilateral organisation;

b) automatic granting of credits by the surplus countries to the EPU, and by the EPU to the deficit countries. These credits were limited, however, to a proportion of accumulated surpluses or deficits—in the case of deficit countries, the credit component diminished as it approached the amount of a quota, which was set at 15 per cent of total trade with the region; and

c) the channelling of part of Marshall Plan aid through the EPU in order to allow a higher degree of deficit financing for some countries (including a significant aid component), without placing the entire burden of financing on the surplus countries.[9]

This latter feature, coupled with the expansionary conditions which prevailed in the world economy in the early 1950s, facilitated the operation of the agreement. Under the current circumstances in Latin America, such conditions cannot be assumed, thereby making the design of an adequate payments system much more difficult.

Keynes' proposal and the EPU came under attack from orthodox thinkers of the time, on the grounds that the availability of automatic credit would promote expansionary policies in deficit countries, thus generating a global inflationary bias. This criticism, which inevitably leads to the principle of conditionality, gradually gained ground, especially in the policies of the International Monetary Fund (IMF).[10] Thus, when the problem of a suitable payments scheme for Latin American Integration was posed in the late 1950s and early 1960s, the orthodox position was dominant.[11] The problem which was then posed was similar to the one which confronts us today, but it referred more to the confidence which potential debtor countries should have in the opening up of trade to partners in the integration process, and certainly did not have the same dimensions as the present difficulties, in terms of the magnitude of the intra-regional surpluses and deficits of some countries.

The arrangement which emerged did not do much to inspire the confidence of the deficit countries in the integration process, since it came close to a pure clearing union with frequent settlement of accounts in hard currencies, freedom to carry on transactions outside the scheme and, at first, no mechanism to finance debtor balances beyond the two months between clearings. Thus, the payments system did not contribute in any sense to the diversification of trade. Rather, it was a relatively orthodox solution, which worked well enough, due to the small magnitude of trade in the first few years and, as we saw previously, to the unique circumstances of the international economy in the 1970s.

The alternatives for action

Marginal adjustment to the present system

Given that the magnitude of the intra-regional trade crisis in the Latin American countries, there appears to be a consensus on the need to expand the possibilities offered by the current system.[12] Nevertheless, the alternatives offered by the Santo Domingo Agreement are very limited. No country at present holds substantial foreign exchange reserves and thus there is no willingness to channel meagre international assets.[13] Therefore, the resources which would permit increased coverage under the Santo Domingo Agreement would have to come from outside the region. However, it would be possible simply to face the fact that the mechanism is incapable of financing large deficit balances and to utilise its limited resources instead to finance the deficits of small countries for longer periods than are currently allowed. In the case of the Andean group, it is also possible to use the resources of the Andean Reserve Fund not so much to finance general balance-of-payments disequilibria, but rather deficits in subregional trade. It should be noted, however, that a large proportion of the resources of the Andean Reserve Fund are currently committed to the former kind of financing, and that, under present circumstances, a proposal of this nature would end up channelling funds to Colombia, something which might be unacceptable to the other signatories of the Cartagena Agreement.

Action related to the system of reciprocal credits and multilateral compensation could be directed towards increasing existing bilateral lines and extending the compensation period. The proposal for a multilateral use of bilateral credit to avoid anticipated payments (a mechanism which is contained in the present agreement) does not seem to be very efficient. In this sense, it would be more reasonable to increase bilateral credit lines, even to make them unlimited prior to compensation, so as to eliminate anticipated transfers.

Of all proposals for reform within the present system, the Brazilian recommendation, which would allow the cancelling of bilateral balances with debt instruments which could be used multilaterally, is the most ambitious so far.[14] According to this proposal, the present bilateral credit mechanism would be preserved, but it would permit the payment of deficit balances between two countries with debt documents, while simultaneously authorising the receiving country to pay off its debts in multilateral compensation with those papers. This system would lead to the accumulation of payments obligations of deficit countries in the hands of surplus countries. In this sense, the proposal resembles the payments system which we will analyse in the following section. However, its mixture of multilateralism and bilateralism is quite cumbersome. The European experience in this area indicates that the system would force the surplus countries to grant bilateral credit to the deficit countries in amounts which might not be desirable to the former, given the latter's degree of solvency. For this reason, it is much more acceptable for the creditors to channel all credit through a wholly multilateral entity, in which all the countries share the risk that a deficit balance would not be paid.[15]

Thorough reforms

Obviously, marginal reforms of the present system are preferable to no change at all. Nevertheless, except for the last proposal mentioned, none of them suggests a lasting solution to the problem which we analysed earlier —the unwillingness of deficit countries to accept a payments mechanism which implies the risk of losing foreign exchange. Thus, the restoration of intra-regional trade is only possible if the surplus countries accept soft currencies as partial payment for exports and commit themselves, in the short or long run, to equilibrate their own intra-regional balance of payments. Furthermore, an agreement of this sort would provide, under present conditions, an incentive for diversification of trade, and would facilitate the creation of exchanges without the fear that such trade would worsen a critical balance-of-payments position.

The reforms could take two different directions. The first would be the creation of a LAIA payments union, similar to that which existed in Europe in the early 1950s. Under this type of agreement, the surplus countries would automatically grant credit to the union in a common currency (dollars, SDRs or an accounting unit specific to the scheme) for a relatively large proportion of their expected surpluses, while, in turn, the union would grant automatic credit to the deficit countries in the same currency for a large proportion of their deficits. The proportion of deficits not subject to union financing, and thus cancelled in hard currencies, would need to be carefully studied during the negotiations for such an agreement. Possibly a mechanism by which the proportion to be paid in hard currencies increases with the size of the deficit (similar to the one that existed in the EPU), or one in which the rates of interest rise according to the size of the disequilibrium, should be established, as an incentive for adjustment in the deficit countries. In any case, the principle of increasing deficit-associated costs should be applied to the current position of each country, and not to the accumulated deficit. The adoption of the latter alternative would produce a rapid return to the present system, in which deficit countries are forced to finance their entire current account deficit in hard currencies after a certain point. The most desirable system could be a combination of the two principles.

Naturally, the foreign exchange received by the union would be transferred to the surplus countries. However, an essential element of the scheme is the creation of incentives for those countries to equilibrate their own intra-regional balance of payments. This would be achieved by introducing the principle of increasing costs for their current as well as accumulated surpluses, through variable interest rates or proportions of the surplus to be paid in hard currencies. In order to avoid adjustments through export controls, a prior agreement should be signed requiring all countries to adopt measures aimed at increasing their imports from the region. In addition, there is the possibility of adjusting the balance of payments through the capital account, through the purchase of the debt of deficit countries with the union,[16] or the creation of investment incentives for residents of surplus countries in other countries of the region.

A second option for reform would be aimed at allowing the deficit countries to cancel a significant share of their negative balances in their own currencies. In this case, the deficit would be reflected as a liability of the corresponding central bank in its own currency with respect to the union or to other central banks (in which case a larger degree of bilateralism would be maintained). The central banks of the surplus countries would at the same time accumulate assets in the currency of the deficit countries, either directly or in proportion to those collected by the union. As in the previous case, it would be necessary to design mechanisms to ensure that a certain degree of adjustment takes place in the deficit as well as in the surplus countries. Clearly, under this scheme, debtor countries should guarantee that the balances in their currencies held by the union or other central banks would not lose real value, through indexing the balance either to their domestic price level or to the exchange rate.[17]

Needless to say, both systems are heterodox designs, although, in either case, intermediate paths may be sought, so as to make them more similar to the present agreement. The virtue of the first alternative is its similarity (though not complete) to the EPU. In contrast, the second offers greater guarantees to the deficit countries, since the liabilities of a central bank in its own currency cannot be really considered part of the foreign debt of the country, while liabilities with the payments union in the first case are more clearly so. In any case, there are difficulties of implementation, not only in terms of overcoming the criticisms of orthodox schools of thought, but also the real problems which must be resolved in order for these schemes to function. These problems will be addressed at the end of this paper.

The difficulties

Orthodox criticisms

As with their theoretical and practical predecessors, the schemes set out in the previous section will be criticised by orthodox economists for inducing undesirable adjustments in the deficit countries. When considering such criticism it is necessary to bear in mind the facts. The orthodox position has left its mark in Latin America in the effects of the traumatic balance-of-payments adjustment processes and the collapse of intra-regional trade. Although the proposed systems are certainly less than perfect in the ascetic world of neo-classical models, they are valid options, even from a neo-classical perspective, considering the 'imperfections' which characterise the actual working of today's international trade and payments.

Furthermore, one should not lose sight of the fact that the intra-regional deficit or surplus scarcely constitutes a fraction of the global disequilibrium facing a specific country. It is thus unlikely that a government would consciously incur the risks of a global deficit in its balance of payments in order to take advantage of this kind of agreement. Of course, exceptions do exist, such as countries whose intra-regional deficit accounts for a particularly large share of their external disequilibrium (see Table 5). In dealing with such cases, the design of the system could include the setting of limits on the amount which a deficit country may borrow as a proportion of its exports.

Chronic debtors and creditors

The theoretical literature as well as the practical experience of the European Payments Union indicate that the basic problem with a multilateral compensation system is the existence of countries which are far from an equilibrium position in intra-regional trade.[18] Furthermore, the system gains effectiveness in direct proportion to the degree of multilateralism in trade. From both perspectives, the Latin American trade environment in the years prior to the crisis was not especially favorable for an agreement of this sort. Excluding fuels, most of the intra-regional trade was balanced on a bilateral basis. In 1980–81 multilateral balancing represented only 13.5 per cent of total trade. Furthermore, a relatively large proportion of trade (27.6 per cent in 1980–81 and 35.7 per cent in 1981) was neither in bilateral nor multilateral equilibrium. What is more, over 90 per cent of this disequilibrium was associated with the Brazilian surplus (See Table No. 6). Obviously, an important part of the surplus was represented by the Brazilian oil deficit (See Table No. 5). Even so, the conclusion which was arrived at in part 1 of this study is inevitable, namely, that a readjustment in the region's system of payments requires a lasting solution to the Brazilian imbalance.

Initially, however, the problem will take on a different character. The adjustment policies adopted in 1982 converted Brazil into a country with a net deficit within the region. The largest global surpluses in that year

Table 5
Trade balance among LAIA countries, 1980–1982
(Million dollars)

	(1) Trade Balance			(2) Surplus or deficit as % of total exports from the country			(3) Trade Balance: fuels		(4) Trade balance, excluding fuels		(5) Trade balance excluding fuels as a % of exports	
	1980	1981	1982	1980	1981	1982	1980	1981	1980	1981	1980	1981
Argentina	−226.7	−5.2	61.2	−2.8	−0.1	0.8	−239.2	−187.3	12.5	182.1	0.2	2.0
Bolivia	−60.5	−35.9	167.5	−5.8	−4.0	19.4	231.7	315.6	−292.2	−351.5	−28.2	−39.4
Brazil	741.7	1.253.6	−112.4	3.7	5.5	−0.6	−878.9	−1.619.9	1.620.6	2.873.5	8.1	12.5
Colombia	−201.5	−348.9	−337.5	−5.1	−11.8	−11.3	−254.0	−367.8	52.5	18.9	1.3	0.6
Chile	−273.7	−489.7	−109.6	−5.7	−12.5	−2.9	−464.1	−283.7	190.4	−206.0	4.0	−5.3
Ecuador	134.6	147.0	133.8	5.4	5.7	6.3	212.7	161.3	−78.1	−14.3	−3.1	−0.6
Mexico	−149.7	−88.4	488.7	−1.0	−0.4	2.3	249.8	633.4	−399.5	−721.8	−2.7	−3.5
Paraguay	−482.0	−494.1	−324.5	−162.3	−168.9	−98.4	−53.5	−58.6	−428.5	−435.5	−144.3	−148.9
Peru	131.1	−146.3	−228.4	3.9	−4.6	−7.1	18.3	112.7	112.8	−259.0	3.3	−8.2
Uruguay	−241.6	−345.7	−157.1	−22.8	−28.4	−15.3	−116.1	−203.6	−125.5	−142.1	−11.9	−11.7
Venezuela	628.2	553.6	418.3	3.4	2.8	2.6	1.293.4	1.498.0	−665.2	−944.4	−3.6	−4.7
Total surpluses or deficits	±1.635.6	±1.954.2	±1.269.5	±2.1	±2.2	±1.6	±2.005.9	±2.721.0	±1.988.9	±3.074.6	±2.5	±3.5

a BTN 027.
Source: IDB-INTAL, Estadísticas de exportación de los países de la ALADI, 1980–1982, based on export statistics from the different countries.

Table 6
Balanced and unbalanced trade of LAIA, excluding fuels
(Million dollars)

	Average 1980–81		1981	
Total Trade, excluding fuels	8,636		8,601	
In bilateral balance	5,088	58.9%	4,404	51.2%
In multilateral balance	1,168	13.5	1,123	13.1
Compensated trade	6,256	72.4	5,527	64.3
Non-compensated trade	2,380	27.6	3,075	35.7
Brazilian Surplus	2,247	26.0	2,873	33.4

Source: Calculations by the author based on IBD-INTAL, *Estadísticas de exportación de los países de los países de la ALADI, 1980–1982.*

were, in all cases, associated with countries having positive balances in intra-regional oil trade (Mexico, Venezuela, Bolivia and Ecuador, in order of importance). Quite possibly, the situation worsened in 1983. Therefore, the major problem in the negotiation of agreements such as those suggested initially lies in defining what proportion of petroleum trade will be included within the scheme. If this trade is totally excluded, Brazil's participation would not be viable, since it would put that country in the uncomfortable position of granting automatic credits to its buyers, while it has a global deficit in its intra-regional transactions. On the other hand, the inclusion of petroleum in the payments agreement would create an incentive for the region's importers to channel all their fuel purchases through the system. It would also create an absurd situation for the oil-exporting countries, since they would have to grant automatic credits to their intra-regional customers, or to receive soft currency payments, although they have the option of selling fuels outside the region for hard currencies.

The petroleum problem demands careful attention. However, there are various ways to approach the issue, two of which will be mentioned here. The first would consist in defining *ex-ante* all bilateral petroleum transactions to be included in the agreement, i.e., establishing a quota system to be negotiated by the interested parties. The second would be to establish uniformly a larger hard currency component for the payment of all intra-regional oil transactions.

The hard currency component of intra-regional trade

The petroleum case illustrates a more general problem: the payments agreements which we have reviewed assume that most of transactions are not convertible into hard currencies. However, there are at least two elements of partial convertibility in intra-regional trade. The first is associated with that part of the region's exports which could be sold outside the region. The second is tied to be imported component (from the rest of the world) of intra-regional trade.

The existence of this convertible component of trade has two important corollaries. The first is that in agreements such as those proposed in this paper, it would be wrong for member countries (with the possible exception of chronic debtors) to create incentives for exports to be region. In such a case, the country runs the risk of losing hard currencies, both from that portion of exports which could have been directed to the rest of the world, as well as from the imported component of exports to the region. At a global level, this means that intra-regional trade incentives should be granted mainly to the *importers* and not the exporters in each country.

The second corollary has to do with the need to maintain a minimum degree of convertibility in intra-regional transactions. This is especially true of the imported component of trade aimed at import substitution for the region as a whole. At the national level, the substitution process has always been faced with the need to channel foreign exchange to the leading import-substitution sectors at certain times. At the international level a mechanism must be found to channel at least the imported component of these sectors' exports; in the opposite case, the absurd situation could arise whereby a system which is largely designed for joint import substitution would force the countries which could lead this process to restrict their intra-regional exports.

Fluctuations in real exchange rates

Since the 1960s, the problem of unstable real exchange rates has constituted one of the central themes in discussions of alternative systems of payments in LAIA.[19] Recent experience has confirmed this difficulty. The most complex issue is associated with sudden devaluations which change only temporarily the real exchange rates, without achieving lasting changes in the direction of trade flows. This greatly complicates the establishment of stable commercial networks.

The design of specific exchange rate system for intra-regional trans-actions is extremely difficult, and does not really contribute to a lasting equilibrium in intra-regional trade flows or to greater stability of real exchange rates. Furthermore, it should be borne in mind that instruments other than the exchange rate exist for equilibrating intra-regional trade flows, among them payments systems like those proposed here and the management of tariff and quota restrictions. However, it might be desirable to complement these instruments with mechanisms which com-pensate sudden fluctuations in real exchange rates (especially through a system of compensatory taxes and subsidies) and in this way stabilize commercial networks in the region.[20]

Conclusions

The past few years have been tragic for Latin American economic integration. The collapse of intra-regional trade has not only brought the rapid decay of the most visible aspect of this process, but has nullified its supposed creative effects in the midst of a critical phase for the region as a whole. As this paper has shown, the crisis is related to the inefficiency of the current system of payments in the region and to the imbalance of intra-regional trade during the boom. Therefore, action must be taken on both these fronts if the advantages of integration are to be enjoyed. This paper has highlighted the need for a system of payments which provides a guarantee for intra-regional deficit countries that their disequilibria will not contribute to a worsening in their already critical balance of payments. This requires the automatic granting of credit for a significant proportion of their deficits or allowing them to cancel their debts in their own currency. Without concealing the opposition of orthodox schools of thought to the proposed system, or the real difficulties implied in its design and negotiation, we are convinced that the current situation in Latin America will not yield to any 'easy solution' that may be put forward as an alternative, or be resolved by clinging to the present remedies.

Notes

1. IDB-INTAL, *El proceso de integración en América Latina,* 1968/71, Tables II–1 and VII–8.
2. Calculated on the basis of IMF, *Direction of Trade,* 1982.
3. IDB-INTAL, *Estadísticas de exportación de los países de la ALADI,* 1980–1982; we assume that petroleum transactions were not affected between 1981 and 1982.

4. *Ibid*. and data on export and import registration in Colombia, the country through which 90 per cent of Andean trade passes in either direction.

5. Alfredo Echegaray Simonet, 'El proceso de revisión de los mecanismos financieros de la ALADI', *Integración Latinoamericana* (83) September 1983, pp 19–29.

6. See, for example, *El Pensamiento de la CEPAL*, Santiago: Editorial Universitaria, 1969, Chapter 5.

7. See the works quoted in footnote 9.

7. John Maynard Keynes, *Shaping the Post-War World: the Clearing Union, Collected Writings*, Vol. 25. For a more recent view on this problem, see Paul Davidson, *International Money and the Real World*, New York: John Wiley and Sons, 1982.

9. Robert Triffin, *El Caos Monetario*, Mexico: Fondo de Cultura Económica, 1961, Chapters 3–5; William Dielbold, *Trade and Payments in Western Europe, A Study in Economic Cooperation*, New York: Council of Foreign Relations—Harper and Brothers, 1952, First Part; W M Scammell, *International Economic Policy*, 2nd edition, London: Macmillan, 1965, Chapter 10.

10. See, for example, Sidney Dell, 'El Fondo Monetario Internacional y el principio de condicionalidad', *Revista de la Cepal* (13) April 1981, pp 149–61.

11. Barry N Siegel, 'Sistema de pagos de la Asociatión Latinoamericana de Libre Comercio', in Miguel A Wionczek, *Integración de América Latina: Experiencias y Perspectivas*, Mexico: Fondo de Cultura Económica, 1964, Chapter 14.

12. Echegaray, *op. cit.*; Guillermo Maldonado *et al.*, 'América Latina: crisis, cooperación y desarrollo', *Revista de la Cepal* (20) August 1983, pp 77–102; JUNAC, *Bases para una estrategia de financiamiento, inversiones y pagos*, Lima, October 1983.

13. The proposal for a Guarantee Fund is subject to the same problem, since it is in fact, a kind of common reserve fund.

14. Echegaray, *op. cit.*, p 26.

15. Triffin, *op. cit.*, pp 147–8; Diebold, *op. cit.*, pp 22–4.

16. This system existed in the EPU and proved to be very useful.

17. See, for example, José Antonio Ocampo, 'Esquema de un sistema de pagos para el Grupo Andino', *Coyuntura Económica* (50) June 1983.

18. R F Kahn *et al.*, 'The contribution of payments agreements to trade expansion', in P Robson, *International Economic Integration*, Harmondsworth: Penguin Books, 1971, Chapter 12.

19. Sidney Dell, *A Latin American Common Market?*, London: Oxford University Press, 1966, pp 164–9; Gonzalo Cevallos, *Integración Económica de América Latina*, México; Fondo de Cultura Económica 1971, pp 221 and 237. As Cevallos states, the problem was not severe in Central America, given the traditional stability of the exchange rates in that region.

20. Eduardo Conesa ('Un mecanismo equilibrador de las balanzas comerciales recíprocas entre países que desean integrarse económicamente', in *Integración Latinoamericana* (82) August 1983, pp 38–43) has proposed a system of certificates, applicable to intraregional transactions, which exporters would sell to importers of the same country on the open market. In the case of deficit, the value of the certificate would operate as a surcharge on reciprocal trade. As the same author recognises, the maximum amount of the surcharge is the margin of preference from the region. However, the system is not symmetrical in the case of surpluses and relies on adjustments that come about as a result of small variations in effective exchange rates.

7
Collapse of intra-Latin American trade 1980–83: causes and prospects

Dragoslav Avramovic

Trade among Latin American countries, exclusive of fuels, fell by 50 per cent or more between its 1980–81 peak and the present, according to the analysis by Dr Ocampo which is to be found among the other papers in this volume. For the Andean Group, a study by Dr Salgado shows that restrictions introduced in recent years in contravention of the agreement now affect some 40 per cent of total intra-group trade.[1] Such orders of magnitude go part of the way to explaining the depth of the depression experienced by the Latin American countries.

These countries are caught in a triple squeeze. First, their terms of trade, together with those of other developing countries, deteriorated sharply following the catastrophic drop in export commodity prices between late 1980 and late 1982. Only a third of the loss sustained then was recovered during 1983. Furthermore, the prices of their manufactured exports are falling at a faster rate than those of developed countries. This is a result of the severe competition in which most newly industrialising and Eastern European countries are engaged in order to acquire the foreign exchange needed to make their debt service payments and maintain essential imports.

Secondly, appreciation of the US dollar has opened the currency pincers around the Latin American countries. Most of their debts, and food and oil imports, are paid for in US dollars, as is much of their imports of machinery and other equipment and intermediate products. Yet a considerable proportion of their exports are directed to non-dollar markets. Furthermore, dollar interest rates have been particularly high recently. The resulting deterioration of the Latin American terms of exchange has been severe.

Third, the geographical distribution of Latin American exports of manufactures has made them particularly vulnerable to external influences affecting other developing countries. Some 50 per cent of Argentinian exports of manufactures, 55 per cent of Brazil's and 62 per cent of Colombia's are directed to other developing countries within Latin America and elsewhere (Brazilian exports to Africa particularly are of major significance). The proportion has been even higher in the case of the most advanced and newest exports: some 73–78 per cent of plastic material exports from these three countries and Mexico have been directed to other developing countries.[2] The sharp fall in primary product prices and a corresponding drop in the export revenues of developing countries during the present crisis have therefore affected the Latin American countries particularly severely. In contrast, Asian exporters of manufactures seem to have fared better, as their exports are directed mainly to markets in the developed countries which have held up better in the recession, and to developing countries whose import purchasing power has been better preserved than in Latin America and Africa.

It is this mutually reinforcing triple squeeze that has brought about a cash crisis in Latin America during 1981–83 that has been of greater severity than during the Great Depression of the 1930s. In 1983, interest and principal repayments absorbed about 62 per cent of Latin American proceeds from merchandise exports, compared with an average in 1933 of 40 per cent in eight Latin American countries for which figures are available.[3]

Trade within the Latin American integration schemes—the Latin American Free Trade Association (LAFTA), the Andean Region, Central America and the Caribbean—has frequently involved goods of 'lower priority' than those imported from the outside world, in the sense that they could, to some extent, be produced domestically or were less 'essential' and therefore would be the first to be cut from imports in a period of austerity. They may also have included goods whose prices were higher, owing to regional preferences, than those obtainable in the free international market. The 'inessential' nature of these goods and their higher prices might have both been accommodated, however, and trade flows might have been maintained if payments arrangements had been in force which would not have involved an appreciable outlay of convertible foreign exchange. But they were not. The existing schemes allow for only limited amounts of mutual swing credit and multilateral compensation, and once these fairly low credit limits have been reached, and in the absence of special measures to stimulate additional exports from the deficit countries, their need for convertible foreign exchange is as great as in importing from the convertible currency areas themselves.

The net effect is that frequently imports of oil, food, essential raw materials and spare parts, and also debt service, which are all payable in developed countries, are given priority in the allocation of foreign exchange, and imports from the integration areas are reduced or dropped altogether. 'Expenditure switching' away from developing country sources of supply in favour of purchases from developed countries, the priority given to lower-cost purchases of investment and intermediate goods in the world markets and the neglect of import opportunities from the integration areas, if essential goods can be obtained faster in the developed countries, have been frequent phenomena in recent years.[4] Under conditions of severe foreign exchange shortage, exhortations to preserve import flows from the integration areas will have no significant effect: they have to compete in priority, quality, price and delivery time with imports from developed countries which are engaged in a struggle for markets, with everyone trying to preserve his export sales and associated production and employment.

What next?

The present situation cannot be sustained, as it would involve the loss of many developing countries' markets, which it has taken much effort to build up. It would also jeopardise the future of the region's integration schemes: a continuing stagnation of trade could destroy other forms of cooperation which need to be developed in their own right, such as collaboration in specific sectors, the transfer of technology and a common position *vis-à-vis* the outside world on such issues as product markets, services and finance.

The Latin American countries are not the only ones whose trade with other developing nations is in jeopardy. The problem is also encountered elsewhere, and thought has already been given in several quarters to ways in which the situation can be improved. Furthermore, the present unfavourable position may in fact serve to trigger off the development and implementation of trade financing schemes which could make a major and lasting contribution to cooperation among developing countries, going beyond the present crisis. Four recent initiatives deserve specific comment:

a) A proposal has been made for the introduction in West Africa of a scheme of limited convertibility among member countries of ECOWAS (the Economic Community of West African States). A study has been prepared which aims at the development of a multilateral payments system within this group of developing countries, which will at the same time try to preserve the advantages of multilateral trading, while saving convertible foreign exchange.[5]

b) The National City Bank of New York, perhaps the most enterprising and aggressive of major multinational banks in identifying and exploiting new openings, established in 1983 a special company for facilitating so called counter-trade—i.e. barter and similar arrangements—through the offer of trade finance, the marketing of products, and provision of related trade intelligence and other services. This Citicorp International Trading Company (CITC) operates from offices in New York, London and Hongkong.[6]

c) The proposed Bank of Developing Countries (South Bank) of the Group of 77, in the design prepared by UNCTAD at the request of the Group, envisages the financing of exports and the support of payments (clearing) arrangements of developing countries as its fields of lending. (The other fields are commodity stabilisation finance, investment project finance and country programme finance.) Lending operations would be both short- and long-term. The scheme is under active consideration by the Group of 77.[7]

d) A scheme explicitly directed at promoting and financing trade among developing countries has been proposed by Mr Agha Hasan Abedi, president of the Bank of Credit and Commerce International S.A., a rapidly growing institution with affiliates and offices in many developing countries. In this scheme, a consortium of commercial banks, private and public, of developing countries, perhaps also supported by their central banks, would be prepared to settle in convertible foreign exchange the balances arising from the bilateral and multilateral trading of developing countries through its lending. The consortium bank (the Bank of the Third World) would establish a unit of account to facilitate such arrangements, thus laying the basis for an ambitious payments scheme for the developing countries. The proposed institution would also engage in pre-export commodity lending, bridging finance and lending for essential imports. Loans would be short-term.[8]

An essential point in the Citibank activities and of the Group of 77 and the Abedi schemes is that they would operate on a world plane rather than being confined to a particular geographic region. An advantage of such a worldwide scheme is that resources can be shifted from surplus to deficit regions, thus permitting the functioning of the scheme even in the present situation when Latin America as a whole is in deficit and is therefore experiencing difficulties in operating any scheme at all. Of course, continuing deficits cannot be sustained, and measures would have to be taken to balance accounts within the system; but a wider scheme would provide more room for manoeuvre, and also, to the extent that direct investment and long-term lending would be encouraged (as it was in the European Payments Union), the balancing of accounts would be facilitated.

Another advantage of a worldwide scheme is that opportunities for mutual trade and thus for multilateral settlements at a low cost in convertible exchange would be greater than in regional schemes. The sphere within which to optimise trade would be greater: complementarities of developing countries are greater across, rather than within, regions, as has been emphasised by Professor Arthur Lewis in his Nobel Prize lecture on economic cooperation among developing countries.[9]

The Latin American governments will have to decide shortly whether to try to revive regional and subregional payments schemes, or to opt for a worldwide one. The first course has not proved resistant to adversity. Furthermore, when attempts were made in good times to link the regional schemes into a worldwide system, they did not get any further than feasibility studies. Going straight to an overall world system now would appear to have all the advantages and no disadvantages.

Moreover, the development of a worldwide payments scheme among developing countries would in no way interfere with regional and subregional integration. All the existing integration schemes and programmes would continue to operate. Bilateral and regional cooperation would, in fact, benefit from a multilateral payments scheme. To the extent that trading relations among neighbours would be favoured over those with other developing countries because of differences in transport and other costs, the payments scheme would enable such bilateral and regional relations to flourish. What a worldwide scheme would do is not discriminate, in providing finance, against profitable trade with developing countries located in other regions.

Notes

1. See the contributions of Dr Ocampo and Salgado in this volume.
2. François Vellas, 'De nouvelles relations commerciales propres à faciliter le remboursement de lat dette', *Le Monde* (Paris) 24 January 1984.
3. Based on Pedro-Pablo Kuczynski, 'Latin American debt: act two', *Foreign Affairs*, Fall 1983, pp. 19–20, and Dragoslav Avramovic, 'The debt problem in developing countries at end 1982', *Aussenwirtschaft*, March 1983, Appendix Table 5.
4. See the statements at the Cartagena Conference of Messrs Bianchi, Fletcher and Mendez. 'Expenditure switching' is Mr Fletcher's phrase.
5. Professor A Cicin-Sain and Professor J Marshall (UNCTAD consultants), *Study on Limited Currency Convertibility among ECOWAS Countries*, UNCTAD, Geneva, February–March 1983.
6. Citicorp announcement, New York, August 1983. I am grateful to Mr Shahid Jamil, Deputy General Manager of the Bank of Credit and Commerce International, for bringing the Citicorp scheme to my attention.
7. *Report on the South Bank*, Office of the Chairman of the Group of 77, New York, and International Center for Public Enterprises in Developing Countries, Ljubljana 1983. Studies A and B, pp 41–95.
8. Statement by Mr Agha Hasan Abedi at the Third conference of banks from developing countries, Ljubljana, 5 July 1983. See also *South*, August 1983, and BCCI, *The Bank of the Third World*, London, 1983 (mimeo.).
9. W Arthur Lewis, 'The slowing down of the engine of growth', *The American Economic Review*, September 1980.

8

The lessons of economic integration in Latin America: the case of Central America

Gert Rosenthal

Twenty years ago, economic integration was perceived by many Latin American economists as a promising vehicle for enhancing economic and social development in their respective countries. The idea, which appealed to always latent Bolivarian sentiments, was inspired first by a conceptual framework promulgated by the Economic Commission for Latin America (ECLA) and very much in vogue at the time. This assigned great importance to industrialisation as a means of accelerating development and also recognised that fairly ample economic and geographical dimensions were required if industrialisation were to be reasonably efficient. In the second place, the idea was given reinforcement by the relatively successful experience of the integration among the Western European countries.

Today, governments and academics in Latin America continue to pay lip service to the possibilities held out by economic cooperation within the framework of formal integration movements. But there is a general air of pessimism regarding the size of the contribution that these movements may have made so far in the development of the countries of the region. Thus, during the 1970s, the 'crisis' that these movements faced was frequently and widely discussed, and there were calls for their restructuring. In more recent years, notwithstanding the metamorphosis of ALALC into ALADI (the Latin American Integration Association), the subject does not appear to be able to arouse even the interest of university research departments. At least implicitly, these have declared the failure of this experiment in intra-regional cooperation.

This pessimism, however, seems to be premature, at least if the main criterion of economic interdependence—reciprocal trade—is applied. The latter grew significantly between 1960 and 1975, and since then has remained at a constant level as a ratio of total exports. As can be seen in Table 1, this statement is applicable to each of the subregional integration movements within Latin America, and for the region as a whole. In

Table 1

Latin America: exports within subregional schemes, within Latin America, and total exports
(Millions of current US dollars, fob)

	1960	1965	1970	1975	1978	1979	1980	1981[a]	Rates of growth		
									1960–1970	1970–1980	1960–1980
ALADI											
Total exports	7,344.8	9,388.7	12,786.7	29,664.2	44,630.1	60,729.0	79,569.1	85,719.0	5.7	20.0	12.7
Exports to Latin America	—	—	1,583.5	5,031.2	7,174.3	10,011.8	11,962.5	13,431.2	...	22.0	...
Ratio exports to Latin America/total exports	—	—	12.4	17.0	16.1	16.5	15.0	15.7			
Intra-ALADI exports	566.6	841.9	1,266.0	4,010.2	5,838.4	8,574.6	10,879.3	11,933.6	8.4	24.0	15.9
Ratio intra-ALADI exports/total exports	7.7	9.0	9.9	13.5	13.1	14.1	13.7	13.9			
Ratio intra-ALADI exports/Latin America exports	—	—	79.9	79.7	81.4	85.6	90.9	88.8			
Andean Group[b]											
Total exports	3,586.8	4,346.0	5,419.1	12,897.8	16,293.4	23,937.5	30,064.5	29,822.6	4.2	18.8	11.2
Exports to Latin America	—	—	569.0	2,055.3	2,404.2	3,412.9	3,922.8	4,401.6	...	21.0	...
Ratio exports to Latin America/total exports	—	—	10.5	15.9	14.8	14.3	13.0	14.8			
Intra-Andean exports	24.5	52.7	91.6	477.1	684.5	1,075.1	1,182.6	1,513.0	14.1	29.0	21.0
Ratio intra-Andean exports/total exports	0.7	1.2	1.7	3.7	4.2	4.5	3.9	5.1			
Ratio intra-Andean exports/Latin America exports	—	—	16.1	23.2	28.5	31.5	30.1	34.4			

(Table I contd.)

Central American Common Market											
Total exports	444.2	762.5	1,105.4	2,309.4	3,974.0	4,462.5	4,942.5	4,239.0	9.5	16.2	12.8
Exports to Latin America	—	—	313.7	645.9	965.7	1,034.2	1,172.0	1,125.7	...	14.1	...
Ratio exports to Latin America/total exports			28.4	28.0	24.3	23.2	23.7	26.6			
Intra-MCCA exports	30.9	132.8	287.1	541.3	862.8	898.7	994.3	921.9	25.0	13.2	19.0
Ratio intra-MCCA exports/total exports	7.0	17.4	26.0	23.4	21.7	20.1	20.1	21.7			
Ratio intra-MCCA exports/Latin America exports			91.5	83.8	89.3	86.9	84.8	81.9			
Ratio intra-MCCA + Panama exports/Latin America exports			95.3	88.9	94.5	92.7	90.7	88.4			
CARICOM[c]											
Total exports	543.7	750.2	1,000.1	3,028.5	3,190.2	3,908.1	5,498.4	5,137.0	6.3	18.6	12.3
Exports to Latin America	—	—	63.2	259.7	297.6	439.6	593.9	657.4	...	25.0	...
Ratio exports to Latin America/total exports			6.3	8.6	9.3	11.2	10.8	12.8			
Intra-MCCA exports	21.3	27.1	42.3	216.8	204.7	255.7	352.5	379.5	7.1	24.0	15.1
Ratio intra-MCCA exports/total exports	3.9	3.6	4.2	7.2	6.4	6.5	6.4	7.4			
Ratio intra-MCCA exports/Latin America exports			66.9	83.5	68.8	58.2	59.4	57.7			
Latin America[d]											
Total exports	8,532.5	11,518.5	15,212.2	36,182.8	52,712.2	70,265.6	91,325.7	96,585.8	6.0	19.7	12.6
Intraregional trade	749.9	1,275.3	1,969.7	5,964.8	8,536.5	11,583.3	13,882.9	15,357.9	10.1	22.0	15.7
Ratio intraregional trade/total exports	8.8	11.1	12.9	16.5	16.2	16.5	15.2	15.9	...	1.6	...

Source: CEPAL, based on official statistics.

a Preliminary figures.
b Excludes Chile.
c Only includes Barbados, Guyana, Jamaica and Trinidad and Tobago.
d Includes 11 countries of ALADI, 5 of CACM, 4 of CARICOM, Panama and the Dominican Republic.

1960, less than 9 per cent of the total exports of twenty-two Latin American countries was destined for the rest of the region. This percentage had increased to 16 per cent by 1975, and has remained within that range, with only a slight downward trend, ever since. In absolute terms, intra-regional trade increased from US$750 million in 1960 to US$15.4 billion in 1981. In other words, within two decades its value multiplied twentyfold. The subregional area that has recorded the highest rate of growth—and the highest levels of interdependence—has been Central America.

This trade is not simply the result of spontaneous forces, or merely generated by geographical proximity. The existence of preferential trade schemes, within the context of the region's various integration treaties, clearly helped to stimulate it. Thus, in recent years, approximately 90 per cent of the exports of ALADI member countries to the rest of Latin America occurred within that subregional grouping. The same proportion can be found in the case of member countries of the Central American Common Market.

At the same time, it is undeniable that subregional integration movements face many problems. And the utopia of a wider Latin American Common Market is even more remote today than it was when the presidents of the region met in Punta del Este, Uruguay, in 1967 and declared their intention of aiming for this goal. How then does one arrive at a balanced and objective judgment about the potential for the intra-regional cooperation in the 1980s and beyond, based on the rich harvest of experience that has so far been accumulated? The experience derived from the Central American integration process, probably the most success-ful movement of its kind in Latin America, could shed some useful light. As emphasised in the following pages, in spite of the many problems that this process has faced over the years, the Central Americans have shown much perseverance in keeping their regional economic integration scheme together.

The historical background

It is useful to recall the background against which the Central American governments decided to reinforce their regional integration process by implementing, in 1960, the General Treaty of Economic Integration. The region had already accumulated roughly ten years of experience in partial integration, influenced in its conception and implementation by the

Economic Commission for Latin America (ECLA).[1] In those years integration in Latin America was seen basically as a means of facilitating industrialisation for the purpose of import substitution, in countries whose domestic markets were too small to justify productive plants capable of providing the necessary economies of scale.[2]

As part of this background, it is also useful to recall the post-war mood, still present in 1960, that sought the gradual abolition of barriers to trade in order to contribute to the prosperity and economic interdependence of the whole international community. The world powers were willing to support only those subregional integration movements—and even then with little enthusiasm—that complied with the rules of the General Agreement on Tariffs and Trade (GATT), and particularly its Article XXIV dealing with trade restrictions in the context of a customs union. Furthermore, it was a period of prosperity, in which the countries of Central America enjoyed relative internal and external financial equilibrium within their individual style of development. This in turn gave them the leeway to take the risks implicit in signing agreements whose exact economic consequences could not be fully calculated in advance.

In the second place, there was a relatively high degree of homogeneity between the governments of the region, in terms of both economic structures and policies and of the political establishment. Costa Rica was perhaps an exception, which perhaps explains the delay in that country's accession to the General Treaty.[3] But there were no significant political differences between the various governments—exceptionally so, in view of the long and often tumultuous history of Central America.

Thirdly, the conceptual framework that was at least implicit in the design of the Central American integration process—influenced in its economic aspects by the writings of the time on customs unions and as far as international relations were concerned by the neo-functionalist school[4,5]—was conceived in such a way that regional commitments would be adopted in a gradual and progressive (some would say linear) manner. The movement would be in the direction of ever more integrated systems, culminating in the fulfilment of an ultimate goal. It was thus thought that the Common Market was only a first step towards the attainment of a truly regional economy, and that one step would unerringly follow another—Common Market, customs union, economic union—on the road to regional unity.[6] During their progress to this goal it was understood that governments would increasingly delegate functions to regional institutions, thus widening the depth and scope of the integration process, as a result of 'spill-overs' into new sectors of activity submitted to common action, or the extension of activity in a particular sector.

Finally, the integration movement had a small but influential constituency—basically technocrats supported by some academics and industrial entrepreneurs—which was able to translate good intentions into reality through its influence on government decisions. This contributed the goodwill and drive which helped so much in the cooperative effort of the early years.

And the achievements were numerous and productive, at least if measured against two key indicators. First, there was the diversification and modernisation of economies, arising from increased levels of industrialisation. This was facilitated, at least in part, by the expanded market and the moderately protectionist policies that formed part of the integration framework. Secondly, there was the increasing level of economic interdependence generated by intra-regional trade flows (see Table 2). As will be observed, since 1966 this trade has represented annually between a quarter and a fifth of total exports of the five countries.[7] In addition, various regional institutions were established, and some of them—for example, the Central American Bank for Economic Integration—had a significant impact on development.

It is, of course, true that the process did not fulfil all the hopes that some had placed in it, and that it did not fundamentally alter the style of development prevalent in the countries involved—this would have been too much to expect of an integration process of a purely economic character—but the limited target set in the General Treaty of establishing a Common Market was achieved virtually in its entirety and within the stipulated time-scale, and this achievement persists, with important variations which will be examined presently, to the present day.

How the integration process worked in practice

In the 1960s and 1970s—a period of considerable change both internationally and within the Central American countries—the integration process was marked by six salient characteristics. In the first place, as it was perceived as complementary to, and instrumental in, the development of the five Central American countries, it naturally reflected the style of development prevailing in each of those countries. In this respect, it basic-

Table 2

Central America: some economic indicators

(Millions of US dollars)

	Exports			Imports (cif)			Ratio of industrial GDP to total GDP
	Total	Intraregional	Percentage of total	Total	Intraregional	Percentage of total	
1960	440.1	30.3	6.9	514.1	30.3	5.9	12.3
1961	454.1	36.2	8.0	495.8	36.2	7.3	12.5
1962	513.7	44.7	8.7	552.1	44.7	8.1	12.6
1963	589.1	68.7	11.7	652.6	68.7	10.5	13.1
1964	673.4	105.3	15.6	770.5	105.5	13.7	13.4
1965	761.3	132.1	17.4	889.3	132.5	14.9	14.1
1966	834.3	170.3	20.4	937.0	170.3	18.2	14.5
1967	856.5	205.6	24.0	1,030.4	205.6	20.0	15.0
1968	947.3	246.9	26.1	1,046.2	246.9	23.6	15.4
1969	971.8	250.1	25.7	1,065.8	250.1	23.5	15.6
1970	1,098.0	286.3	26.1	1,234.0	286.3	23.2	15.9
1971	1,107.0	272.7	24.6	1,304.3	272.7	20.9	16.0
1972	1,328.8	304.7	22.9	1,411.7	304.7	21.6	16.9
1973	1,663.6	383.3	23.0	1,845.7	383.3	20.8	16.1
1974	2,109.2	532.5	25.2	2,926.2	532.5	18.2	16.2
1975	2,298.7	536.4	23.3	2,945.5	536.4	18.2	16.1
1976	3,007.7	649.3	21.6	3,311.9	649.3	19.6	16.4
1977	4,108.7	785.4	19.1	4,357.7	785.4	18.0	16.8
1978	3,855.3	862.7	22.4	4,743.5	862.7	18.2	17.1
1979	4,456.0	899.2	20.2	4,946.2	899.2	18.2	16.8
1980	4,897.0	1,129.2	23.1	5,502.0	1,099.6	20.0	16.9
1981	4,380.0	924.8	21.1	5,327.0	973.2	18.3	16.4
1982	3,876.0	747.5	19.3	4,202.0	784.3	18.6	16.2

Source: ECLA, based on official figures.

ally responded to the interests of the dominant groups of the Central American societies, although it preserved some of the reformist characteristics that lay behind the original conceptual framework proposed by ECLA. It is no surprise therefore that equity and social considerations were insufficiently taken into account, or that the transnationalisation of the countries' economies was facilitated through an 'open door' policy towards foreign capital. This was a logical consequence of an integration process adjusted to a style of development whose main characteristics are well known, and which, with different nuances, was common to all five countries (Guatemala, Honduras, El Salvador, Nicaragua and Costa Rica). In other words, since the integration process was complementary to the domestic development of each country, it could hardly be expected to correct problems that domestic policies did not confront.

In the second place, because integration was simply a reflection of economic policies adopted in a more or less homogeneous manner in each country, it was the market mechanism that was basically depended upon to assign new activities—or reassign existing ones—in the light of the new expanded market. Although it is true that during the 1960s there persisted some modest efforts at introducing a certain level of consultation in allocating industrial projects between countries, through the so-called Integration Industries Regime—another remnant of ECLA's conceptual framework—these attempts had minimal results. In addition, the complementary efforts of the Central American Bank for Economic Integration to support projects located in the least developed countries of the region were insufficient to avoid a concentration of new industrial activities in the more highly developed countries.

This does not mean that a purely *laissez faire* policy was pursued, since moderately protectionist customs barriers were erected and fiscal incentives were offered for industrialisation, but, apart from these attempts to alter the prices of goods processed in the region relative to those in the international market, some governments, as well as private industrialists' organisations, resisted the measures. In their opinion, they would mean that the siting of activities would be directly influenced by non-market criteria (including the need to have an equitable geographical distribution of the new activities spawned by the Common Market).

Thirdly, since the General Treaty has come into operation, governments have displayed considerable pragmatism and flexibility in the application of the rules pertaining to the Common Market. The General Treaty and other regional agreements contained rules that subsequently proved to be very burdensome—many decisions required legislative approval in all five countries, which led to delays measuring years, not months, in their application, and they did not contain escape clauses. Governments therefore found solutions through 'agreed violations', as circumstances required. In some cases, the violations were adopted without agreement. The process has revealed a surprising capacity to adapt even to the most adverse circumstances, as will be seen.

In the fourth place, and perhaps due to the relative homogeneity that existed between the governments of the region, it was possible to separate, at least partially, developments related to economic integration from those that are usually the concern of the foreign policy of each country. In other words, it was possible to separate the economic from the political spheres. For example, the responsibility for the functioning of the Common Market was assigned to the ministers for the economy, who met in the intergovernmental forums established by the General Treaty, while the foreign affairs ministers met in the context of the Organisation of Central American States (ODECA). Furthermore, the 1960s, at least until 1967 or 1968, were virtually free from political conflict between the governments of the region. Even when the first differences between El Salvador and Honduras arose, over massive migrations, these were effectively isolated from the sphere of economic cooperation.

Fifthly, a symbiotic relationship developed between the 'inward growth' strategy implicit in economic integration and the industrialisation it fostered, and the 'outward growth' strategy traditionally associated with the development model of the five countries. The integration process was never conceived as an instrument to reduce Central America's participation in international trade (although it was conceived as a way of gaining greater autonomy in the development of that trade). In fact, as intra-regional trade and the level of industrialisation grew, so did trade with third countries. The ratio of imports from the rest of the world to GDP for Central America increased from 15.8 per cent in 1960 to 26.0 per cent in 1980. In addition, due to the high level of economic interdependence that developed between the countries of the region, a close interaction developed between the levels of trade with third countries and the levels of intra-regional trade. During periods of prosperity in the traditional export sector, intra-regional trade grew very rapidly, while during periods of international recession that trade lost its dynamism, although less than that of total trade, thus allowing it to play a compensatory role in the cycles related to the external sector. Furthermore, the Common Market became a test for the export of manufactured goods within the region—goods that subsequently would be able to compete in international markets. In summary, a complex reciprocal relationship was established between intra-regional and extra-regional trade.

Finally, although the integration commitment was of both a global character—the call was to accord free trade and adopt a common tariff—and of a specific nature—to execute joint industrial projects, such as a regional road or telecommunications network—the emphasis was on the perfection of a free trade zone and other global commitments. For example, it was expected that the common action adopted by each country to create a single regional economic unit would imply a reallocation of the countries' existing productive activities and a different mode of allocation of those activities at the regional level, without any of the countries being able to foresee how all this was going to affect it.

In sum, during the 1960s, against the background of a continually expanding international economy, relatively homogeneous governments in the region, a conceptual framework that saw integration advancing in progressive stages towards the achievement of a single economic unit, and a small but influential constituency in favour of the Common Market, the Central American integration process evolved in a relatively stable environment.

The beginnings of doubt

Beginning in 1971, when the US government decided to break the link between gold and the dollar, the international framework began to change rapidly. The period of expansion in international trade, which had already been put to the test during the second half of the previous decade, now faced new challenges, which were seriously to affect the fortunes of the international economy, and, in turn, the economies of the Central American countries. One of the many immediate consequences was that, faced with ever-growing restrictions in their traditional export sector, the countries of the region showed an increasing reluctance to meet their integration commitments regarding unlimited free trade.

In addition, there was an internal event which translated itself into a qualitative change in the conditions that had prevailed in previous years—

the armed conflict in 1969 between two member countries of the Common Market. The fact that the integration process survived with few substantive changes is eloquent testimony to the degree of interdependence that the five countries had already achieved, but the interruption of trade between El Salvador and Honduras in 1969, and the virtual withdrawal of Honduras at the end of 1970 from the majority of its multilateral commitments, signalled the formal suspension of the intergovernmental forums established in the General Treaty.[8] At the same time, the disappointment that prevailed in circles associated with the integration process convinced many that the only way to salvage the original impetus of the 1960s was through a global restructuring of the regional commitments.[9]

As a result partly of these two factors, questions were raised in some circles as to the validity of the conceptual framework that had guided the process during the 1960s. After more than a decade of experience at integration, not only in Central America but in other parts of Latin America and the rest of the world, it was beginning to become evident that, contrary to the forecasts of the theoreticians, none of these movements had witnessed a progressive expansion of their integration commitments, nor had the governments concerned delegated more activities to the regional institutions. Rather, in the majority of the movements, the pre-established goals had only rarely been achieved—as, for example, in the case of LAFTA—and in the more successful exercises, such as Central America's, the movements had simply found a sort of point of equilibrium at which they tended to rest.[10] In the specific case of Central America, the 'crisis' of integration did not refer so much to the breach between the original goals and achievements, as to the breach between achievements and expectations. There was no progress towards a full customs union, and even less towards the formation of a single regional economy.

Thus, it followed that in Latin America a more pragmatic approach to integration became increasingly popular. This new orientation, which some called 'informal integration' or 'integration by project', sometimes abandoned global approaches and goals, simply replacing them—or completing them—with joint activities in fields which permitted cooperation between two or more countries. This approach undoubtedly influenced the thinking behind both the Latin American Economic System (SELA) and the Second Montevideo Treaty, which established the Latin American Integration Association (ALADI). Even if the ideas had not yet been accepted in Central America, they were the subject of intense debate.

In summary, during the 1970s, contrary to the experience of the previous decade, doubts arose regarding the general orientation of Central American integration. This had two contradictory consequences: on the one hand, it underscored an intense debate on the 'restructuring' of the process, which in itself sometimes contributed to the hampering of specific action aimed at overcoming the 'equilibrium' sticking point at which the process found itself. On the other hand, it contributed to the abandonment of some of the fixed rules of the existing juridical framework—unilaterally suspended by Honduras at the end of 1970—and facilitated an increasing level of pragmatism intended to maintain the levels of economic interdependence achieved in previous years. As an example, although intra-regional trade grew at a lower rate than it had in the 1960s,[11] it nevertheless increased, while the movement continued to exhibit signs of vitality.

Yet, as a result of phenomena described above, the basis of mutual confidence and motivation that had helped so much to give the integration process its initial impulse was being eroded. In its place, there appeared the gradual bureaucratisation of some of the regional institutions in charge of promoting integration, a growing scepticism in various strata of the population regarding the prospects of integration, and open questioning, in some circles, of its potential benefits.

During a brief period there was even a possibility that events in the political sphere would spill over into the economic one, putting an end to the successful separation of political differences from the functioning of the Common Market. The cause was, of course, the armed conflict between El Salvador and Honduras. This disrupted economic relations between two countries which had had a long tradition of economic interdependence, even predating the formal arrangements of the 1950s—a disruption which persisted until 1981 when bilateral trade was re-established on a tentative basis. However, as already stated, the conflict was unable to interfere with the multilateral arrangements between the two countries and the other three members of the Common Market, and even a moderate trade flow between the two affected parties—through third countries—continued. So, in practice, a grave political conflict was unable to alter significantly the functioning of the Common Market along the lines foreseen in the General Treaty.

Towards the end of the 1970s, further major events had a decisive influence on the course of Central American integration, and are altering the basic characteristics of the process. Among these, two stand out. They are the rapid deterioration of the international economy, as a result of stabilisation policies and austerity measures adopted by various industrialised countries, especially the US, and the increasing heterogeneity of the governments within the region, with the appearance of a regime born of a popular insurrection in Nicaragua.

Regarding the first, from 1979 onwards the countries of the region were already facing serious problems in their foreign trade. These problems arose, first of all, from a contraction in world demand for the majority of the region's goods and from the deterioration in the region's terms of trade, especially in 1979, resulting in large part from the increase in the price of the region's liquid fuel imports. To these negative circumstances was added the erratic behaviour of the capital account. Large capital outflows occurred, encouraged by non-economic factors, while the region faced increasing difficulty in mobilising new capital from an international financial community increasingly concerned about its creditworthiness. In addition, higher interest rates in the international capital markets increased the burden on the public external debt. The situation deteriorated progressively in subsequent years: for the region as a whole, the gross domestic product in 1979 grew at a real rate of 3.6 per cent; that rate fell to 1 per cent in 1980, and it became a negative 1 per cent in 1981 and a negative 3 per cent in 1982. The crisis was of such magnitude that real per capita income in Costa Rica, Guatemala and Honduras now barely reaches the 1976 level, while, in the case of El Salvador and Nicaragua, it is equivalent to the levels achieved during the first half of the 1960s.[12]

The second development has multiple implications. Not only are there diverse governments in the region, pursuing different objectives in economic policy and separate paths towards their attainment, but important political differences have appeared, and these threaten to spill over into the area of economic cooperation. In addition, intense conflicts in other countries of the region, especially El Salvador, and the highly visible presence of diverse international interests, which have injected an East–West dimension into those conflicts, have greatly exacerbated the differences between the governments of the region.

These two new phenomena or, at least, their qualitatively different intensity when contrasted with previous years, could alter the whole face of the integration movement and even—although it is not likely—interrupt the economic interdependence achieved between the five countries during the previous 20 years.

It has already been pointed out in previous pages that a symbiotic relationship has historically existed between the 'inward growth' strategies that facilitated industrialisation through integration, and the 'outward growth' strategies associated with the traditional character of Central America's participation in the international economy. During the past three years, hand in hand with a progressive contraction in aggregate demand, almost all countries have been forced to restrict their global imports, sometimes including those originating in the rest of the region. Furthermore, the shortage of foreign exchange has been so acute in some countries that their respective central banks have been unable to settle their obligations arising from deficits in intra-regional trade accumulated in the Central American Clearing House.

None of the above necessarily implied a reduction in the level of economic interdependence between the countries of the region. On the contrary, collective action could help to mitigate the recessive trends originating in the traditional external sector, and intra-regional trade could once more play its past compensatory role in the cycles of trade with third countries.

In effect, to deal with the situation, the region's countries resorted to a number of bilateral and multilateral mechanisms, with which they acknowledged their desire to preserve their interdependence, in recognition of the role that integration has to play in the development of their economies. The Central Banks of surplus countries involved in intra-regional trade extended credit lines to deficit countries for more than US$300 million during the period 1980–82. At present (November, 1983), about US$250 million of those obligations are outstanding, which means that the capacity of central banks to continue extending credit is nearing its limits. It is nevertheless worth noting the magnitude of the financing operation undertaken by the central banks of countries that, in the political sphere, have major differences. As to the multilateral dimension, in 1981 the five governments of the region established a mechanism—the Central American Common Market Fund—to finance the deficits arising from periodic liquidations of balances in the Central American Clearing House. Furthermore, the five countries have undertaken joint efforts in the international financial community to find the resources to capitalise this fund.[13] These efforts have so far been relatively unproductive.

In summary, during the period 1980–82, the governments of the region made a considerable effort to maintain the levels of intra-regional trade, so that it could continue to play its traditional role in compensating for short-falls in trade with third countries. However, in 1981 this trade was already losing its impetus, no doubt owing to the global balance-of-payments problems confronting the countries, and in 1982 this trend was aggravated (see Table 2). Even though, until 1982, the contraction of intra-regional trade was not significantly higher than the contraction in global trade, it is not certain that this situation can be maintained. This does not mean that intra-regional trade will cease, but its evolution will naturally depend on the capacity of each country to import from the rest of the region, which in turn is a function of each country's exports to the region. In other words, the limit of intra-regional trade could be decided in the years to come by the availability of foreign exchange to the countries in deficit.

The above implies that one of the basic advantages of the integration process in the past could be lost, since intra-regional trade would fail to compensate for the contraction of trade with the rest of the world. At the same time, intra-regional trade could itself be adversely affected by the crisis that most countries face in the external sector, joining the phenomena that have contributed to the recession in the region.

The increasing level of political heterogeneity in the region could also significantly change the characteristics of the integration process, for both economic and non-economic reasons. This heterogeneity has itself contributed substantially to the present political differences, which have themselves been exacerbated by the attentions of diverse outside interests. This raises doubts whether in future it will be possible to separate economic integration from the sphere of foreign policy. It is no secret, for example, that there has been armed confrontation on the border between Nicaragua and Honduras, and that profound differences have arisen between El Salvador and Nicaragua, on the one hand, and Costa Rica and Nicaragua on the other.

Up to the present, however, in spite of such tensions, the region's governments have demonstrated their ability to continue operating in the economic dimension. In spite of the fact that mutual confidence, and the credibility of the process, have been further eroded, trade goes on. Governments continue to act jointly to overcome common problems—for example, the financing of intra-regional trade—and to take part in inter-government meetings, whether they are between economics ministers, central bank presidents or even foreign ministers (in relation to the initiative towards political détente proposed by the governments of Colombia,

Mexico, Panama and Venezuela). It is reasonable to assume, however, that the capacity to keep economic cooperation separate from political tensions has its limit, and that the region is much closer to that limit today than at any time since the Treaty was signed.

It is impossible to predict what that limit is. Undoubtedly, armed aggression against a country—an extreme but not an altogether impossible circumstance—would signify the end of this particular experiment in multilateral cooperation. A continued polarisation of positions between countries could have the same effect. At all events, to the considerable social and political costs of a spill-over of any differences between governments one would have to add the economic cost inherent in the loss of the benefits brought by integration. Fortunately, however, the high level of economic interdependence that has already been attained has so far proved to be an effective barrier to any such spill-over.[14] In this regard, Central American economic cooperation could eventually contribute significantly to détente in the political sphere, not only because of the concrete benefits that economic interdependence brings, but, because, having learnt to cooperate in the economic sphere, governments might also learn to co-exist in the political one.

But growing heterogeneity among governments has another implication for the style of integration that may develop in the future. As already stated, the integration process is a tool of development, complementing the efforts undertaken in individual countries. As long as the objectives of the five countries were more or less similar, it was not difficult to conceive of an integration process that reflected development patterns prevalent in each of the countries. However, in contemporary Central America, there are governments which pursue differing economic policies. They differ especially in regard to the relative importance assigned to distributive policies, the role of the public sector in the economy, the degree of determination shown in the application of economic policies, the role of popular participation, and the characteristics of their external economic relations.

This by no means suggests that heterogeneity in the application of economic policies is incompatible with an integration process, since there is sufficient community of interest between all countries for integration to accord with some of their objectives. What it does mean is that, from now on, integration must be perceived somewhat differently from the past. In other words, if any doubt still remained in the 1960s, it is now abundantly clear that any hope of reconciling all areas of economic policy of all the countries, with the aim of reaching, gradually but progressively, some kind of regional unity, must be abandoned. What is required, rather, is to identify areas of common interest between economies whose goals may be different, but which may be susceptible to joint efforts to achieve those goals.

The challenge of the future

Faced with the great political and social tensions in some countries, and the serious conflicts that exist between governments, the outside observer might conclude that the Central American integration process has lost all meaning. Certainly, the tensions have altered the relationships between the region's governments—survival takes precedence over economic development—and the mutual trust needed for carrying out an integration programme is being increasingly eroded. However, the degree of economic interdependence reached by the end of the 1970s was of such magnitude that the integration process continues to show a fair degree of vitality. About 20 per cent of the total exports of the five Central American countries is traded between them; the fortunes of each country's manufacturing sector depend to a high degree on the functioning of the free trade scheme, and the region's governments continue to show some inclination to co-operate in such important fields as energy, transport, foreign trade and external financing.[15]

The main problem is undoubtedly that of finding some way of relieving the grave social and political tensions that some of its countries face domestically and that Central America faces as a whole in its international relations. Given the present levels of polarisation and the conflicting external interests playing a part in the region, this will not be easy. Inevitably, the topic of economic development will continue to be relegated to second place for some time to come.

It is foreseeable that Central America will continue to be a region that comprises heterogeneous governments and political systems, but nevertheless preserves strong common interests. The fact that governments have different objectives and instruments of economic policy by no means excludes the possibility of promoting economic cooperation between them; it only means that the approach in the 1980s and beyond must be changed. It is no longer feasible, for example, to think of a gradual and progressive coordination of all areas of economic policy with a view to achieving a single economic unit. This would clearly reveal irreconcilable differences between domestic and regional economic activities.

In other words, recognition of the complementary and instrumental nature of the integration movement implies the abandonment of the goal of reconciling the economic policies of all the participating countries, in all their aspects. On the contrary, in order that joint endeavours of value to each of the parties concerned may be carried out, areas of common interest must first be identified, recognising that some problems that the countries face are common to all. Examples of common efforts that do not necessarily require global commitments abound. Among them is the nurturing of intra-regional trade under a preferential regime. In addition, countries could continue to promote regional industrial and agricultural projects; they can cooperate in the field of energy—for example, by linking up their electricity distribution systems; they can jointly develop part of their physical infrastructure and transport services, and they can cooperate in finding ways of better exploiting the opportunities offered by the international economy. None of the above involves commitments that require countries to subordinate their national development goals to abstract regional aims, but they do confer on integration the role of supplementing development within the framework of each country's objectives. An approach of this kind also would make it possible to extend the geographical sphere of cooperation to include, for example, Panama and even other Latin American countries.

A style of integration that has limited objectives requires a high degree of flexibility in the application of regional commitments, and levels of consultation which permit countries to take account of what regional cooperation has to offer in achieving their national development goals. It also requires regional institutions that can identify projects and programmes susceptible to cooperation and that can promote their implementation.

All of this is readily achievable not only by the Central American countries, but by other subregional groupings in Latin America. It is surely reasonable therefore not only to continue the efforts to preserve the economic interdependence that has already been achieved, but also to try to take greater advantage of the potential that those efforts imply.

Notes

1. In Resolution 9 (IV) of ECLA, approved in June 1951, the representatives of the Central American countries asked the Secretariat of ECLA to support the efforts of the economic cooperation committee, made up of the economics ministers of the region.
2. 'Integration (in Central America) has been conceived in a limited fashion, oriented especially towards integration in the industrial sphere'. CEPAL, *La integración económica de Centroamérica: Su evolución y perspectivas,* (E/CN.12/CCE/33/Rev.2), 1956, p 6.
3. The General Treaty was signed by representatives of the governments of Guatemala, El Salvador, Honduras and Nicaragua on 13 December 1960. Costa Rica acceded to it on 23 July 1962.
4. See, for example, James E Meade, *The Theory of Customs Union,* Amsterdam: North Holland Publishing Co., 1955; and, Jacob Viner, *The Customs Union Issue,* New York: The Carnegie Endowment for International Peace, 1950.
5. Ernest B Hass, *Beyond the Nation State: Functionalism and International Organisation,* Palo Alto: Stanford University Press, 1964.
6. Bela Balassa, *The Theory of Economic Integration,* Homewood, Illinois: Richard D Irwin, Inc., 1961.
7. The decline in that relative participation during the period 1976–77 was not due so much to a loss of dynamism on the part of intraregional trade but rather to the exceptional prices for coffee prevalent in international markets, which inflated the value of extra-regional exports.
8. The so-called 'Central American Economic Council', made up of the economics ministers of each country, and which the General Treaty established as the force in the integration process, thus ceased to function. In its place, the governments first established the so-called 'Normalising Commission of the Central American Common Market', and, later, simply the meetings of the economics ministers. However, reciprocal trade between most countries—Honduras being the exception—continued to follow the rules of the General Treaty.
9. This led the governments to establish, in 1973, a 'High Level Committee for the Restructuring of the Central American Common Market.'
10. See: CEPAL, *Centroamérica: Evolución Económica desde la Posguerra* (CEPAL/ME/ODE/34/ Rev. 1), January of 1980, Chapter III.
11. During the period 1960–68, intra-regional trade grew at yearly compounded rates close to 30 per cent, both in current as well as constant values, while during the period 1969–1978, the rate of growth reached 15 per cent yearly in current values and approximately 6 per cent in constant values.
12. CEPAL, *La crisis en Centroamérica: orígenes, alcanes y consecuencias* (E/CEPAL/G.1261), 22 September 1983.
13. That is the purpose of the forum organised by the Inter-American Development Bank, which convened its first Special Meeting of the Development Programme of the Central American Isthmus in Brussels, 13–15 September 1983.
14. In this respect, the spokesman for the Central American countries at the Brussels meeting (note above) pointed out: 'Outright necessity also made us separate economic activities from politics—to such an extent, that neither ideological differences nor the diversity of political systems have been capable of impeding the progress of integration. Even the armed conflict between two countries in 1969 did not cause irreparable damage to the multilateral scheme.'
15. For example, in the second half of 1983 alone, in spite of growing tensions between countries in the political and military spheres, the energy ministers met to adopt a Central

American Energy Programme; the transport ministers met to consolidate the Central American road network and to agree on measures designed to facilitate intra-regional transportation; electricity projects continued to be developed, including one which allows for the exchange of electricity between Honduras and Nicaragua; the already mentioned Special Meeting of the Development Programme of the Central American Isthmus took place; the new president of the Central American Bank for Economic Integration was unanimously elected; two meetings of the airlines of the five countries were held to explore forms of promoting mutual cooperation, while the meetings of ministers and vice-ministers for the economy and presidents of central banks continued with relative normality.

9

Experiences in regional integration and cooperation: the case of the Caribbean Community and Common Market (CARICOM)

William G Demas and Jasper Scotland

Up until the 1950s, the Caribbean territories had already shared a common bond, as colonies of a European power. During that period, even if the idea existed that stronger ties between the Caribbean economies could help in their development, no positive action was taken to promote such cooperation. The Federation set up in 1958 was the first definite step, but it broke up in 1962. Then, on the premise that some form of economic integration was essential to the survival and development of the region, the Caribbean Free Trade Association (CARIFTA) was formed in 1968.

This was the first of a number of significant steps on the road to increased cooperation and integration. A subregional integration institution, the East Caribbean Common Market (ECCM), was also established in 1968 and an agreement setting up the Caribbean Development Bank was signed in 1969 (it began operations in 1970).

CARIFTA, it should be mentioned, had a special focus—free trade—and was envisaged as a first step towards deeper forms of economic integration. In 1973, it was replaced by the Caribbean Community and Common Market (CARICOM). A brief outline of some of the major provisions of the Treaty establishing CARICOM is essential in any assessment of the English-speaking Caribbean's experience of integration and cooperation.[1]

The Treaty provides for the setting up of a Common Market. One of its major objectives is 'strengthening the coordination and regulation of economic and trade relations' among participating countries. It envisages 'sustained expansion and continuing integration of economic activities' and the benefits of its particular form of integration must be 'equitably' shared, taking into account the special needs of the relatively less developed member states. The Treaty goes beyond mere trade liberalisation and the consequent beneficial shift in the division of labour among members of the Common Market. It provides for, *inter alia*: cooperation in customs administration; a common external tariff; a common protective policy; some coordination of economic policies and development planning; harmonisation of fiscal incentives to industry legislation practices; and cooperation in the areas of monetary, payments and exchange rate policies. But its provisions go beyond the economic sphere. One of the major stated objectives is the coordination of the foreign policies of member states; another is the pursuit of what the Treaty calls 'functional cooperation', which refers to cooperation by member states in the operation of certain common services, in education and shipping, for example, and several other socioeconomic and cultural activities.

CARICOM, then, is not simply a trading arrangement or even a mechanism for promoting cooperation in production, based on the creation of a Common Market. In addition to integration of national markets and cooperation in production, the CARICOM states also undertook to co-operate with each other in certain functional areas, as well as in other economic, political, financial and monetary matters.

The structure of CARICOM

The Caribbean Community comprises thirteen states: Antigua and Barbuda, Bahamas, Barbados, Belize, Dominica, Grenada, Guyana, Jamaica, Montserrat, St Kitts-Nevis, St Lucia, St Vincent, and Trinidad and Tobago. All except the Bahamas are signatories to the Common Market provisions of the Treaty. In the CARICOM context, Barbados, Bahamas, Guyana, Jamaica and Trinidad and Tobago are referred to as 'more developed countries (MDCs)' and the others as 'less developed countries (LDCs)'. These terms are obviously only relative. Except for Belize, the LDCs form a subregional integration grouping known as the Organisation of Eastern Caribbean States (OECS). The OECS, established in 1981, replaced the cooperation arrangement previously known as the West Indies Associated States (WISA). The East Caribbean Common Market (ECCM) arrangement, established since 1968, continues to operate under the aegis of the OECS.

The salient activities of the OECS are:

1) The promotion of economic integration through the ECCM, which promotes intra-OECS trade liberalisation, the coordination of external

tariffs and, to some extent, cooperation in subregional industrial and agricultural development;

2) the issue and management of a subregional currency through the East Caribbean Currency Authority which, since October 1983, has become the East Caribbean Central Bank;

3 the coordination of judicial activity at the level of the West Indies Associated States Supreme Court;

4) the coordination of civil aviation through the Directorate of Civil Aviation (DCA); and,

5) the establishment abroad of joint overseas Missions and Embassies.

The OECS is a subregional grouping of the less developed CARICOM states.

The main organs of the Caribbean Community itself are: the Heads of Government Conference (the Supreme Organ), the Common Market Council (with one ministerial representative from each member state), and the Secretariat (the administrative arm headed by a Secretary-General). Other institutions created by the Treaty include standing committees of ministers responsible for each of the following areas: finance, education, health, labour, agriculture, foreign affairs, industry, transport and information. The institutions formulate policies of a regional nature, subject to the general directives of the Heads of Government Conference.

The Community established relations with several 'associate' but autonomous institutions such as: the Caribbean Development Bank (CDB), the Caribbean Examinations Council (CXC), the Council of Legal Education (CLE), the University of Guyana (UG), the University of the West Indies (UWI), the Regional Shipping Council (RSC) and the OECS.

CARICOM objectives

CARICOM's three basic objectives may be summarised as.

1) Economic integration through the workings of the Common Market;

2) functional cooperation in sectors such as transport, education, health, labour and information; and,

3) coordination of foreign policy.

Economic integration activities

The principal instruments of the Common Market are the trade liberalisation regime, the agricultural marketing protocol (AMP), a common external tariff, a common protective policy; the harmonisation of fiscal incentives to industry; regional industrial programming; monetary, payments and financial cooperation; cooperation in production generally and through joint ventures; some coordination in agricultural development; and coordination of external trade and external economic relations.

The CARIFTA arrangement which preceeded CARICOM helped substantially in freeing intra-regional trade. Between 1967 and 1973, the proportion of intra-regional trade to total trade increased from 3 per cent to about 5 per cent. By 1982 it was nearly 9 per cent. Over 90 per cent of the items traded intra-regionally were free of trade barriers. This growth in intra-regional trade took place in spite of difficulties encountered by the integration movement when, in the late 1970s, two MDCs—in defence of their balance of payments and in accordance with treaty provisions—imposed global quantitative restrictions, with telling effect on intra-regional trade. Implementation of the Common Market provisions has not, however, been as scheduled, and some of the lags and shortcomings are examined below.

The agricultural marketing protocol (AMP) signed at the same time as the CARIFTA agreement and continued under the aegis of the CARICOM treaty, contains several provisions for the intra-regional marketing of agricultural products. Prices were fixed from time to time for a range of agricultural products, and exports or imports were mutually agreed upon for surplus or deficit countries respectively. The protocol was accompanied by a guaranteed market scheme (GMS) for products produced in the LDCs. Transport difficulties, inadequate market information, and the absence of efficient production plans which would lead to greater specialisation in agricultural production, particularly in the LDCs, caused the operations of the AMP and GMS to be less effective than originally envisaged. However, as a result of the two instruments, a limited volume of trade in agricultural products between the member states has been maintained and developed. The AMP is now being re-examined with a view to making it more effective.

The common external tariff (CET) is not yet 'common'. The four MDCs agreed on a common external tariff which came into force on 1 August 1973. But this has not yet achieved the targeted harmonisation with the CET of the LDSs and Belize.[2] Further, even the harmonisation between the tariff of the MDCs is of limited effect. That is because of the conditional duty reduction and exemption list which effectively enables the national government, and not the Common Market Council of Ministers, to set tariffs for almost all imported raw materials, intermediate goods and capital goods. Commonality therefore tends to be the exception rather than the rule.

No positive action has yet been taken towards formulating and implementing a common protective policy based on the harmonisation of quantitative restrictions in order to promote the development of, and protect, specific regional industrial and agricultural activities. And the economic and political difficulties facing national governments during recent years appear to be reducing the likelihood of early agreement on the implementation of this measure. As will be pointed out below, implementation of the agreed change in the rules of origin to facilitate a substantial transformation in the industrial processes carried out in the region has also encountered operational difficulties. More recently, the trade liberalisation process has also been plagued by the foreign-exchange difficulties of most of the constituent states of the Community.

In 1981, the rules governing the duty-free treatment of regional products were changed to induce producers to undertake more processing in the region and to encourage greater use of indigenous raw materials. Certain difficulties have arisen over the administration of the rules-of-origin criteria and the certification of goods entering intra-regional trade. These have led to some slowing of trade liberalisation.

Further, the balance-of-payments situation in several MDCs has led to currency devaluations and import restrictions which have tended to militate against the hitherto relatively free flow of regional products. In 1979, the region established a clearing and payments mechanism, the CARICOM Multilateral Clearing Facility, to which detailed reference will be made later, which assisted considerably in facilitating intra-regional trade. But, in the first quarter of 1983, the payments mechanism suspended operations, primarily because a major participating country had exceeded its credit ceiling and the mechanism became illiquid. This development, too, has caused a slowdown in the growth of intra-regional trade exchanges.

The CARICOM arrangement envisaged industrial development of the region through the pooling of markets, some programming of industrial production and joint production, and the development of export-oriented industries, and its contribution to industrial progress in the region cannot be dismissed as negligible. Manufacturing production has increased during the last ten to fifteen years. It now accounts for between 10 per cent and

20 per cent of total production (GDP) in many CARICOM States. Much of that production is geared for the regional market and has been in response to a regional import-substitution strategy. Some states, particularly the LDCs, have attracted 'enclave-type' or 'off-shore assembly' industries, perhaps as a result of the regional agreement on the harmonisation of fiscal incentives, a scheme with has worked reasonably well. Industrialisation in at least one state has been based on its demonstrated capacity to develop some production of light manufactures for sale within CARICOM and to third country markets.

But regional attempts to programme industrial production have been disappointing. The sub-regional ECCM industry allocation scheme covers some 30 small industrial activities, of which about eight have come on stream, but the broader regional exercise of industrial programming has made little progress. A comprehensive study of a framework for regional industrial programming has been undertaken, which considered relevant criteria for the selection and location of industries. It identified a cluster of industrial activities which, with regional collaboration, could be pursued in the short, medium and long term. The activities included food processing, textiles and clothing, wood and furniture, building materials (clay blocks, bricks and structural steel), leather and footwear, pulp and paper, and petrochemicals. However, the decisionmaking process for the implementation of a rational approach to regional industrial programming has, for a variety of reasons, been slow and halting.

Considerable technical work has been done in the field of agriculture. A regional food and nutrition strategy has been developed and spelled out, and the Caribbean Food Corporation was established to rationalise and develop regional agricultural production. However that organisation has got off to a slow start.

One mechanism, which has been on the books in the region for some time now and has the potential for advancing the cause of industrial programming, is the CARICOM enterprise regime, which contemplates the establishment of various regional enterprises (in manufacturing, insurance, banking, construction, consultancy services, etc.). The principles underlying the concept of a CARICOM enterprise regime have been firmly accepted, but the concomitant steps for implementation of the regime have been slow.

Monetary and financial cooperation activities

In the area of monetary and financial cooperation, too, there have been several developments. The central banks and monetary authorities have built up a significant rapport, and engage in frequent informal consultations. Coincidentally perhaps, by 1976 the six individual currencies of the region had adopted a common intervention currency, the US dollar, and thereby avoided day-to-day variations in exchange rates between the regional currencies, though each country is free to change its 'parity' at any time.

The region's central banks and monetary authorities collaborated from 1980 in the issue and administration of a CARICOM traveller's cheque. Those institutions have also been involved in the establishment of a multi-lateralised regional payments and clearing scheme—the CARICOM multi-lateral clearing facility (CMCF)—which has helped to conserve scarce foreign exchange and has facilitated payments arising from intra-regional trade and other transactions. In each of its first four years of operation, the facility saved the region US$200 million in foreign exchange. And there is no doubt that its existence was of critical importance in sustaining and developing significant levels of intra-regional trade. Indeed, when the facility was forced to suspend operations in early 1983—primarily because one member state had exceeded its credit limits and was unable to settle the required 50 per cent of its outstanding balance—regional trade suffered serious setbacks. Steps are currently in train to reactivate the CMCF.

The Caribbean Development Bank (CDB) has also contributed in no small way to regional financial cooperation. To date, the Bank has mobilised from both within and outside the region nearly US$500 million in financial resources for the support of development projects. In fact, some 70 per cent of its lending on concessionary terms has been to the LDCs. Trinidad and Tobago, the only country in the region which because of its oil-producing capacity was not adversely affected by the oil crisis of the 1970s, also provided generous financial support to its CARICOM partners in the period 1973–82. However, because of a declining trend in that country's foreign reserves, this level of financial support to its regional partners has abated in the last two years.

The CARICOM regime contemplated significant developments in the flow of capital between states, particularly from the MDCs to the LDCs. Such developments have not taken place, chiefly because of the exchange control regulations of member states. Exchange control policy at the national level has been insulated from the various regional attempts to coordinate financial policies. The weak foreign exchange situation of most member states no doubt militates against regional efforts to encourage a freer intra-regional flow of capital.

With regard to the treaty provisions for consultation on economic policies and the coordination of development planning, progress has been markedly slow. Although the Treaty obliges member countries to 'seek to progressively coordinate their trade relations with third countries or groups of countries', there are instances of significant national trade agreements with third parties which are not even reported to regional partners, as the Treaty requires. However, it has to be pointed out that the region has participated en bloc in the ACP/EEC negotiations leading to the signing of the Lomé Conventions, and the region's initial response to the Caribbean Basin Initiative (CBI) showed signs of a high degree of collaboration and coordination. It is as yet too early even to speculate whether the initiative, as it is being implemented, will prove to be a cohesive or a divisive force for regional cooperation and development.

Functional cooperation

The Caribbean Community has made giant strides in the area of functional cooperation. There is a wide variety of regionally engineered policies, programmes and projects in the field of health, for example. The regional University of the West Indies continues. The Caribbean Examination Council (CXC) has also successfully established a system of secondary school examinations which will soon fully replace the previous reliance on British educational institutions for the testing of secondary school graduates. Several programmes and projects have been established—through the CARICOM Secretariat and the CDB, for example—for the provision and development of the technical assistance required by the various CARICOM states, particularly the LDCs. There is some cooperation (certainly not enough) between national radio and television broadcasting establishments; and the establishment of the Caribbean News Agency (CANA) has assisted in the flow of news and information about member states to each other.

In the field of culture and sports, mention must be made of the Caribbean Festival of Creative Arts (CARIFESTA), which has played a significant role in bringing together the artists of the region every two years. There are desks at the CARICOM secretariat dealing with women's affairs, labour relations and youth and sport. Significant regional cooperation is also in evidence in a wide variety of other areas, such as regional library development, meteorology, the creation of a restricted postal union, the 1980 population census and the establishment of a Caribbean Common Market Standards Council. Functional cooperation between the CARICOM States is an essential element in the regional structure. Its importance ought not to be overlooked.

Coordination of foreign policy

CARICOM states have coordinated their positions in various international forums on a wide variety of issues. Among such issues are the Convention on the Law of the Sea; apartheid; territorial claims by third countries on Belize and Guyana; the ACP/EEC negotiations; the Caribbean Basin Initiative; and the signing of economic cooperation agreements with Canada and Mexico. Inasmuch as coordination of foreign policy does not necessarily mean harmonisation, there have been occasions when individual CARICOM states have adopted different stances on international issues. However, it is probably no accident that, since the establishment of CARICOM, international recognition of the external legal personality of CARICOM has been on the increase.

Some conclusions

Advocates of regional trade liberalisation and market integration may learn some useful lessons from the CARICOM experience. First, there seem to be inherent limitations in reliance on trade liberalisation as a means of promoting the economic transformation of small developing countries. The region has a combined population of about 5.5 million, and a combined gross domestic product of about US$13 billion. Production possibilities are competitive—with little complementarity. The scope for a diversified economy, which can produce certain basic consumer goods as well as most capital goods and inputs for production, is limited. Hence, the CARICOM economies continue to rely heavily on imports of essential consumer goods, production inputs, capital goods and technology. Increasingly, it seems that the sub-regional import substitution process in the CARICOM sub-region needs to be accompanied by greater efforts at promoting exports to countries outside CARICOM.

Secondly, the ink was barely dry on the Treaty of Chaguaramas before crisis beset the world economy in late 1973 and wreaked havoc, particularly for the developing economies of small oil-importing states. As a result, for the past ten years, in spite of CARICOM, the region's economy has remained virtually stagnant. International developments led to a serious slowdown in the region's export and tourist sectors. Terms of trade have deteriorated and external finance has become not only scarcer, but more expensive. Integration schemes, even if they work reasonably well, are not insulated from international economic dislocation.

Thirdly, while intra-regional trade has increased since 1968, expectations that the Common Market would lead to a higher degree of cooperation in production between the states are largely unfulfilled. The regional economy remains structurally weak and undiversified. In particular, the agricultural sector is as weak and dependent as it ever was (though it would be premature to write off continuing attempts at cooperation in production in the sub-region).

Fourthly, however, there is no gainsaying the fact that the level and effectiveness of functional and other forms of cooperation between the CARICOM states has benefited both individual members and the region as a whole. A greater degree of coordination of foreign policies, especially in the trade and economic fields, has been achieved—although the situation is by no means ideal in these respects.

Inter-regional cooperation

So far, we have concentrated on what may be viewed as a somewhat parochial assessment of the workings of the CARICOM integration exercise. But it is recognised that CARICOM is a small English-speaking sub-region which forms part of a wider multilingual Latin American and Caribbean region, in which there is tremendous scope for economic, technological, political, social and cultural cooperation. Most independent CARICOM states are members of the Organisation of American States (OAS), the Latin American Economic System (SELA) and the Inter-American Development Bank (IDB). In the United Nations, the Commonwealth Caribbean countries are included in the Latin American region as members of the Economic Commission for Latin America (ECLA) and its subgroup, the Caribbean Development and Cooperation Committee (CDCC). Colombia, Venezuela and Mexico are regional members of the Caribbean Development Bank.

A variety of options for greater Caribbean and Caribbean/Latin American cooperation present themselves. A Group of Caribbean Experts who reviewed the progress of the grouping up to 1980, pointed out opportunities for both 'deepening' the cooperation mechanisms among CARICOM states and 'widening' the movement through the extension of trade and other relations with non-CARICOM Caribbean states and the rest of Latin America.

A symposium held in Barbados in 1983 to review CARICOM progress in its first 10 years of operation also considered the question of CARICOM relationships with the wider Caribbean and Latin America. In this context, particular note was taken of the provision in the articles of the new Latin American Association for Development and Integration which would permit its member states, in specified conditions, to negotiate nonreciprocal preferential trading arrangements with less developed countries in the Americas. Within this framework, an economic and technical cooperation agreement between the Andean Group and the Caribbean Community is a possibility worth pursuing.

There seems to be a degree of consensus that there is scope for further cooperation in the Caribbean/Latin American region in areas such as trade, technology, project development, the creation of jointly financed enterprises and monetary and financial matters. It appears, however, that, as in the case of the evolution of cooperation between the CARICOM states, a process of institution-building is needed as a preliminary to the development of integration and cooperation mechanisms at the levels of the wider Caribbean and Latin American region.

In this context, too, the scope for cooperation among developing regions (or South-South cooperation) is vast. The CARICOM experience has demonstrated that a region can achieve at least some gains, economic and political, through integration and cooperation. However, in the face of serious international crises, such gains may be much less than they could otherwise be. Perhaps it is fitting to conclude by quoting in full some of the recommendations of the Group of Caribbean Experts on the question of CARICOM relations with the Third World:

> The external trade and financial requirements for development in the region will call for even greater and more concerted efforts by the Caribbean countries to increase their contributions to developing countries' initiatives to establish a New International Economic Order. In particular, CARICOM should lend its full weight to efforts to:

a) Achieve greater stability in export earnings from commodity trade by the negotiation and the renegotiation of commodity agreements, the establishment of the Common Fund and the provision of more adequate facilities for compensatory financing;
b) roll back protectionism in the industrialised countries with respect to unprocessed, semiprocessed and processed products;
c) promote concrete international action to assist developing countries to overcome the international obstacles to achieving greater domestic processing of their own raw materials for export and greater participation by them in the international marketing and distribution of their products;
d) conclude the negotiations on a code of conduct for the transfer of technology;
e) support greater participation by developing countries in maritime and air transport, particularly with respect to the movement of their own cargoes;
f) secure larger and more predictable flows of concessionary finance on improved terms and on both a programme and project basis. In this connection, the CARICOM countries should make special efforts to seek better international understanding and support for the special needs of island developing countries, even when they fall into the category of so-called middle-income countries;
g) mobilise a larger flow of risk capital for productive investment and negotiate a code of conduct for the operations of transnational corporations in developing countries; and,
h) reform and restructure the international monetary system.

Notes

1. It should be noted that there is a difference between regional (or subregional) cooperation and regional (or subregional) integration. Both connote collaboration between states or regions, but integration is the more intense form of collaboration. In fact, integration schemes usually involve the participants giving up some degree of sovereignty in the interests of the attainment of predetermined goals. Accordingly, economic integration mechanisms aim at creating an economic unit larger than the sum of the economic units of the participants.
2. Harmonisation with these was programmed for 1981 (except in the case of Montserrat for which the correspondent date is 1985).

10

The Andean Pact: problems and perspectives

Germanico Salgado Penaherrera

The Cartagena Agreement: basic principles, evolution, achievements and problems

The Cartagena Agreement, which unites the countries of the Andean Pact, was signed in May 1969 in Cartagena, Colombia. The Council, the Pact's administrative body, was immediately constituted and began to function alongside the Commission—the decision-making body, made up of government representatives—towards the end of 1969 in Lima, Peru, which was chosen as the headquarters for these institutions. They have now been in existence for fourteen years, a long enough period of time to be able to make a serious evaluation of the long-term perspectives for this attempt at regional integration.

The Cartagena Agreement was a direct outcome of the frustration felt by some members of the Latin American Free Trade Association (LAFTA) over the way that that form of regional integration had worked in practice. The countries concerned were those of medium economic importance within the LAFTA (Colombia, Chile, Peru and Venezuela), and two of the so-called relatively less developed countries (Bolivia and Ecuador). The LAFTA was created in 1960 with the aim of achieving within the space of twelve years a free trade zone according to the classical definition.

As might have been expected given its structure, the system worked to the advantage of those countries in a more advanced stage of industrialisation, which, because of their larger internal markets, had been able to go further in the import-substitution process. These were Argentina, Brazil and Mexico. The benefits of the system to them are shown by the figures for the expansion of trade, and participation in complementarity agreements, in the vast majority of which these three countries were involved. As a result, negotiations within the Association stagnated, with the weaker countries (the small and medium-sized countries) blocking any advance.

Of these countries, the Andean nations wanted to form a group which would bring about more rapid and complete integration, with leaving the LAFTA—thus they called themselves a 'subregional' group. The aim was to give the group as a whole sufficient weight to be able to negotiate on more equal terms with the major countries in the LAFTA (Argentina, Brazil and Mexico). This implied a more ambitious form of integration than what had been achieved so far, despite great efforts, through the Association, emphasis on the industrial sector, through joint planning in areas of major concern (consumer durables, intermediate products and capital goods), and a system which would ensure 'harmonious and balanced development' for all member states, which basically means first of all the existence of effective preferential treatment for the weaker countries in the group.

The initial responses to the frustration caused by LAFTA, and the need to reconcile the different interests of the more and less developed nations in the group determined the basic features of the structure of the system of integration which was built into the Cartagena Agreement. To give a brief summary, its original characteristics were:

1) The creation within a period of ten years of an economic union of a new kind. This was more than a customs union, since it involved harmonising policies in fields such as technology, foreign investment, and industrial policies. Nevertheless, it could not be called a common market, since there were no specific provisions for the free movement of productive factors.

2) The basic aim was to create economic conditions and the necessary means for joint industrial development. It was not simply a question of coordinating the industrial policies of member states, but of drawing up an industrial strategy and policies for the sub-region which would also have to be planned or 'programmed'. This planning would have to take into account the need both for justice and effectiveness.

3) Two systems were used to create a market, involving the removal of internal barriers to commercial exchange, and the erection of common protective barriers against third parties. The first was the automatic and lineal liberalisation of tariffs, accompanied by a two-stage process of progressively building up a common external tariff; the second involved joint industrial planning, which also used the mechanism of liberalisation–common external tariffs, but in this case to support the distribution across different countries of industrial

projects, through the sectoral programmes for industrial development.

4) The principle of balanced and harmonious development should be respected throughout the process of integration and in the operation of the main programmes. An entire chapter of the Agreement was dedicated to the question of support for the weaker countries (Bolivia and Ecuador). This chapter established a series of favourable conditions for these countries, including a longer list of items excluded from the common tariff policy, a longer period in which to liberalise tariffs and bring themselves into line with the common foreign tariffs, etc. But the chief mechanism of the Agreement for evening out differences in the level of development of the member states was the sectoral programmes for industrial development.

5) A number of objectives for the coordination of economic and social policies were specified. Insofar as policies directly affecting trade were concerned, the terms and nature of the coordination were defined very precisely. The Agreement did not set terms and was less precise in relation to other areas, with one very important exception: policies towards foreign investment were to be drawn together and a common position established within a year.

6) The creation of a set of strong institutions which would have a real influence over the development of the process of integration. Firstly, there was the Commission, the decisionmaking body, which was composed of ministers of the member states. Then there was the Council, whose powers represent one of the most important innovations differentiating the Agreement from the LAFTA and other forms of integration. The Council has virtually exclusive power to put forward proposals, as well as the power to make resolutions regarding certain issues, and to ensure that the Agreement is observed. It never carried out this last function, since it was clearly the role of a judicial agency, whose creation became necessary because of subsequent developments which demanded a means of resolving disputes: this agency, the Andean Court of Justice has now been set up, and will begin to function in 1984.

7) In the Agreement the member states did not state a preference for any one political system. The Agreement was purely economic, and was considered to be compatible with different political systems.

During the first years after the Agreement came into force, there was tremendous vitality. The governments of the member states showed political will, and the process of integration moved forward, meeting the demanding deadlines laid down in the Agreement. Trade between countries multiplied, and despite all the difficulties which arose during the negotiations, the first Sectoral Programme for Industrial Development, dealing with the metal-working industry, was agreed in 1972. Venezuela, which had initially remained outside the Pact, asked to join, and this was negotiated during 1973.

However, there soon emerged the difficulties which led to the Andean Pact's current problems. To summarise, these are the main problems which have faced the Andean Pact, and which explain the progressive loss of vitality in this attempt at regional integration:

1) Radical changes in the economic policies of some member states in relation to the openness or liberalisation of their economies to foreign interests particularly in the case of Chile who eventually withdrew from the Pact. Even among those Governments which did not take a neo-liberal position, there were growing differences in approach to economic policy in relation to levels of protectionism and the priority given to import-substitution: the kinds of economic policy pursued by members became more varied.

2) Repeated failure by all members to observe the articles of the Agreement, either because these had not been incorporated into national law, or because those articles that had become law were not observed. Initially, the problem arose only in relation to specific issues; it took on massive proportions after 1980, and beame especially acute more recently with the reduction in trade caused by the international economic crisis.

3) Difficulties in the preparation and negotiation of the Sectoral Programmes for Industrial Development. Although the Council tried from the start to put forward programmes covering broad fields, which offered potential for all countries, there were exceptional problems in negotiation. In more than one case this led to solutions being found which were unsatisfactory in terms of increased efficiency. Only three programmes have been agreed: the programmes for the metalworking industry (1972), for petro-chemicals (1975) and for the automobile industry (1979), as well as the outlines for an iron and steel programme, which has not progressed enough to allow any action to be taken. Two of these three programmes have

been partially put into practice. All three have had to be reformulated, one in order to bring in Venezuela, who was not a member of the Pact when the metalworking programme was agreed, and the other two because the international crisis and the increase in petrol prices have profoundly altered the economic and technological characteristics of the petro-chemical and automobile industries. The changes in these two programmes have still not been agreed. In fact, at the present moment the balance between the different systems which the Agreement had anticipated has been destroyed, with the automatic reduction of tariff barriers taking precedence: this can be seen clearly in the unwillingness of the weaker nations to complete the reduction of tariff barriers and the establishment of common external tariffs.

4) Political and territorial disputes between member states. Political differences came to light when Andean integration gave itself a politically democratic character, while developments in one member state went against democratic principles. In practice, this country was not involved in negotiations for several months. A territorial dispute, with the serious problems that this entails for economic integration, occurred when there was armed confrontation between Peru and Ecuador. The international situation in recent years has had a negative and quite significant influence at every stage.

The present situation and proposals for reactivation

The effect of these problems has been to bring key negotiations between the Andean Pact countries to a total standstill over the definition of the market (common external tariff, liberalisation and industrial programmes). Although there has been progress in other fields, there is a general feeling of discouragement and more recently a real reduction in trade which has made the sense of crisis more acute.

Member states have drawn up a candid and precise analysis of the present situation under the title 'Plan for a Reorientation of the Process of Andean Integration', which was recently approved. The report states:

The Andean Pact is at present being affected by a number of disruptive factors, which are clearly holding up its development, and are now putting at risk the community structures we have worked so hard to build. Today we can see problems over the issue of freeing trade, difficulties in putting into practice programmes for joint industrialisation, a lack of definition over questions like the common external tariff, and the failure of member nations on many occasions to respect their obligations under the legally-binding statutes of the Cartagena Agreement.[1]

Many of the major problems have remained unresolved for a number of years, despite the ongoing and determined efforts of the agencies of the Agreement, in particular the Council which has prepared evaluations, drawn up programmes of action based on these, and most recently put forward for consideration by the Commission, the 'Plan for a Reorientation of the Process of Andean Integration' mentioned above, and following on from this a series of strategy documents.[2] The Commission has not ceased to function, except during the turbulent period following Bolivia's temporary withdrawal and the inevitable interruption of business caused by the conflict between Ecuador and Peru. Since May 1979 the Heads of State of the member nations[3] have met six times, and on each occasion one of the main themes has been how to reactivate the process.

It is a measure of the stubbornness and difficulty of the problems facing the Andean Pact that these have not been resolved in spite of this ongoing institutional activity, and the influence of another group of institutions which in their own way are demanding solutions to these problems: i.e., the Andean Parliament, the professional, employers' and workers' organisations, etc. Objectively, one cannot deny that the Pact has made progress even in this period of growing difficulties. It has a long list of achievements in a number of spheres: negotiations over foreign affairs with the US and the EEC, the coordination of positions in other international forums, among them the ALADI itself, serious efforts to work out joint action in the sensitive field of agricultural policy, real achievements in technological policy, and even joint investigations which offer great promise for the future.

But the failure to make progress in the main areas of policy regarding the creation of an open market and joint industrialisation has detracted from the effectiveness and importance of what has been achieved in other fields, has aggravated a crisis mentality, and has increasingly weakened faith in the future of the Pact. Moreover, as has been mentioned, events contribute to deepening concern and discouragement. Trade between member countries, which for the first ten years of the Pact's existence grew at an average annual rate of 28.2 per cent,[4] showed virtually no increase after 1979, and in the first few months of 1983 showed symptoms of severe contraction. The serious financial crisis which all members are experiencing has brought not only devaluations which have radically altered the relationship between prices, but even the imposition of restrictions which violate the Agreement; these restrictions, according to the Council, today affect 40 per cent of trade between member countries.[5] All of the countries have been affected by the reduction in trade within the group, but for the countries with less relative development, this reduction in sales comes on top of their dissatisfaction with the results of the industrial programme, and contributes to a feeling that they are suffering comparative disadvantage and damage, which is precisely what the founders of the institutions of the Agreement of Cartagena had sought to avoid.

Faced with this complex situation, the agencies of the Agreement have put forward the 'Plan for a Reorientation of the Process of Andean Integration', which will be put into practice through the agreement of strategies for each of the so-called 'major areas for priority action'. It is probable that the method of carrying this out will be for the elements of these strategies that are approved to be formulated as decisions of the Commission. Three strategies have already been approved (those relating to farming, industry and the creation of an open market) and others are being discussed. According to the Plan, there are eight priority areas[6] and we will try to provide at least some indication of the principal points of the proposals and their objectives, with the exception of those three areas in which the key problems of this process of integration arise, as we have indicated above. These three fields are trade, industry, and the special terms for Bolivia and Ecuador, the two relatively less developed countries, which receive preferential treatment under the terms of the Agreement. Here it is essential to go in depth into the proposals in order to understand the possibilities they offer of resolving the central problems in the Agreement. These three areas will be examined in the following section; the remainder will be briefly discussed afterwards.

Proposals for action in critical areas

Formation of a larger market and strengthening of commercial activities

Emphasis is put on completing the programme for the freeing of the market, extending some time limits, making the treatment of excepted areas more flexible, and regulating the use of safeguard clauses. In relation to the adoption of a common external tariff, the aim of the first stages is reduced to 'revising or adjusting' the levels of the common minimum external tariff, with the creation of a common tariff with upper and lower limits left until a later stage, and the period in which it is to be carried out unspecified.

Clearly the idea of perfecting the customs union has been abandoned, at least in the short term. This is reflected in the greater flexibility which is proposed for harmonising policies which directly affect the common external tariff, such as non-tariff measures, traditional rules, and industrial development legislation, and in general, all exceptional tariff systems. Given this relative softening of the terms of the Agreement in relation to the classical means for developing an integrated market, the strategy puts significant emphasis on less orthodox means of increasing trade, which are referred to as 'new forms of commercial exchange'[7] (agreements over state purchases, regulated commerce, such as compensated exchange, and trade in agricultural surpluses and shortfalls), and in general on the promotion of trade, and the increase in trade relations with third countries. This is symptomatic of the desire which exists today to go beyond the limits of the purely formal integration process and make better use of its potential for joint action. Later we will assess how far this is possible, and its likely value.

Integration in the industrial sector

This is the sector in which we can see most clearly the change in the objectives of the Cartagena Agreement over the years. As has been mentioned, the high priority given to industrialisation in the Agreement is well known. This was the basic motivation behind the setting up of the Andean Pact, and can even be seen in the lack of formal rigour[8] with which other areas of activity are treated in the same text of the Agreement. Furthermore, according to Article 32, the aim was to 'embark upon a process of industrial development in the sub-region, through joint planning', that is, introduce a common industrialisation policy, in which for a number of reasons the sectoral programmes for industrial development were to play a vital role.

The documents we are now discussing show a considerable change from this concept. In the 'Plan for the Reorientation of the Andean Process of Integration' the importance of industry within the Andean process is mentioned alongside other factors: while it is not denied, its status is reduced.[9] The document is still more explicit about the character of the industrial policy when it states that 'it is not the intention of the strategy to establish a uniform or all-encompassing pattern of development for the Andean Pact countries'. It subsequently adds that 'New actions taken at the sub-regional level must take into account national programmes and priorities, identifying the common denominators of national policy as the basis for joint initiatives'.[10]

This pragmatic approach is undoubtedly the result of past experiences, but it is a clear indication of the possible irrelevance of mechanisms of joint planning, and especially the sectoral programmes for industrial development, given the new approach which the strategy proposes for the Andean integration process. In fact, only one, and as we shall see, not the most important of the areas covered by the industrial strategy refers to this sectoral programming. The central aim in this area is to 'adjust and perfect the sectoral programmes for industrial development', but this involves only those programmes approved so far (metallurgy, petrochemicals, automobiles and steel). The reference to 'new possibilities for planning' which is also included in this section of the strategy covers only the mandatory (under the terms of the Agreement) allocation to Bolivia and Ecuador of some industrial projects which have been taken from the list of the so-called 'goods not in production', which are normally areas of little economic importance, or which are technologically difficult to introduce. In general, the emphasis in planning is on the project and not on the sector as a whole, and there is a desire to limit the allocation of projects to the two weaker countries, and then only in a restricted field and on a once-off basis.

The emphasis on the project and the omission of any reference to the idea of distribution within the sector is seen in a second part of the strategy entitled 'Areas of new industrial opportunities', although here priority sectors are established (agroindustry, capital goods production, electronics and communications).[11] Of the three parts of this strategy which remain to be covered, the first and clearly the most important in relation to the overall approach of the document is the 'consolidation of existing industry by improving its competitiveness and encouraging its development'. The focus is on those sectors which are going through crises, and quite rightly, the immediate priority is seen as being to regain and extend markets, with countries outside the Pact as well as member states. Emphasis is also put on the importance of the rationalisation programmes which were included in the Cartagena Agreement but which have not yet been put into practice, mainly because of the lack of trading mechanisms (such as preferential tariffs, common external tariffs, etc) which could be incorporated into the PSDIs.

Finally, the strategy puts forward proposals for actions to support industrial development, through studies, analyses and the preparation of projects, a policy for business and technological development, horizontal cooperation with third countries, etc.

Application of the special rules for Bolivia and Ecuador

In the preceding pages, we have already described the special function within the Agreement of the preferential treatment for Bolivia and Ecuador. The most effective means of achieving this was intended to be the industrial planning and the direct allocation of industries by sectors which this entailed. Analysis shows that the results of the application of this treatment have been negative, and the agencies of the Agreement have not attempted to hide this.

The Plan for a Reorientation states plainly that 'the results achieved have not lived up to early expectations'.[12] The Council of the Agreement's document 'Principles for a strategy for the application of the Special Rules for Bolivia and Ecuador' attributes these results to the 'limited' application of the joint industrial programme.[13]

One of the most serious aspects is that among the reasons for this limited application which has not produced satisfactory results, the failure of other countries to carry through their commitments, even in the sphere of industrial planning, bears a major responsibility, as the Council itself has said in the document recently quoted.[14] This led to the liquidation of a number of enterprises, and the consequent loss of credibility by the PSDI. There have also been other problems, stemming from the internal conditions in the relatively less-developed countries such as their limited capacity to initiate and carry through projects; nevertheless, it is reasonable to conclude that even given this last limitation, if the other countries had met their commitments in terms of joint planning and freeing of trade, this would have encouraged investments and a significant flow of trade, which would undoubtedly have lessened the sense of frustration of the weaker countries.

As might have been expected, the relatively less-developed countries have in their turn been unwilling to comply with their obligations to introduce an automatic and linear freeing of tariffs, and have requested the Commission that this tariff removal be postponed. Their frustration has increased the difficulties in negotiating other measures, such as the Common External Tariff, and the two countries are taking the attitude that it is not advisable to proceed with the creation of a larger market while this system of preferences, which has proved to be so weak in practice, remains. As in the case of many attempts at regional integration of developing countries, differences in the distribution of costs and benefits has become the main force blocking the process of integration.

This is why it is so important for the Andean Pact countries to re-orientate and improve the system of preferences. Without for the moment making any judgement about its success in achieving this, this is the aim of the strategy put forward by the Junta. This includes systematic references to the nature of the preferential treatment which will be given in each of the areas of joint action which make up the process of integration. The treatment basically consists of commitments to take preferential joint action (technical support, carrying out of studies, drawing up projects, access to greater resources from the CAF and the Andean Investment Fund, emphasis on promotion, etc) in order to enable projects to be carried out, or to encourage the solution of certain problems such as Bolivia's lack of a coastline. By their very nature, these are fairly general commitments which reflect intentions rather than definite obligations which have to be carried out in a specific way. The exceptions are in the spheres of trade and industrial integration.

In the programme for the removal of restrictions, the postponement by the two weaker countries of their participation is made formal; the mechanism established for this programme is the partial removal of tariffs, whose continuation will be dependent on future evaluations. The mechanisms for implementing the trading policy are also made more flexible—among these are the lists of exceptions and the application of national regulations.

In industry, preference in joint action follows the pattern discussed above of making general commitments to provide support through joint action (through the identification and encouragement of projects, technological and institutional support, financial assistance, priority in rationalisation programmes). There are specific references to the 'preservation of viable allocations and cooperation in achieving these', and to the 'establishment of reserved markets'. This second question would have to be explained in detail in order to give an idea of its effectiveness; the first clearly refers to existing allocations under the PSDI and those items in the list of goods 'not yet in production'.

We should remember that in the industrial strategy it is argued that in modifying the PSDIs already approved, preferential allocations should only be retained for 'viable and priority' areas of production in Bolivia and Ecuador. This question has already been discussed in the Commission of the Agreement, in relation to the programmes for metallurgy, petrochemicals and steel, following consultations by the Council with member states. These consultations[15] and the subsequent discussion of the issue by a Working Party of the 39th Extraordinary Session of the Commission which did not lead to any firm agreements[16] indicate the considerable problems which will be faced in determining which are the 'viable and priority' projects for Bolivia and Ecuador.

It is apparent, therefore, that given the present attitude of members, little can be expected from the PSDIs approved so far for the Special Rules for Bolivia and Ecuador, since the difficulties of reaching meaningful agreements will be still greater, if such a thing is possible, in the case of the automobile programme, for which no proposal for modification has yet been put forward.

Proposals for other areas of joint action

As well as the proposals mentioned above, the Plan includes suggestions for other areas in which joint action might be worthwhile. Put together, these make up a long list of proposals, simply to name which would take up several pages. Here we will only mention the spheres of action, and make a few comments on their importance, because unlike the three areas discussed so far, these do not constitute the basic problems for the integration of markets which have led to the present stagnation of the Andean Pact. These proposals would undoubtedly be very beneficial if they were put into practice, but in our opinion, they represent secondary forms of cooperation, and if progress is made in the task of integrating markets, there should be little problem in introducing a good many of the ideas proposed. There is one exception, and that is the areas of transportation, and road transport in particular. The Andean Pact has not been able to take any significant measures in this sphere. It is obvious that if the problems in the negotiations between the countries are resolved, the expansion of the Pact's trade will make it necessary to find immediate solutions to all the issues involved in the improvement of transport, which is one of the areas of the strategy which we wish to mention in this section.

The other areas are: foreign relations; the integration of farming and fishing; investments, finances and payments; science and technology. The Pact countries have already done some work in all these areas, and the foundations have been laid for more concentrated activity in the future. In one area—that of investments, finances and payments—joint institutions have been created (the Andean Development Corporation and the Andean Reserve Fund) which have provided support for the Pact. Now these institutions need to increase their own resources to prove their ability as financial intermediaries by arranging loans on a scale adequate to meet the demands of the present situation.

In the sphere of foreign relations, the plan represents an attempt to systematically employ the strength given by negotiating in conjunction. This has already been carried out in the agreements with the United States and the EEC, and now it is necessary to extend these kinds of agreements and diversify the range of countries with whom they are made. The natural priorities for this area must be ALADI, the organisation which succeeds LAFTA, and a number of other Latin American countries.

In the spheres of both science and technology and the integration of farming and fishing, the Andean Pact countries have done some useful work. Now they must increase their work in these fields. In relation to the first, the Andean Pact was the first attempt at integration in the developing world to give serious consideration to the question of technology, making a systematic investigation of the field, and even carrying out its own research projects (the Andean Programmes for Technological Development). Today the aim is to put into practice a genuine policy for shared technology. In relation to the integration of farming and fishing, there is good reason to call for a form of horizontal cooperation which will allow each country to introduce farming and fishing policies of its own which will help to ensure a 'secure food supply'. The question of trade in farming and fishing products is mentioned in the strategy, but clearly without any hope that these suggestions will be carried out shortly, or to any significant extent. Instead, there are many other areas in which joint action or mutual support could be beneficial without creating conflicts (regulations on animal and vegetable hygiene, campaigns to eradicate infections, research, training, etc).

The immediate future for the Andean Group

I feel some disquiet in embarking on this final section, which will inevitably have to combine arguments or recommendations with predictions. This implies being able to give an answer, which may be extremely arbitrary, to many questions about the immediate future internationally and in each of the member countries, as well as making a subjective evaluation of the experiences and interests of each of them. The risk of arbitrariness is unavoidable here, since any option will be based on the perspectives and possibilities of the Andean Pact.

The atmosphere for negotiations within the Pact is today, in spite of frustrations and suspicions, a positive one if judged in terms of the work carried out and the concern of the countries to find a solution to this stagnation and deterioration. Even accepting that there is a generally *positive* attitude of concern to overcome this 'impasse', it has to be said that the overall context of the negotiations is difficult, both because of objective factors, and because of the evaluation made by each member of their experiences during the life-time of the Andean Pact.

One of the most important objective factors accentuating the problems of the Andean Pact, and as a consequence influencing the climate of negotiations, has been the international scene, with the particular repercussions this has had for the Latin American financial crisis and the crisis in the balance of payments. The contraction of the economies of the industrialised nations between 1980–83 has had, as is generally recognised, a devastating effect on Latin America and, therefore, the Andean Pact countries.

Even if the economic recovery in the US is consolidated this year, and that brings in its wake a recovery in the other industrialised countries, a development which is probable, but not certain, the economic and financial problems in Latin America and the Andean Pact countries will continue to be pressing and urgent for several years because of the heavy financial obligations of the region. We may foresee a continuation of policies designed to restrict imports and predict that the instability of international exchange rates will be reflected in devaluations on a large scale, given the relationship between these measures and inflation, which shows no signs of falling significantly in the near future. Such a situation is clearly not ideal for negotiations over the integration of markets and production. Experience shows that these require a minimum space to enable medium- and long-term objectives to be identified.

I know that my opinion goes against current expectations about the response to the crisis that can logically be expected from our countries. This response would favour closer cooperation between Latin American countries which would enable them not only to reduce the effects of the present situation, but also to give their national economic policies more autonomy. This view has been put forward in a recent series of regional economic meetings which culminate in the Latin American Economic Conference which is taking place while these words are being written. But despite this, I believe that at least in the immediate future these calls for closer links of integration and cooperation will nevertheless carry little weight when it comes to making decisions over crucial problems in the Andean integration process. In taking these decisions, the traditional positions of member states, coloured to some extent by the experiences of the past and the restrictive situation created by the international situation, will be of more importance than arguments about the clear benefits of future cooperation. This is not to deny that the logic of cooperation may be followed in many areas (financial questions, the administration of trade, relations between countries, etc) and below we shall indicate some of these areas; but I am not convinced that this logic now prevails to the extent of creating a climate for negotiations which would allow the reconciliation of differences which is crucial if the Andean Pact is to advance in the process of regional integration according to the basic principles of the Cartagena Agreement. I believe that the crucial issues contained in the Plan for Reorientation, which have been briefly examined in preceding pages, will be discussed and decided upon without the above-mentioned response to the crisis having a significant influence.

The Plan for Reorientation is, as our summary suggested, really a list of everything that could reasonably be done jointly by a group of countries which have already gone some way towards integration. The Cartagena Agreement's original objective was to achieve a far-reaching integration of markets and production. It is worth asking, therefore, which aspects of the Plan are essential for this level of integration. This will allow us to assess if in the form in which it is set out, the Plan will in the first place lead to the kind of integration which the Agreement had intended, or to a process with different characteristics; and secondly to see whether its proposals are viable given the present situation in which the Cartagena Agreement finds itself. Once we have an answer to these questions, we will be able to risk an opinion on the viability and significance of the other measures of cooperation.

Earlier in this paper, we gave a summary of the proposed strategy in three areas which we consider crucial in continuing the process of integration, and it is not surprising that these are also the areas in which we find the most difficult problems for negotiation. These three areas are: the creation of a larger market, integration of industry, and the special regulations for Bolivia and Ecuador, the two weaker countries, or those with relatively less development.

The proposals for the creation of a larger market—which, it should be said, represent a realistic identification of those areas in which, in the best of cases, there may exist a possibility of agreement—imply a considerable softening of the terms of the Agreement, both in respect of the time in which these must be carried out, and of the area to be covered by the tariff reduction, at least during the initial period. The same thing can be seen in relation to the common external tariff, an instrument of integration which to begin with will be simply a common minimum level, which will later move within the so-called 'margins'—that is to say, will move between maximum and minimum levels. In both cases, the Plan for Reorientation suggests, in vague terms and clearly as a distant goal, a later stage when progress will be made towards a complete removal of tariff barriers between nations, and the countries will agree on a single common external tariff, which were the initial goals of the Agreement.

In real terms Andean integration will no longer aim for the special brand of economic unity which we talked of at the beginning of this paper. Its aspirations now lie in an intermediate path between a partial free-trade zone and a customs union. The concept of a 'margin' within which the foreign tariff will operate is particularly worrying, because in order for it to exist, a series of regulations will have to be introduced which will cause conflict during negotiations (over traditional tariffs, and over rules of competition, etc) and will be extremely difficult to make effective. Given that integration will take this form, with differences remaining between countries in the level of protection imposed against the products of countries from outside the Pact, it will moreover be virtually impossible to deal with certain questions which, at least from a technical point of view, are unavoidable in a process of integration, such as the minimum harmonisation of monetary and exchange policies. The programme mentions these questions, but this is quite obviously merely a formal gesture.

The aim of the Cartagena Agreement was undoubtedly not this kind of integration, but that is not to deny that its achievement would be an important step forward. The real question is whether even this lesser form of integration is viable in the present situation. One can only give an answer—which in any case inevitably risks being subjective—when one has made an analysis of the three key areas, which of course are closely linked.

The second area is that of industrial integration, the most precisely-defined aspect of the integration of production contained in the Cartagena Agreement. Here the application of the new strategy would mean a major shift away from the original approach of the Cartagena Agreement, as we have already pointed out. We see to begin with a desire to reduce the importance given to industrial development within the process of integration; the strategy goes on to state plainly that it will not attempt to impose a 'uniform and all-embracing' policy, that is, a common industrial policy of the kind foreseen by the Agreement, but rather to find 'common denominators' within national programmes, which will provide the basis for measures to increase integration. Finally, despite assurances that sectoral planning for industrial development will continue, it is apparent that it will virtually cease to involve the larger countries, and will play merely a residual, almost formal role in relation to Bolivia and Ecuador.

I believe that this formal shift in priorities should be understood first and foremost as an effort to widen the sphere of joint action, and prevent excessive emphasis on a sector which up till now has proved the most difficult and prone to conflict. We should just make one rather obvious comment, that the motivations for the integration of developing countries like those of the Andean Pact, lie basically in the desire to enjoy the advantages of large-scale production for industrial development, and that the results of the process will be evaluated principally by looking at the indicators for trade in industrial products, investment and technological change. If industry has been an area of conflict within the Andean Pact, that is because expectations have focused on this area, and it is here that the first real effects of the integration of markets and production have been felt. Farming has not been a problem up till now, because there have been no real expectations for this sphere, and the mechanisms of integration have not been employed in it. Had this not been the case, farming would have caused more conflict than industry, as is happening in the EEC, even despite the fact that in developed economies agricultural production has relatively considerably less importance than in countries with a large primary sector. We could go so far as to say that in practice the change in priorities is merely formal, and that in fact Andean integration will continue to be assessed by its members principally in terms of its achievements for industrial development.

The other two changes in the original approach of the Agreement are far-reaching and deserve a closer critical examination. The decision to abandon the goal of a common industrial policy and the use of sectoral programming of industrial development as a means of achieving this goal means that at least for the three largest countries, Andean integration will return to the old pattern of integrating markets and production by using the market as the single means of distributing resources. As we have said, the Cartagena Agreement was originally based on the decision to reserve an area of industrial development—at that time expected to cover those industries of greatest complexity and potential—for control by a special mechanism which would determine where development would take place, and consequently the allocation of investment. The disappearance of this area removes from the Agreement a mechanism which in the first place had been intended to neutralise to some extent the natural advantages or disadvantages of member countries and to prevent or reduce the scale of the classical conflicts that occur in any attempt at integration among developing countries. It deprives it in the second place of a way of rationalising, as far as possible, industrial development within the new economic unit. As we said above—and we will now see that this is equally true for the relatively less-developed countries—it is market forces which decide not only the flow of trade, but also of investment. Naturally, this will not be either a wholly open market, nor one that is uniformly protected, but instead will be a market with much more limited scope than had originally been intended, yet which will nevertheless have exclusive control over the distribution of resources.

We believe that these are the fundamental aspects of the proposals for industrial strategy which need to be borne in mind. The rest of the proposals —rationalisation programmes, support for projects offering new opportunities in industry using advanced technologies or in priority areas, joint investment, or the use of Andean multinational enterprises as a means of advancement—involve horizontal cooperation, which could theoretically occur without integration, even though in practice they would be more effective and equitable as part of a dynamic process of integration.

Numerous worthy reasons can be given for this change in the principles of the Cartagena Agreement. We do not intend to repeat here what has already been said about the tremendous difficulties confronted in negotiations over the PSDIs or the disruption which the negotiations caused in the efficiency of the programmes; but I feel that the countries should at least try to salvage those programmes already approved, with their considerable powers of allocation, as far as possible improving them and making every effort to carry out their resolutions.

The position of the two relatively less-developed countries and the whole body of preferential treatment established for their benefit are also affected by this change of principles. The strategy proposes that some of the areas of production allocated to them under the PSDIs already approved should be retained. The discussion within the Commission of specific proposals for changes is clear proof of the difficulty in reaching significant agreements over particular points. The terms of negotiation are totally different from those of the original programmes, and today negotiations take place over isolated projects which will benefit individual members. This brings all the irritation, and in the long run little of real importance, as usually happens where negotiations are one-sided.

We have already discussed the implications of the preferential treatment for tariff removals and the common external tariff. The proposed strategy takes a flexible approach towards the two relatively less-developed countries as regards their removal of tariffs, and probably also their adoption of the two types of common external tariff. If these proposals were accepted by the Commission, this flexibility could help to some extent to counterbalance the concern which Bolivia and Ecuador may feel at the virtual annihilation of the system of industrial planning in the areas which offer most potential for them. But at the same time, the preferences given under the trading rules may make the other countries much less sympathetic to the aspirations of these two countries and less concerned to act in their favour, either in the allocation of the few projects in the PSDIs already approved, or in the other areas of preferential treatment which depend basically on unilateral decisions by other members to offer their cooperation. In fact, despite the potential breadth of the system of preferences proposed in the strategy—there is practically no area in which no mention is made of some kind of measure to benefit the two countries—in only very few cases is there a clear and firm requirement that members put these preferences into practice, as had existed with the PSDIs or the commercial preferences. The implementation of the other measures of support will depend on the good will of the rest of the members and their ability to offer effective cooperation, which is frequently doubtful. In the past, support has been given in financial matters, and a few other fairly isolated cases; but their own problems and limitations make it very unlikely that a system of preferences could be made to work on this basis. Looking at the expectations and concerns which exist today, it is clear that neither of the two relatively less-developed countries see this as sufficient compensation for removing virtually all the industrial planning powers, which they had quite understandably considered the essence of the system of preferences. This explains their insistence on including the allocation of industrial projects within the packet of support measures which are under negotiation at present.

With all modesty, we believe that this analysis provides the basis for making a realistic evaluation of the future of the Andean Pact. We start from the premise that today it is more important than ever to keep alive the movements for integration which have appeared in Latin America. For a number of different reasons, they face a difficult situation, and there may be circumstances in which the only way to keep them 'alive' is to leave them ticking over until better times arrive. I hope that this will not be the case for the Andean Pact. The Cartagena Agreement could be implemented less energetically than was originally hoped, yet still be of use to all the members. It is essential that the benefits be shared by all. If the Pact is going to work at half strength, as appears inevitable, it will be disastrous if the process of integration deepens contradictions between members. The distributive effects of the process should be monitored more carefully than ever to prevent any of the members, whether or not these are the relatively less-developed countries, from being marginalised from the development taking place in the more dynamic sectors, and to prevent them from feeling that they are bearing unjustifiably high costs in relation to the benefits received. Some difficult decisions will have to be left until conditions have improved, and the Pact returns to a system which is more able than at present to find ways of compensating for the sacrifices it demands.

Finally, it is vital that the Andean Pact regain what could be called its 'credibility'. The creation of the Court of Justice is a new development which should allow violations of the Agreement to be drastically reduced. To keep the Pact alive for the moment demands above all that commitments be kept, once, as the Council has proposed, their irrelevant or inapplicable clauses have been removed.

These considerations are particularly important given the nature of the change in direction proposed by the Plan for Reorientation and the strategies which we have discussed above.

The first proof of viability must be the completion of the negotiations at present going on in the Andean Pact. As we have seen, the Gordian knot can be found in the three key areas of creating a larger market, industrial development, and the special rules for Bolivia and Ecuador. Because of the terms under which the negotiations are taking place, they are likely to be extremely laborious and to demand substantial concessions by members, especially in the allocation of industrial projects of real relevance and importance to Bolivia and Ecuador. To fail to make these concessions would be like limiting the integration process to the biggest countries. This is an alternative which cannot be ruled out, since the larger countries are certainly a more homogenous group, but it is an alternative which would have very serious political and economic costs, and which would have to be considered carefully by all members. For the moment, we will not even consider it, on the basis that the aim is to maintain the present structure of the subregion.

Even if the negotiations are completed, the challenge will remain of making the process of integration described schematically above function. There are two aspects of the process which should be borne in mind. First of all, it is a process which will use the mechanism of the market both in relation to the flow of trade and in the allocation of investments. Given the great differences between members, the effects of this will tend to concentrate benefits. In the second place, this market mechanism will operate within a fragmented or limited space (where there are exceptions, sensitive products, safeguard clauses), where competition is likely to be distorted because of the lack of a common external tariff. These factors will limit the tendency to concentrate benefits mentioned previously, but will equally create numerous possibilities of conflict and will demand complex administration. Here the speed and efficiency of the Andean Court of Justice will be put to the test. The survival of the Pact will be conditional on its work.

In short, we believe that the integration of markets and production can proceed using this system; but the need to maintain a minimum balance and reduce conflicts over routine activities will be reflected in serious limitations on the extent and pace of the process of integration. I believe that the Andean Pact's Plan for Reorientation has taken this inevitable result into account, and that is why it is emphasising a range of complementary measures for cooperation or joint action in areas which go from foreign relations to science and technology. As long as the core of the process of integration of markets and production is maintained, it will be much easier to arrange cooperation between members and draw third parties into negotiations. If this does not happen, and the present stagnation and frustration with the process of integration continues, it is very unlikely that even the most worthwhile attempts at cooperation will be carried out.

It is not the place here to examine one by one the long list of tasks which come out of the strategies. In every sphere it would be possible to make progress on a number of the ideas put forward. In some cases it is essential for the process of integration that progress should be made, as in the case of transport. In other areas like financing, a relatively developed form of organisation already exists and could be made to work more energetically. Finally, there are other areas like science and technology in which the increased degree of cooperation implied by the proposals would provide the process of integration, which by now is lacking in fresh ideas, with new goals and aspirations. In almost all of these areas, the Andean Pact could also encourage action at a Latin American level. Great potential undoubtedly exists, but if this is to be realised, the process of integration must first of all be salvaged; without neglecting other areas, this must for the moment be the Andean Pact's main focus.

Notes

1. Council of the Agreement of Cartagena, 'Our Nation is America', 1983, p 15.
2. The principles and main arguments of the strategy documents referred to are given in the following documents which the author has been able to consult: Jun/dt. 205/Rev. 2; COM/XXXIX–E/dt. 7; Jun/dt. 212; Jun/dt. 204. This last document is dated September 1983, and the others, November 1983.
3. Exceptionally, the place of one or other Head of State has been taken by a delegation of officials, with the status of personal representatives.
4. 'Our Nation is America', p 40.
5. *Ibid.*, p 40.
6. They are as follows: 1) foreign relations; 2) farming; 3) trade; 4) industry; 5) financing and payments; 6) trade and technology; 7) physical integration, boundaries and tourism; and 8) special terms for Bolivia and Ecuador.
7. Document: 'Outline for a strategy for the formation of a larger market and the strengthening of commercial activity', JUN/dt. 205/rev. 2, p 37.

8. Less precise measures relating to commitments, or no indication of the time-scale within which these are to be adopted.
9. 'It is thus vital to move towards a more balanced integration of trade, farming and industry', p 23.
10. *Op. cit.*, p 46.
11. Outline for a subregional strategy for integration in the industrial sector'. COM/XXXIX–E–dt 7, November 1983, p 32.
12. *Op. cit.*, p 68.
13. JUN/dt.–213, November 1983, p 7.
14. *Ibid.* 'Failure to respect the commitment agreed by the other countries under the Pact, which affected both the exclusive nature of the allocations granted to Bolivia and Ecuador and also the freeing of trade', p 12.
15. 'Reports on consultations with member states on the modification and completion of the PSDI's. COM/XXXIX–E/dt 5; November 1983.
16. 'Report of the Working Party of the Commission on the adjustment and completion of the PSDIs in metallurgy, petrochemicals and steel'. COM/XXXIX–E/dt 6. November 1983.

11
Latin America—the hour for unity

Elvio Baldinelli

Latin America is at its hour of crisis. Massive debts, whose causes will be outlined below, are threatening to drain its commercial life-blood and crush the social aspirations of its peoples. As is frequently the case, however, adversity is a powerful force for unity. And it is through unity that it may be possible to solve the continent's problems. How this could be done is examined in this paper.

To know the present and to penetrate the future requires an assessment of the immediate past. A number of events in the world economy have affected Latin America in recent years, but most notable was the frustration of the region's hopes of increasing exports to the developed world, which had until recently been enjoying extraordinary prosperity. The world recession which depressed prices and reduced exports contributed significantly to the high indebtedness of most Latin American countries.

Between the last years of the 1950s and the beginning of the 1970s the developed world experienced unprecedented economic expansion, encompassing all the industrialised countries and lasting for almost a quarter of a century. Contributing to this prosperity were the will of the peoples devastated by war to strive for their countries' reconstruction; the application of technical developments to the needs of mass consumption; the existence in Europe of large rural populations which met the needs for labour of expanding industries, and, in no small measure, the gradual elimination of the trade barriers which existed between 1918 and 1939, thus facilitating a rapid growth in international trade.

The developing countries, including those of Latin America, benefited from this expansion. The greater demand for raw materials, food, energy and light industrial goods not only gave an impetus to these economies, but also, most importantly, gave rise to the hope—almost the certainty—that poverty would be left behind in the wake of the seemingly endless prosperity of the developed world.

The disastrous consequences of the acute protectionism of the 1930s had taught the world a hard lesson. Thus, at the end of World War II, the principal industrialised countries, on the initiative of the US, drew up the principles of the General Agreement on Tariffs and Trade (GATT), whose aim was to eliminate protectionism by applying the principles of reciprocity and non-discrimination to their trade dealings. However, the efforts of GATT were impeded by grave defects, such as the failure to liberalise trade in agricultural products and, in 1962, by the signing of agreements on cotton textiles which dashed the hopes of many developing countries of exploiting a clear advantage in this area by exporting products made from local raw materials with a high content of unskilled labour.

Then, when the economic crisis of 1973–74 struck the industrialised countries, protectionism made its appearance. This was not in the traditional guise of import duties, but in the form of non-tariff restrictions— an approach appropriately dubbed the 'new protectionism'. Thus the hopes of the developing countries were frustrated.

The industrialised countries not only protect their agricultural production, but also subsidise the exports of their produce, thereby curtailing Latin American sales of sugar, milk products, cereals, cotton, oils and meat. These subsidised exports are possible owing to an amendment to the GATT code of conduct secured by the US more than twenty years ago. The result is that today a strict regime for industrial exports co-exists with a totally lax one for agricultural products. Thus, while the industrialised countries were experiencing their unparalleled growth, the developing countries which traditionally exported temperate climate agricultural products were suffering difficulties and setbacks which were particularly hard to bear both socially and politically, since they occurred amid the expansion and opulence of the developed world. In this small group were several Latin American countries, including Argentina, Paraguay and Uruguay, as well as the sugar and cotton exporting nations.

It was a mistake on the part of the signatories of GATT not to have listened to the repeated protests of this small group of countries. To have tolerated an injustice favouring the agricultural sectors of some countries to the detriment of entire communities elsewhere was a precedent which led to the general relaxation of the principles of GATT, thereby opening up the way to the 'new protectionism'.

The new protectionism

For some the economic crisis began in 1973 and still continues. For the rest it began the following year, finally affecting all countries without exception. Today there is an international consensus that, although what initially unleashed it was the increase in the price of petroleum, there was no single cause. The reasons are many and complex, some of them deeply rooted and of long standing. Some believe that they are a product of the times and will soon pass—they instance the high cost of energy, high interest rates, the decline in investment, the halting of industrial expansion and high government spending for social purposes. Others think that there are also structural causes whose elimination will not be too easy. They point to the attitude prevalent among the new generation in the industrial countries who insist on combining high consumption with less work.

Government officials, as well as economists, in the developed world recognised from the first that the recession, and its sequel—unemployment —could not be fought with greater protectionism. This would only cause acrimonious commercial warfare, magnifying the crisis even more, as happened in the 1930s. Yet in spite of this sensible view of the situation among responsible people, protectionism made its appearance. As we have described, this did not take the traditional form of high import duties, but was under the guise of non-tariff restrictions. It would seem that there was a belief that this form of non-tariff protection was of a transitory character, in contrast to the tariff approach. It was forgotten that nothing is so permanent as what is introduced to solve a temporary problem.

The 'new protectionism' is far-reaching in its effects, embracing exports both from the EEC to the US and from the US to the EEC. Exports from Japan to every destination are affected. It touches exports of agricultural products from both the developed and the developing countries, as well as the manufactured products of the so called 'low income' countries. The forms which this protectionism takes are also varied. In some cases it is expressed in the form of government subsidies which support dying industries; in others, it shows itself simply as a vigilant attitude to imports, which acts as a warning to those who are gaining markets. There are also 'voluntary' agreements, at a private, as well as at an official, level, which limit exports to quotas that are reported to the GATT. And there are technical measures, as well as outright abuses of the procedure, to counter the supposed flooding of the home market with low-cost merchandise. The sectors which have been most affected by this are textiles, clothing, shoes, steel, naval construction, electrical appliances and, in the agricultural sector, beef production.

As already mentioned, one of the consequences of the period of expansion in world trade which followed World War II was that developing countries cherished the hope that they would be able to expand their own exports of light industrial goods, while in the meantime the industrialised countries would increasingly concentrate on the production of technologically sophisticated articles. But the 'new protectionism' persuaded the world's poor countries that there was little sense in investing in industries for export, since as soon as their sales reached a significant level the markets were closed to them.

The industrialised countries nevertheless made some attempt to halt the progress of the new protectionism, recognising that the present situation was far from being as serious for them as that reached in the 1930s. In the so called 'Tokyo Round' of negotiations which took place under the aegis of the GATT, they committed themselves to reducing tariffs for the year 1987 by nearly 6 per cent *ad valorem*. But they were not so successful when it came to agreeing on a new code for subventions and compensatory levies in relation to agricultural products, nor when they tried to prevent non-tariff restrictions. Aware of the dangers of protectionism, the industrialised countries agreed to reduce import tariffs even further, but left the door open to other forms of protection as damaging as the import duties, if not more so.

Latin America's food export problems have their origin in the economic expansion of the industrialised countries, principally during the 1950s and 1960s, when industry demanded enormous amounts of labour, resulting in a depopulation of the land. This should have been good news for the Lain American region, but it was instead the origin of great difficulties. The industrialised countries resolved, for various non-economic reasons, to maintain a certain level of self-sufficiency in food and therefore so arranged matters that agricultural workers would receive wages equal to those of urban workers. The method selected to achieve this was a policy of high prices for the consumer, or direct subsidies, or a combination of both. At the same time political pressure exerted by the farmers frequently resulted in prices going far higher than could possibly have been justified by production needed to cover only part of consumption. On the other hand, the technological revolution in farming after World War II was producing even larger levels of output.

These factors in the case of the US, added to the natural efficiency of agriculture in that country, translated themselves into enormous surpluses of cereals and cotton, which the US government had to export at prices lower than prevailing levels. These sales did not accord with the GATT code of conduct in regard to subsidised exports, and it was for the purpose of legalising its position that in March 1955 the US secured the amendment relating to agricultural produce.

The European Economic Community meanwhile gradually became self-sufficient in more and more areas of agriculture by means of subsidies even higher than those granted by the US. In many cases, such as sugar, cereals, milk products and meat, it became a significant exporter, thanks to the application of ample financial resources which were the result of industrial growth and the laxity of GATT.

Thus Latin America lost part of its European market. And not only that: the exports from the US, Canada and the EEC led to fewer sales by the Latin American countries in the rest of the world and at lower prices than they might otherwise have expected. This had adverse effects on their balance of payments, as well as on the income of the producers, who were thereby frequently prevented from taking advantage of modern technological developments, such as fertilisers and mechanisation.

The US is now finding that its policy of subsidising its agriculture and the export of cereals at low prices has become a burden. The increasing exports of the EEC, following the amendment to the GATT code, depressed international prices even more, increasing the US's loss of revenue. In view of this, the US Administration now regrets having secured the amendment in the first place.

For its part, the EEC is reaching the limit of the funds available for financing its agricultural policies and some governments (the United Kingdom and, latterly, the Netherlands) do not appear to be keen on continually increasing the resources devoted to agriculture.

An amendment to the code regulating subsidies which would end exports of this kind, or at least limit their volume, would prompt a general rise in prices in the international markets. This would not only benefit the public revenue of the US, Canada and the EEC, but would also bring relief to the economies of the countries producing at market prices, such as those of Latin America, as well as Australia and New Zealand. Latin America has neither the political nor the economic clout to exact an amendment of its own to the GATT code, but were it to coordinate its efforts with other countries, such as the US which now seems to want to amend the code, and some sectors of the EEC which believe that subsidies have gone too far, then there might be a positive conclusion. The Latin

American Economic System (SELA) has an important role to play here.

One day, then, the industrialised countries might well decide to amend the code relating to agricultural production. But this may take years. That is why, while a solution is awaited, and while all necessary steps to that end are taken, it is only sensible to evolve ways of preserving Latin America's existing markets and of recovering those which have been lost for sugar, cotton, oils, milk products, cereals and meat. This policy should be developed within the terms of GATT, for though GATT might not be altogether fair in relation to subsidies, it is in other matters—apart from the fact that for countries in the position of the Latin American ones the existence of even an unfair trade regime is better than none at all.

If the Latin American countries subsidised the sale of some of their own agricultural products sufficiently to recover the markets that had been taken over by other countries as a result of subsidies, they would in fact be acting within their rights according to GATT. They should not introduce open market exports, however, but should duly select the markets and the degree of subsidy.[1] Such sales would be carefully regulated by the authorities in charge of the operation, so that the subsidy granted would suffice only to recover the lost market and not go beyond that. This would not only avoid unnecessary expenditure but—and this is more important— it would not provoke internal price rises.

Indebtedness of the developing countries

The increase in the price of oil from US$1.80 per barrel in June 1973, to US$9.50 in June 1974, enormously boosted the revenues of the members of OPEC. The surpluses of these countries surpassed US$8 billion in 1973 and US$70 billion in 1974. Some of the OPEC countries with large populations had no problem in finding a use for these larger revenues (they increased their imports), but there were several Arab countries with small populations which found themselves with huge surpluses on their hands.

The industrialised countries realised that they would have to buy oil from countries that did not need to buy their own goods in return. The orthodox solution to this maladjustment would have been to reduce oil imports, but this would have inevitably meant an even more acute economic recession. An alternative was to give those countries the opportunity to invest their surpluses in a way that would secure them a lucrative income, and this was the solution adopted.

A relatively small amount of the OPEC money was channelled into the purchase of businessess and properties abroad. For example, the purchases included 15 per cent of Daimler Benz's shares and 25 per cent of Krupp Group stock, both in Germany, as well as the Manhattan Tower in Paris and an island off the coast of South Carolina in the US. But the bulk of the money went to banks in Europe and the US. As is well known, these banks lent a substantial part of the funds to the developing countries and to the Eastern bloc. For their part, these countries used a large part of the loans to pay for their imports from the industrialised countries.

This was the so-called 'recycling' process. The industrialised countries could not sell goods to some of the Arab countries to balance their oil imports, so they effected sales to the developing countries. They, in turn, requested loans from the big banks to pay for them and the source of this money was the Arab surpluses arising from oil.

It is interesting to note that ten years ago the developing countries asked the industrialised world for a massive transfer of funds to aid their growth. But the request was turned down, in spite of repeated appeals. Yet, years later, the transfer did take place, not, however, through governments or the international credit organisations, as would normally have been expected, but through the private banks, and this not by design, but by accident. The explanation for this 'miracle' transfer of funds is that, had it not taken place, the industrialised countries would not simply have faced a crisis which was limited to a slight reduction in the growth of their gross national product: they would have had to cope with a disaster on the scale of that of the 1930s.

Nevertheless, these loans have turned out to be one of the major economic problems of the present time with, in March 1981, Poland and then successively Mexico, Argentina, Brazil and Romania informing their creditors that they were not in a position to pay at maturity. And these are not the only countries with excessive debts: about forty countries are each indebted to private banks for more than US$1 billion and thirty more individually owe more than US$250 billion.

Altogether, the developing nations and countries in the Eastern bloc owe government agencies, international bodies and private banks approximately US$650 billion. It is a serious situation for some of these countries, because not only can they not make the required repayments of capital, but they are unable to pay all of the interest either. As a result, they have to take out further loans to pay the interest, and their indebtedness increases.

Neither are the banks in a particularly comfortable position. Their exposure in respect of the Eastern bloc countries and the developing world has reached US$350 billion, which represents more than double their capital assets, while the interest accruing from this sum exceeds their joint profits. If a solution is not found, the international banking system could collapse, throwing the world into an acute depression of many years' duration.

Public opinion in the industrialised countries puts the blame for this situation on the banks for lending their money too easily, but also on the developing countries for indiscriminate borrowing. Undoubtedly, both bear some blame, but, in fairness, all the circumstances leading to the situation need to be examined. At the time the loans were contracted, nobody imagined that the recession in the industrialised countries would be so long-lasting. Then, as now, the opinion of some government officials and economists was that the crisis could end at any moment. Nor could anyone foresee that interest rates would increase from a real 2 per cent to between 5 per cent and 10 per cent. No one thought that the imports, which had already been reduced by the industrialised countries before the recession, would be cut back even further following the appearance of the new protectionism, nor that the prices of agricultural products in the international markets would suffer from subsidies granted by the industrialised countries.

The routes to follow

The Latin American countries have frequently adopted austerity programmes suggested by the International Monetary Fund which have involved reducing imports to a minimum so that they can at least manage to pay the interest on their borrowing. They have cut wages in real terms and pruned public investment in order to reduce economic activity and permit a reduction of purchases abroad. The three countries with the highest indebtedness—Brazil, Mexico and Argentina—have managed to reduce their joint imports from US$55 billion in 1981 to an estimated low of US$40 billion in 1983.

Sacrifices such as these arise from a recognition that ignoring a debt means the loss of credit and throwing away, for many years to come, the chance of attracting overseas investment. This, in turn, entails the sacrifice of living standards and development opportunities. Another consideration is the natural wish to preserve one's dignity and to pass on intact to future generations a heritage of faithful compliance with financial commitments.

Many observers think that the current efforts of the Latin American governments, the commercial banks and the international credit organisations, combined with the growth in exports stimulated by the economic upswing in the US, will be enough to overcome the crisis. In this scenario, confidence will be restored, capital that had moved abroad will return, new foreign investments will be attracted and prosperity will dramatically reappear. Others are not so optimistic, however, and fear that the revival in the US will induce even higher rates of interest, destroying the gains made through exports, and leading, as described above, to even greater indebtedness. During coming months the Latin American countries will once again be discussing the refinancing of their debts with their creditors. They will be finding out whether there is light at the end of the tunnel or if all their efforts have proved fruitless. Should the latter prove to be the cause, it would not be surprising if the politicians decided that there were few worse things than to lose power under suspicion of being more sensitive to foreign interests than to their own—and opted to stop paying. The degree of indebtedness is not the same for all countries in the area, but if one or two of them chose not to continue paying, it would be very difficult for the rest not to follow.

Such a catastrophe could be avoided if the industrialised world were to revert to the principles that inspired the creation of GATT, by reducing protectionism and acknowledging reciprocity and non-discrimination for both industrial and agricultural products. It would also help if economic policies were adopted which would permit a return to normal interest rates. None of this is easy to achieve in the short term, but if, for example, governments were to subsidise the interest being levied on the loans provided by their countries' institutions, they would demonstrate their determination not to let Latin America sink into hopelessness.

Obviously, the politicians of the industrialised world do not win votes by transferring money to foreign countries, but it should be borne in mind that neither is there any prestige to be gained by simultaneously jettisoning both the money one has lent and one's friends. If any preventative action is to be successful it must be undertaken now, however, while the attitude of the Latin American politicians is one of struggling to meet their commitments. Once they give up, nothing further can be done.

Bilateralism in Latin America

The crisis in external payments which is affecting almost all the Latin American countries, along with the emergence of the new protectionism, has led to the resurrection of the system of preferential regional schemes. Both under the former LAFTA (Latin American Free Trade Association) and in the LAIA (Latin American Integration Association) preferential margins agreed by the contracting parties were intended to stimulate exchanges based on the principle of reciprocity in trade expectations. Tariff advantages are agreed on the understanding that there will be reciprocal benefits in the deal, but lack of parity in the rates of exchange and their constant fluctuation, combined with different levels of external tariffs, make these expectations illusory. Their credibility is exhausted when, as in the past year, direct controls on imports are multiplied as a result of the financial crisis affecting the region.

As long as these conditions prevail, it seems hardly useful to persist in preferential margin negotiations in the hope that the resulting trade relations will be fair, since neither the governments nor the entrepreneurs involved, really believe they will be effective. Moreover, the payments situation is so involved for all parties concerned that they are naturally unwilling to favour imports that do not carry with them the certainty that they themselves will be able to export to a similar value.

Table 1 shows the proportions of the global exports and imports of eleven countries comprising LAFTA/LAIA which make up their regional trade. During the period covered, intra-regional trade increased in relation to the countries' global trade both in terms of imports and exports, but the increases were only marginal and far short of the level required to meet the countries' present pressing needs.

In several Latin American countries there is a large industrial labour force, which cannot be fully employed owing mainly to the squeeze in the external sector. An expansion of regional trade could bring increased employment, bigger output from established industries and increased substitution of imports from third countries. But to make this possible, there would have to be arrangements to ensure balance in the transactions.

Bilateral agreements for balanced trade

Basic components of an agreement of this kind would be a list of products to be exported and a complementary one of those to be imported, indicating in the latter case the customs tariff to be applied, which would not be less favourable than that applying to third countries. For each bilateral agreement there would thus be a list of items to be exported and another of goods to be imported, which might or might not coincide.

The procedure adopted for dealing with the imports on the respective lists could be modified at the discretion of the importing country, without prior consultation with, or the approval of, the other party. This flexibility is possible because a country wishing to expand its exports by means of such an agreement will need to seek ways to increase its purchases, contrary to what happens now in LAIA.

In the bilateral trade and payments agreements which functioned until the end of the 1950s, the central banks agreed on a reciprocal credit arrangment to facilitate operations and to avoid unnecessary payments of foreign exchange. These credits are not necessary today and the payments would continue to be made in the usual way and using the normal instruments. On the other hand, both parties would negotiate an 'agreed imbalance' for a specific amount which might represent, for example, the estimated value of one month of trade. Should the exports of one of the parties exceed the value of the imports of the other, the losing country would have the right to cease issuing import licences for products covered by the agreement until the balance had been reestablished. In this way, there would be no outstanding credit balances which are the cause of so many problems under other bilateral trade and payments agreements.

Information regarding the progress of the agreement could be obtained from the letters of credit or bills negotiated through the commercial banks or from the documentation held at the customs. This information should cover imports as well as exports, in f.o.b. dollars, so that a correct comparison can be made. Both parties should exchange information via telex to check the compatibility of the balances. Trade in goods not included in the lists would not be taken into account.

Limitations on bilateral agreements

The use of the bilateral instrument should be limited to trade between the countries of LAIA. Also, it would not be convenient to abandon multilateralism in commerce with the industrialised countries and the Eastern bloc, as the freely convertible foreign exchange resulting from this trade can be used for the payment of service charges on loans or to buy goods wherever the price and quality are right. Moreover, the rules of GATT acknowledge bilateralism between the countries of the LAIA, but not with the industrialised countries and it might be thought prudent to respect the prevailing order, because, though on occasion it might operate somewhat unfairly, it is better than no order at all.

There should be limitations on bilateralism in respect of products, however. Exports that find sufficient markets in other parts of the world, or that may be readily exchanged for freely convertible foreign currency, should not be included. It is products which are difficult to sell in the industrialised countries, such as manufactured goods, that should be exported under bilateral agreements. There is a simple way of promoting trade under bilateral agreements in the case of products that can be imported from third countries on payment of a customs duty. That is to include these products in the lists, but with a lower levy. Such products would then be rerouted through the agreement.

However, half of all the purchases of the Latin American countries enter without the payment of import duties. In these cases (frequently capital goods) the only preference the countries of the region could accord might be to authorise such imports only when they are made under bilateral agreements. To prevent the danger of price abuse, which has so far blocked the growth of regional trade in capital goods, the Latin American Institute of Iron and Steel (ILAFA) has proposed to LAIA that when state enterprises examine international bids and find that the price offered by a Latin American firm is not more than 8 per cent above the lowest bid, the contract should be awarded to that firm on condition that the price is made equal to the lowest bid. This procedure is not applicable to imports of capital goods by the private sector, however, as the latter generally does not employ the bid system, and here there is no alternative but for the relevant authorities to approve the price of each transaction. This might involve a lengthy bureaucratic procedure, but it would be justified, as the present scarcity of foreign currency and of credits for the purchase of equipment looks likely to last for several years.

Since the emergence of the payments crisis in Latin America a wide range of so called luxury goods, or non-essentials, has made its appearance, the introduction of which has been forbidden. If these were to be exchanged under bilateral agreements, it would not be so much a case of substitution of imports, as with capital goods, as of benefit to the consumer in terms of price and quality arising from a wider variety of supply. Moreover, there would be no competition from third countries, as the goods are generally produced within the region, and the activity would also benefit the local industry.

Continuity of operations

One of the most serious drawbacks with bilateral trade and payments agreements after World War II was the lack of continuity due to the suspension of import licences whenever adverse balances occurred. The following are some of the means that might be adopted to reduce this risk. When one of the parties to a bilateral agreement exports more than it imports, thus upsetting the 'agreed balance', it could seek to increase its purchases by including new products in its list of imports or by increasing the margin of preference for those already on the list. It could inform the other party of the measures adopted and request a special extension of the amount of the agreed balance until the new concessions are converted into actual trade transactions.

However effective this procedure might be, however, there would still come a time when the trade between the two countries concerned reached a ceiling and one of the parties would be exporting more than the other. Suspension of import licences in this instance would be very damaging for products that require distribution, advertising and stocks of spares. The situation is not so serious with commodities, as their substitution from other sources is easy, as is their rerouting to other markets, or with quasi-commodities such as steel and aluminium for construction, etc. In order to reduce the damage caused by such an interruption of exports, therefore, the governments signing the instrument might agree to list, in order of priority, the products which would be the first to be banned.

Another procedure would be for the countries of the region with bilateral agreements to compensate for trade imbalances by means of crossflow arrangements among themselves, thus giving the agreements a certain degree of multilateralism.

Bilateral agreements of this kind might help to lessen the sacrifices that the Latin American countries have to endure in order to overcome the problems they experience in the external sector. They therefore merit the special attention of the authorities. If the scheme were to be successful it might be worth exploring how agreements of this type might, without conflicting with the rules of GATT, be reached with other, non-Latin American, developing countries, such as Spain, Israel, Yugoslavia and India. This would increase the opportunities for exporting manufactured goods and certain raw materials and agricultural produce.

About a third of the exports of the OECD countries and 40 per cent of those of the US are to the developing countries and 17 per cent of these are in Latin America. An energetic substitution of imports by Latin America and other developing countries might have the double advantage of not only alleviating their payments situation but also convincing the industrialised countries that the nations of the world are interdependent, and commercial policies cannot be adopted that take into account the interests of only one of the parties.

Conclusion

Several factors were influential in enabling Europe to achieve a high degree of economic unity after World War II and a not inconsiderable capacity for coordinating action in the political arena, but there is no doubt that the determining factor was a shift in the balance of power as a result of the war. Until 1939 the principal European powers had considerable individual influence. The United Kingdom was the leading naval power in the world and its empire numbered hundreds of millions of people living in numerous countries. The colonial empires of France, the Netherlands and Belgium were also extensive, and Spain, Portugal and Italy had considerable territories, too, while Germany was building the powerful military machine which was to lead to the outbreak of war. At the end of World War II the centre of gravity had shifted to the two great super-powers, the US and the USSR. The European countries ceased to be the political, military and economic axis of the world and were fast losing their colonies. They had become second- and third-rate powers, far behind the two principals.

It is difficult to conceive of a Europe with its present level of unity if the countries in it had retained something of the power they had held before. It was not until Europe's politicians realised that they would not regain their former influence in the world unless they joined forces that they decided to forget old rivalries and even the fresh wounds of war. Thus it is today that the EEC has become the first power in commerce in the world and makes its weight felt both in its bilateral and global relations.

Latin America has so far shown little commitment to unity, concentrating its efforts mainly on bilateral relations with the industrialised countries, to which it directs a major part of its exports and from which it receives not only industrial goods but also new technology, fashions and culture. As long as this commercial relationship with the developed world functioned well, individual countries preferred to enhance it, rather than establishing links with other countries in the region.

Today the countries of Latin America are no longer exporting to the developed world, not even to the extent necessary to maintain the living standards of former years. The acuteness of the crisis and the fact that it threatens to last for many years only increases the advantages to Latin America of unified action, bearing in mind that the conditions in the continent are basically similar to those that induced the European states to join forces with each other. Nothing unites mankind more than adversity, and in this Latin America is no exception.

Table 1
Latin American regional trade as a percentage of global trade
(Percentages on the total)

Year	on Exports	on Imports
1972	11.6	10.8
1973	10.9	11.3
1974	10.7	11.1
1975	12.6	10.2
1976	13.6	12.5
1977	14.3	13.4
1978	13.1	11.7
1979	14.5	13.3
1980	14.0	12.5
1981	13.3	13.3
1982	12.2	14.8

Source: LAFTA and LAIA Secretariats, based on data from the member countries.

Notes

1. Subsidies for open market exports are those which are applied to a product whatever its destination. The EEC generally does not grant open market subsidies, but rather for selected markets, for instance, it does not subsidise exports of meat to South America.

12

The disintegration of the integration process: towards new forms of regional cooperation

Luciano Tomassini

Those who judge the schemes of Latin American integration in the light of the expectations they originally raised agree that for a long time now these processes have either reached a standstill or are in a state of crisis. In contrast, those who observe these phenomena from a less orthodox standpoint tend to recognise that over the course of the last decades the interrelationship of the Latin American economies has not ceased to deepen, although this did not always happen in the ways that were envisaged at the outset. To resolve this apparent contradiction one must go beyond the concepts that inspired the first schemes of integration and accept that during the last fifteen years there has been a transformation in the context and orientation of the Latin American economic cooperation process and consequently in its modes of operation. This essay seeks to provide background information and elements of judgment which will help to describe and explain this phenomenon.

Latin American economic integration was conceived as an element of the development strategy applied by the countries of the region during the postwar years. This in its turn was largely determined by the type of external linkages imposed on these countries by the international economic context and by their degree of development during this period. Subsequently, both the external context and the degree of development of the Latin American countries changed substantially and this was accompanied by modifications—at different rates and in different directions —in the economic policies of these countries. Nevertheless the prevailing integration paradigm, which responded to the earlier circumstances, was not revised to the same extent, and the schemes based on this model stagnated while new forms of cooperation arose in the Latin American countries.

At least at the rhetorical level, economic integration in Latin America came to be regarded as an end in itself, regardless of the economic policies followed by the participating countries in each particular stage. Hence an increasing confidence was placed in the instruments proposed by the prevailing integration model and incorporated by the different schemes. It was customary to ascribe the integration crisis to an insufficient or erroneous application of these mechanisms, attributable to an inadequate understanding of their advantages or to the lack of political will. The fact that the Latin American theory of integration is considerably different from the conventional theory of economic integration or customs unions tended to highlight the importance of the aforesaid instruments, instead of emphasising the *de facto* solidarities that were so important in the European experience. Consequently, there is as yet no analytical framework to explain the rise and assess the importance of those non-traditional forms of cooperation which have prevailed in recent years. This has helped to dull the understanding of the subject and to weaken the dynamism of the other options.

This paper starts with the assumption that the tempo and modes of integration basically depend on the development strategies and forms of external linkage adopted in each period by the countries participating in the process and, therefore, on the characteristics, limitations and opportunities posed by their external context. In other words, the integration processes must be adapted to the national development strategies and to the circumstances of the international economy, and not vice-versa. It also begins with the supposition that the stagnation of the said mechanisms in Latin America is not the result of a crisis of integration but of development, and that their utility and reinforcement will depend on their adaption to the modes and perspectives which this process presents today, as is pointed out in a recent important analysis on the subject.[1] Clearly then, it is as harmful to cling to the instruments prescribed by the traditional integration model, once this has ceased to be functional in the new domestic and international circumstances, as not to recognise the full extent of the potential offered by the new forms of cooperation that have arisen in the wake of these circumstances. There is a need to overcome the rigidity that characterised the Latin American integration schemes in the past and to strengthen the trend towards flexibility in these new processes which are already observable among the Latin American countries.[2]

It is useful to draw attention to the fact that, for the reasons given above, this trend towards 'flexibilising' the integration process in Latin America has long been ignored or has become merely the object of a timid acceptance. The first document by ECLA (probably the institution that has had most influence on the conceptualisation of Latin American integration) which makes a major analysis of these trends and presents systematic information on the new forms of cooperation on specific aspects arising out of them dates from 1980. A more recent study from the same institution, in amplifying the analysis of the subject, considers it desirable to state that 'it has been thought useful to include in this paper some examples of these new forms of association among Latin American countries ... with a view to drawing attention to the tendencies which, though still only faintly, are beginning to indicate that they may acquire greater importance in the future' and, in continuation, considers it necessary to point out that the mention of these examples 'does not replace the overall analysis of regional integration and cooperation'.[3]

The reflections which follow attempt to make some contribution to this trend. The second part refers to the evolution of the traditional paradigm of Latin American economic integration in the light of its original conception. The third part explores the changes observed in the international and Latin American context that have had the greatest influence on the evolution of this process. The fourth part presents some information on the new forms adopted by regional economic cooperation, largely in consequence of the changes previously indicated. In the last section some conjectures are formulated on the prospects that cooperation among the Latin American countries might hold out in the light of these tendencies.

The failure of the Latin American integration paradigm

Conceived in the decade of the 1950s, economic integration was a requisite of the development model that in one way or another the Latin American countries had been applying since the 1930s crisis and the war. The rationalisation for it was provided by studies carried out by Dr Raúl Prebisch and ECLA during that and the following decades. This model was associated with the pattern of external links of the Latin American economies prevalent at that time, within the framework of an international division of labour which assigned to the peripheral economies the role of producers and exporters of foodstuffs and raw materials, and to the central economies the role of suppliers of the manufactures and capital goods required by the periphery. This form of international insertion implied a continuing deterioration in the terms of trade of the developing countries in their relations with the developed economies. To alter its position within the international division of labour Latin America had to follow the course of industrialisation, a process which, taking into account the circumstances prevalent at that time, had to be carried out under the aegis of important substitution.

As the bulk of technical progress took place in the manufacturing sector, highly concentrated in the large industrial centres, productivity, and hence average incomes, tended to increase more rapidly in these than in the periphery. Moreover, the development of the peripheral countries tended to be unilaterally concentrated in the primary exporting sector, while the moderate growth and diversification of their demand for industrial goods was largely satisfied by imports from the centres. Since the income-elasticity of manufactured products is much greater than that of commodities the terms of trade tended to adversely affect the primary products. As a result countries of the periphery had to make a systematic transfer to the centres of a considerable part of the benefits derived from the limited improvement in the productivity of their commodity export activities, and the gap between the two groups of countries continued to widen.

In these circumstances, the 'external barrier' loomed as the main obstacle to the development of the periphery. The industrialisation of the developing countries appeared in the light of this analysis as the only way in which, through changing the specialisation of these countries in the international division of labour, they could improve their terms of trade and retain a larger share of the fruits of technical progress. The drastic reduction in the value of their exports as a result of the 1930s crisis and the further difficulties in importing caused by the war gave these countries new incentives to adopt policies of protection and stimulus to the creation of an industry which, during an initial stage, was based on import substitution and 'growth turned inwards'.

But the import-substitution strategy had certain limitations. For one thing, production costs rise as the protection of national production increases; in fact, as import substitution attempts to go beyond a relatively 'easy' stage to embark on more complex products, the lack of economies of scale becomes a serious barrier and the quantity of productive factors required per unit of growth increases, together with the costs of the process. Furthermore, in a period of very scant resources for development financing, the 'inward oriented' growth model was not only incapable of generating the external resources needed by the Latin American countries but was also faced with growing difficulties in further reducing imports, since the countries found themselves obliged to replace the import of relatively simple products by that of the capital and intermediate goods which were needed to deepen their development and which they could not produce locally. Finally, a policy formulated to cope with the problem created by the disarticulation of international economic relations during the whole of that period seemed fated to be wrecked against that 'external barrier'.

Economic integration seemed to offer a solution to this problem. On the one side, it provided these countries with the possibility of increasing their exports to the regional market in the case of products that they had not been able to sell in the world markets owing to the standstill in international trade. On the other side, it enabled import substitution to be conducted more efficiently at the regional level, through the utilisation of the economies of scale made possible by a wider market. Economic integration, therefore, seemed destined to fulfil the double role of finally compressing the coefficient of imports through the creation of economies of scale and of increasing exports to the regional market, thus augmenting the availability of external resources. The integration schemes instituted during that period—the Latin American Free Trade Association, the Central American Common Market and, subsequently, the Caribbean Community and the Andean Pact—were created in response to these objectives.

Economic integration was the natural follow-up to the strategy of 'growth turned inwards' pursued in that period by the Latin American countries, and was conceived as a method of removing the 'external barriers' to development by deepening import substitution. The need to reduce that external obstacle impressed on the Latin American theory of integration a special trait, which is its insistence on the contribution of this process to the amelioration of the countries' balance of payments, whether through the reduction of their imports or the increase of revenues deriving from their exports to the regional market. The theoretical bases of Latin American integration did not completely coincide, therefore, with the basic theory of customs unions which had guided European integration and which was claimed to be the inspiration of the Latin American process. The Latin American conception of integration placed more emphasis on the need to contribute to the attentuation of the restrictions of the balance of payments and much less on the benefits that might accrue from the possibility of taking advantage of economies of scale and achieving a better combination of the productive factors in a genuinely enlarged market. As a result of this, it also put more emphasis on the commercial aspects of the process than on its implications for infrastructure and the productive sectors, and—within that perspective—on intra-regional trade rather than on external economic relations.[4]

As a consequence of this bias, in the long run Latin American integration was aimed to replace imports of goods that could be produced within the region with those of capital and intermediate goods and basic inputs. This led to changes in the composition rather than in the quantity of imports, permitting a reallocation of the foreign exchange in favour of the exporters of capital goods in the industrialised countries. At the same time, the increase in the exports of Latin American countries to the regional market had to be accompanied by an increase in their purchases from that same market, at a higher cost than that indicated by world prices, in order to maintain reciprocity in trade transactions, which was a major requisite of the prevailing integration model. But although this implies that there was more deviation than creation of trade, the deviation achieved was also insufficient, since the imports made from the region tended to be more competitive from the standpoint of the local producers and hence were more successfully resisted. Another problem lay, of course, in the dependence of exports to third countries in relation to the deviation of trade in favour of Latin American providers.

The foreign exchange liberated by the substitution of competitive imports at the regional level was used to augment imports of non-competitive goods, such as equipment and intermediate goods; the increase in revenue coming from exports to the regional market was to some extent offset by the greater cost of the product which, to maintain reciprocity, it was necessary to import from the countries of the region; and the substitution of imports obtained from third countries by products deriving from the regional market tended to limit the income obtained from exports to the rest of the world. These circumstances eroded the expected impact of economic integration on the balance-of-payments difficulties of the Latin American countries and weakened the viability of the existing formal integration schemes, stimulating the search for new forms of cooperation.

This process was accompanied by deep changes in the circumstances in which the Latin American countries developed during the postwar period and by the modifications which these countries had to introduce, with different nuances, in their economic policies and strategies of external insertion.

The changing context of regional economic integration

The international system within which the development strategies of the Latin American countries were designed and their integration schemes launched during the postwar period underwent a complete transformation towards the end of the 1960s.

The structure of world power, which during the whole of the postwar period remained rigidly bipolarised and strongly influenced by the Cold War, began to show a significant change with the relative decline of the power of the US; the rise of tensions within the trilateral system and, very particularly, within the Atlantic Alliance; the internal difficulties experienced by the Soviet bloc and the erosion of the model that this represented; the growing degree of development and external projection achieved by some Third World countries and, in general, the trend towards the fragmentation of the international system—all of which introduces a much greater degree of fluidity into international economic relations.

There is a shift from a world dominated by considerations of strategic security and by the confrontation of the two superpowers towards another characterised by a certain degree of *détente* and by a more favourable atmosphere for prosecuting other interests—economic, technological and sociocultural—in international relations. The fragmentation of world economic and political power is accompanied by the growing complexity and dispersion of strategic conflicts. This process is also stimulated by the emergence of global problems—such as that of energy, the environment, stagflation or external indebtedness—on the solution of which depends the well-being of ever-increasing sectors of the national societies. These trends would seem to reveal the transition from an international system dominated by the concepts of 'power' and 'security', such as that which, broadly speaking, dominated the postwar period, to another based on relations of 'interdependence' and oriented towards the maximisation of 'well-being' within these societies.[5]

One might venture here the hypothesis that, in consequence of the trend towards the fragmentation of world power and the diversification that has taken place within the national societies, international relations at the present time, as opposed to the past, 1) are characterised by a growing number of centres of power, 2) whose external dealings aim at satisfying a much wider range of objectives than in the past; 3) evolve around a much more diversified and complex and less hierarchical agenda; and 4) are administered by new and multiple state and private agents which 5) bring into play non-traditional power resources in a variety of areas which are much more numerous, changeable and intertwined than before.[6] In addition to that, since the end of the 1960s the world economy has entered into a state of profound transition or crisis, whose structural, and not merely cyclical, character can no longer be denied. This crisis has had a severe effect on the developing world, and particularly on the Latin American countries, which had attained a greater degree of integration into the international economy. This transition was due in part to the changes in the preferences of the public in a growing number of social sectors as a result of the profound socio-cultural transformations which are altering the ways of life of industrial societies and diffusing attitudes less interested in having more of the same and more directed towards values linked with the quality of life.

These trends are associated with the decline of productivity in the industrialised countries; with the fall in investments and in the profitability of business enterprises; with the appearance of idle capacity in a growing range of industrial branches; with the slower tempo of technological innovation; with the rise in the operating costs of the productive systems, and those of social security and of the state; and in general, with the loss of competitiveness in a growing number of productive activities.

Thus a new international division of labour is beginning to rise, the future pattern of which is not yet clearly envisaged, but which is already provoking severe tensions among the developed countries and which could change the traditional forms of insertion of the developing countries into the world economy.

The development strategies on integration schemes of Latin American countries had been established during the postwar period. Now that the international setting and the development styles which prevailed during this period are crumbling, major changes should be introduced in both internal strategies and international links of Latin American countries, comprising its integration schemes.

To deal with these changes the Latin American countries had to make major adjustments. These adjustments were more painful in the case of those developing countries which had been more closely integrated in the world economy, which were more vulnerable to its transformations, and which lacked the resources to palliate the adverse effects of the transition experienced at global level on their economic growth, or to finance the reforms which this made necessary. These countries attempted to ease the adjustments, in different ways, through the massive use of external indebtedness. This was made possible by the extraordinary amount of liquidity which became available to the world economy from the beginning of the 1970s. After almost half a century the private financial markets began to reappear, primarily due to the weakening of the dollar, but also because of the surpluses accumulated by OPEC which were subsequently recycled by the private banks.

It is evident that the view the Latin American countries took of the 'external barrier' during the postwar years began to change after the end of the 1960s, when international economic relations gradually became more fluid, confronting them with a new balance of risks and opportunities. At the same time, the role that regional cooperation might play has also changed, becoming less focused on the removal of the aforesaid barrier, but on the deepening of development and on the strengthening of the external insertion of the Latin American countries.

It is true that in the last year regional economic integration has been invoked again as an umbrella against the impact of international crisis on the Latin American economies. But it is also true that integration has been the first casualty left by the crisis, that its role as an umbrella always will be a weak one, and that this role by no means could be played without a context of international participation and greater internal growth.

In that sense, the striking growth rate attained by an ever-increasing number of developed countries over the past twenty years and their progressive integration in the international economy has created profound changes in their economic, political and social systems, and in their linkages with the industrialised countries. The share of the relatively more industrialised developing countries in the imports of manufactured goods from the OECD rose from 2.6 per cent to 8.1 per cent between 1963 and 1977.[7] A World Bank report prior to the 1980s crisis indicated that the share of the developing countries in world exports of manufactures had risen from 6 per cent in 1960 to 10 per cent in 1966, and estimated that it would reach 16 per cent in 1990.[8] The share of manufactures in the total exports of the developing countries (excluding petroleum) grew from 10 per cent in 1955 to 20 per cent ten years later, and to around

40 per cent in 1975.⁹ Moreover, industrial products, whose share in the global exports of Latin America was only 5 per cent in the 1950s, now represent something in the region of a quarter of these exports.

During the last three decades Latin America has evidenced what may be considered a very dynamic economic growth. The gross domestic product rose at an average rate of 5.5 per cent per year, higher than the growth rate of the industrialised countries with market economy, and more intense than that of other developing regions of the world. As a result of this, the product of the region increased five-fold between 1950 and 1980, while the production of steel and energy grew ten-fold and that of capital goods fifteen-fold.

This rate of economic growth was accompanied by an intense process of investment and the productive and technological transformation of their economies. The industrial base of the region showed a remarkable expansion and diversification. This enabled domestic production to satisfy practically the whole demand for consumer goods and the greater—and growing—part of the demand for basic intermediate goods and capital. Although the processes of integration played an important part, a considerable proportion of the said growth was found to be outside the preferences granted within the framework of the formal integration schemes. More important was the vigorous expansion and diversification of Latin American exports to the rest of the world from the middle of the 1960s and the increasing incorporation of manufactured products in these exports. At the same time agriculture was transformed, at least in its modern or commercial sector, with the introduction of modern production techniques and advances in the organisation of agricultural enterprise and in the marketing of its products, with a closer integration into the rest of the economy. In addition, infrastructure was considerably enlarged, particularly in relation to transport, communications and energy, and there was an expansion and modernisation of banking and financial services. Through these advances the national economies substantially increased their sectorial integration and interdependence.

The institutional development of Latin America in the postwar period was considerable and was firmly linked with the processes of industrialisation and urbanisation which, having started earlier in several countries, were greatly intensified during these years.

Per capita income expanded at an average annual rate of 2.6 per cent in the course of these three decades, doubling itself in absolute figures and achieving a per capita average of some US$1,300 at the beginning of the present decade. It is noteworthy that this rate of income growth was much higher than that recorded in the now industrialised countries during the period that might be considered their own development stage, that is, during the time of the industrial revolution. Certainly this did not alter the fact that income distribution continued to be extremely unequal, and that this inequality even increased, although it is also certain that the origins of inequality in Latin America stem from deep and tenacious historical roots and that its maintenance should be in part explained by decelerated population growth.

The notable strengthening of the productive forces of the Latin American countries was accompanied from the middle of the 1970s by decided efforts on the part of most of them to open their economies, with different rates and methods, both on the commercial and financial plane, and to integrate themselves more closely into the international economy. At the commencement of the 1980s the Latin American market as a whole represented a demand of over a billion dollars and had become a factor not to be despised from the standpoint of the progress or economic reactivation of the industrialised countries. All this tended to change the orientation of the development strategies of the Latin American countries.

Although this transition has often been presented as a conflict between rival schools of thought, it will perhaps be realised with hindsight that in practice it was a question of stages in the economic development of the Latin American countries and not of alternatives. The strategy of import substitution was the only valid option open to them at a given moment in their history, considering the stage of development that they had reached and the existence of an adverse external situation. Frequently, this strategy served as a basis not only for their industrialisation but also for the consolidation of their own nationalities. Besides, not only were they unaware at the time of a necessary contradiction between the domestic and external markets, but the former often served as a springboard for entering the international markets.

The fact is that, since the middle of the 1960s, the Latin American countries have begun to apply at different tempos and in different ways— some of them obviously exaggerated—new development strategies based on the liberalisation of the international market and the opening of their economies to the external world.

These changes were bound to affect the importance and goals assigned to integration and cooperation in Latin America, as was underscored by the President of Colombia, Alfonso López Michelsen, in contrasting the development models applied by most of the medium-sized countries of the region until midway through the 1960s (and which he associated with the thinking of CEPAL) with the 'Asiatic model' which began to gain ground after World War II in other regions of the world, and in formulating the question as to whether these countries, not now at national but at regional level, could barricade themselves again 'behind the walls of an excessively high common external tariff and thereby return to the import-substitution model' followed in the past.[10] Subsequently, the same type of doubt was broached, implicitly or explicitly, from various angles.

Finally, the fact that the changes introduced into the development strategies of the countries of the region, in response to the new international and domestic circumstances described above, led to a greater divergence or heterogeneity among these policies, in comparison with the prevalent postwar situation, was another element that put pressure on the process of Latin American integration. The same effect resulted, and with more reason, from the growing instability and diversity arising among the political régimes of the Latin American countries during the past decade and, in particular, the coexistence of democratic systems of government with régimes based on the doctrine of national security, which, by definition, viewed with suspicion the possibility of making long-term commitments with other countries that might reduce their margin of external manoeuvre.

Hence there is a lack of real substance in the traditional explanation of the failure of integration schemes in Latin America, according to which this is due to the lack of 'political will' in the member countries, expressed in the chronic non-observance of the commitments undertaken within the respective agreements and in the insufficient use of the instruments set up by these agreements. As was stated in a recent report, 'to seek the causes of the weakening of integration solely in the functioning of the regional or subregional institutions or in the legal instruments governing them would undoubtedly be to take an inadequate view of its complex and diverse origins'.[11]

The evolution of these strategies—in response to new circumstances—from a model of 'growth turned inwards' to a more open type of growth, and the increasing heterogeneity that arose among them as a result of the differences in the approach or the tempo of the responses given by

the different countries to the same circumstances, constituted the main
cause of the weakening of the formal integration schemes and of the rise
of new forms of Latin American cooperation. This is the conclusion reached
by a senior analyst of these processes when, after discarding other possible
explanations, he declares that 'the conflicts between the said strategies
are as responsible for the failure of the integration exercises in Latin
America as the incorrect design of the schemes', and he points out the
inadequacy of the traditional instruments, based on trade liberalisation,
in helping to solve the current problems of economic development in Latin
America.[12]

To sum up, having placed great emphasis on the need to contribute
to the solving of the balance-of-payment problems of their member
countries, the Latin American integration schemes, considered as a
prolongation of the import-substitution policy, showed themselves to be
incapable of surmounting the 'external barrier'. As the Latin American
countries reached a higher stage of development and were more closely
integrated into the international economy—which at that time had become
in fact more permissive or fluid—they began to apply policies aimed at
the expansion of their exports and to obtain external financial resources
more successfully, or so it seemed, than in the past. Eventually the financial
aspects of this external opening pared to the forefront, so that today the
current account of the Latin American economies has ceased to be
dominated by the trade balance, depending basically on financial transactions. In these circumstances the external trade of the Latin American
countries is not the vehicle to solve unaided, to a significant degree, their
external financial problems; on the contrary, it is probable that these
problems will come to be decisively important in the structure of trade.
The former appreciation particularly apply to intra-regional trade. This
seriously limits the possibilities of integration schemes of a commercial
nature, whose potential contribution to the solution of the balance-of-
payment problems of their member countries was overestimated, and makes
it necessary to seek in regional economic cooperation an instrument which
will help to strengthen the productive capacity and competitiveness of the
Latin American economies at the real level.

From this standpoint, regional cooperation can help to promote a more
complementary and sustained development of the Latin American
countries, not only through trade preferences, but also through the reinforcement of the regional infrastructure, more efficient systems of pay-

ment, greater access to credit, a more interrelated institutional system, a greater mutual awareness among economic agents operating in the different countries and, above all, a growing technical complementarity and a greater development and integration of their productive sectors. The fact that over recent years the countries of the region have known how to take advantage of the opportunities open to them on these diverse fronts explains the rise of the new forms of cooperation described in the following sections.

The new ways of Latin American cooperation

The aim of this essay was to show how and why, alongside the multi-lateral integration schemes based on the application of general instruments, there have emerged, and with more vigour, new forms of cooperation based on specific actions, covenants and projects agreed between pairs or groups of countries. To describe this phenomenon the terms 'real' or 'informal' integration are used, as distinct from the schemes formally agreed in the treaties, or a contrast is established between 'integration' in a strict sense and 'cooperation' in the broader sense referred to above. What follows is an account of the latter phenomenon, particularly in the fields of trade, infrastructure, the productive sectors and development financing.

It is now clear that the increase in intra-regional trade—roughly from 8 per cent to 16 per cent during the seventies—is due only in part to the preferences granted within the framework of the formal integration schemes and in large measure to the improvement of the national mechanisms for export promotion, to the conclusion of bilateral trade agreements and to other factors which have facilitated reciprocal trade. Although only some of these factors have been directly or indirectly linked with the functioning of the integration schemes, while others have arisen independently, one would have to speak here of the 'hidden benefits of integration'.[13] These benefits, through not being always susceptible to adequate quantification, have not been appreciated in their real dimension. In general, they are connected with certain institutional improvements in the field of foreign trade, with a greater value being placed on the Latin American market, with a deeper knowledge of the realities of the other countries of the region, and with the development of a greater interdependence among the economic policies of the different countries.

The instruments of trade liberalisation incorporated in the existing formal integration schemes were complemented during the past decade by the resurgence, though in limited form, of bilateral trade agreements, particularly between countries situated in the southern cone of the continent. In many cases the formalisation of these agreements took place within the ALALC framework. An initial procedure, and probably the most advanced in this field, is represented by those agreements that set up a programme of trade liberation of a bilateral nature, with greater margins of preference and speedier schedules for the signing parties than those established by ALALC. These instruments include the agreements made between Argentina and Uruguay in 1974, between Uruguay and Brazil in 1975 and between Brazil and Paraguay in that same year. Another form of procedure in this field is represented by agreements aimed at intensifying, through tariff and non-tariff concessions, the interchange of products included in special lists, in cases where reciprocal trade in these is of interest to the signatories; these include the agreements signed between Bolivia and Paraguay in 1974, and between Chile and Paraguay, Bolivia and Uruguay and Chile and Uruguay in 1975. A third procedure, which has given rise to a greater number of agreements, consists in commitments made between Latin American countries to supply basic products over several years; these agreements, which represent the main types of integration in the food and agricultural field, enable major trade flows to be established and production to be better planned by creating greater certainty as to the subsequent placement of the products. Brazil, for example, has actively promoted this type of agreement and has current commitments for the acquisition of wheat in Argentina and, on a lesser scale, in Uruguay, along with natural gas and, eventually, metallurgical products, nitrogenised fertilisers and cement in Bolivia. A fourth and very promising method of commercial cooperation which is being tried out by a number of Latin American countries consists of agreements aimed at promoting direct purchases between public enterprises situated in those countries.

The establishment of systems of external trade financing and of payment compensation among Latin American countries has made a significant contribution to the expansion of their reciprocal trade. At present there are three mechanisms of this type in force: the ALALC payment agreement, which includes the Dominican Republic, and which in 1979 transferred credits to a value of $1,600 million, making possible a volume of financial operations exceeding $6,400 million, which represented three-quarters of the intrazonal trade in that year; the Central American Chamber of Compensation which in 1979 liquidated transactions amounting to $1,037 million, covering not only the whole of the subregional trade but also other financial transfers in addition; and the CARICOM system of multilateral compensations, which in 1978 totalled transactions for $263 million.

The integration of the physical infrastructure of the Latin American countries has made sustained and notable progress during the last two decades, particularly in the fields of transport, communications and energy, facilitating the expansion of their reciprocal trade and the complementarity of their productive sectors.

Road transport is the only type of transport that is almost totally integrated throughout the region, although the use of this medium is very unequal, being highly concentrated in some subregions. The railways links, in contrast, are more restricted to the southern cone of the continent and although in general the national railways show a reduction in their networks in service, this is offset by the increase in the tons of freight transported. River transport is much used in the River Plate and Amazon Basins. At present the effort of the countries in the transport sector is directed not so much to the enlargement of the physical infrastructure as to the better use of existing facilities through the establishment of swift transit lines by means of the employment of intermodal transport practices, modern technologies (as, for example, the use of containers) and administrative procedures for the speeding up of freight transport. There is still much to be done, however, to improve the competitiveness of the regional services as against those offered by third countries and to capture a larger share of the extensive international market of freightage and insurance, in which in 1982 the region paid $8,000 million to foreign firms solely in respect of seaborne freight.

In the energy sector, joint action has traditionally been confined to the generation of electricity. During the last two decades there has been continued expansion in the linkage of the national electricity systems, and a marked increase in the number and scope of binational projects aimed at exploiting the hydrographical basins shared for hydroelectric purposes. One can mention the Itaipú works between Paraguay and Brazil (which at the beginning of the 1980s involved investments of over $10,000 million), and those of Salto Grande between Argentina and Uruguay, among those which are at a more advanced stage of execution, and those of Yaciretá and Corpus between Argentina and Paraguay, Laguna Mirín between Brazil and Uruguay and Puyango-Tumbes between Ecuador and Peru, among the more important projects at various stages of development. In the hydrocarbon sector, during the more recent period, some Latin American oil-exporting countries set up the Energy Cooperation Programme for the Central American and Caribbean countries, instituted in virtue of the San José Agreement, and thanks to this and other bilateral and multinational initiatives an extensive network of agreements and action programmes has been established throughout the region, which should enable it in the future to grapple more effectively with the problems that arise from its great financial, commercial and technological vulnerability in the energy sector. The Latin American Energy Cooperation Programme (PLACE), of the Latin American Energy Organization (OLADE), constitutes an ambitious initiative in this field.

One of the fields in which economic complementarity among Latin American countries through specific cooperation measures seems to have acquired greater dynamism during recent years is that of the productive sectors. The failure of Latin American integration has often been attributed to the fact that the expanded markets created by this process have been exploited by direct foreign investment channelled through the great transnational enterprises operating in the countries of the region. This phenomenon has hampered the appreciation of the growing importance of entrepreneurial cooperation among Latin American countries, whether through multinational investments of regional origin or through arrangements aimed at combining markets, technology, entrepreneurial capacity and other productive factors.

The data on direct investment of intraregional origin are not reliable. At all events, the process manifests a striking dynamism, since the investments of Latin American origin seem to have grown at a more rapid rate than the direct foreign investments from outside the region. What is more important, the intra-regional investments have shown great flexibility in their modes of operation, and seem better adjusted to the development requirements of the countries of the region. The traits which characterise these investments include the diversity of the organisational forms through which they are channelled, their tendency to be associated with national capital, the frequent participation of public enterprises in the larger investments and a better sectorial distribution of these investments as a result of the similarity between the economic structure of the investing and receiving countries within the region.[14]

The foregoing illustrates the growing importance of technological complementarity among the countries of the region. Tradtionally, the technology required for their development originated in the industrialised countries, which in exchange for its transfer obtained monopolistic returns that placed a heavy burden on the Latin American countries. For a long time the greater part of the analyses of this problem described the technological challenge of the Latin American countries in terms of the acquisition of reasonably well-selected foreign technology at the least possible cost. More recent approaches reveal that a large number of problems whose solution is vital for the development of the countries of the region are only recognised when the said foreign technology is incorporated into their productive processes, or even when the scientific research—international or national—has to provide applied technological solutions.[15] At these levels the Latin American countries are called upon to play a much more active part than in the past. Besides, the more advanced countries of the region now possess a technological and professional capacity sufficient to produce a domestic flow of knowledge complementary to that imported, which can facilitate the autonomous application of the scientific research to the elaboration of technological solutions, the selection and adaptation of foreign technologies in terms of local requirements and the disaggregation of the 'technological packages' usually offered by the industrialised countries, thus permitting the construction of new technological combinations that incorporate a large component of national technology and are more suited to local needs. The interchange of knowledge and technological complementarity among Latin American countries plays an important role in this process.

The mechanisms of financial cooperation have been particularly important in Latin America. Mention has already been made of the systems of foreign-trade financing and payment compensation in relation to the instruments for the promotion of Latin American intra-regional trade. Here reference will be made to the systems of financing disequilibria in the balance of payments, to the development banks and funds and to other institutions for financial and monetary cooperation.[16]

The mechanisms for financing disequilibria of balance of payments were conceived as instruments complementary to those provided by the systems of payment compensation. The latter operate on a short-term basis, during which the trade balances have to be compensated, thus creating the need to have credits for larger amounts and for a longer term in order to cope with the deficits generated by the regional interchange, which, in general, aggravate the structural disequilibrium of the balance of payments of the Latin American countries. This situation led to the Agreement on Latin American Financial Assistance (Santo Domingo Agreement), the purpose of which is to complement the ALALC system of payment compensation; the Central American Monetary Stabilisation Fund, and, later, the Central American Chamber of Compensation, the Andean Reserves Fund, and the Regional Stabilisation Fund of the member countries of CARICOM.

The institutions for financing development operating in the region are of long standing and very important. Fundamental among these is the Inter-American Development Bank, whose origins, history and influence would require a special study. Subsequently, and with the support of the IDB, there were established the Central American Economic Integration Bank, the Andean Development Corporation, the Caribbean Development Bank, and the Financing Fund for the Development of the River Plate Basin. Reference has also been made to the financing facility agreed between Venezuela, Mexico and the Central American and Caribbean countries with regard to their energy requirements. Although the Venezuelan Investment Fund is a bilateral mechanism, it shares with the aforesaid multilateral institutions its emphasis on the financing of regional integration projects.

In conclusion, mention should be made of other institutions associated with financial and monetary cooperation which, because of their functions, could not be classified in the aforementioned categories. These include the Latin American Export Bank (BLADEX) the Latin American Bank Acceptances System (ABLA), the Andean Trade Financing System (SAFICO) and the Latin American Arabian Bank (ARLA-BANK).

The trend towards the 'flexibilising' of the integration process, which has led to the new forms of cooperation mentioned above, has found an institutional expression in the creation of the Latin American Economic System (SELA), in pursuance of the Panama Convention of 1975. In contrast to the formal integration schemes existing at that time, SELA was conceived as a flexible mechanism, capable of promoting a wide—or practically unlimited—range of forms of cooperation on specific aspects. It is noteworthy that at the time when SELA was constituted the idea of creating a mechanism of that type was, so to speak, 'in the air'.[17] SELA embraces all the countries of the region, including Cuba and the English-

speaking Caribbean countries, and has in general two important functions:
1) to coordinate the position of the Latin American countries in their
external relations—a function previously performed non-institutionally by
the Special Commission for Latin American Co-ordination (CECLA)—and,
2) to foster measures of cooperation among the Latin American countries—
or among some of them—in specific sectors. The main instrument available
to SELA for promoting this last type of action is the Action Committees,
the creation of which is proposed by the Permanent Secretariat of SELA
to deal with specific issues and which function with the participation of
the countries interested and with considerable autonomy. The results of
SELA's work have probably been below the expectations that its great
flexibility raised at the outset. This is largely due to the fact that, being
a much more political instrument than the integration schemes, from
the very beginning it lacked at that level the support of the countries of the
south of the region and, quite early in its career, it also lost much of the
initial support of the two countries that had had the greatest influence
on its creation (Mexico and Venezuela). This is certainly connected with
the trend towards a growing heterogeneity and fragmentation among the
Latin American countries, which was referred to above. Nevertheless,
owing to its structure, SELA continues to be, at least in principle, an
appropriate instrument for promoting the cooperation of the Latin
American countries through specific actions.[18]

Some final reflections

Latin American economic integration, in its traditional forms, did not
achieve the goals expected of it in its initial stages and ended by 'dis-
integrating' into diverse forms of economic cooperation, more narrow in
scope, when the development strategies that had produced this process
were modified as a result of the changes that occurred, from the beginning
of the 1970s, in the regional and international frame of reference of the
Latin American countries. In effect, integration had been a kind of
prolongation of the 'growth turned inwards' strategy that prevailed during
the postwar period and began to lose its functionality when, one after
another, the countries of the region started to review this strategy in the
light of the growing attraction exerted by the policies of openness to
external trade and finance which, at different rates and in different ways,
were adopted by most of the countries during the 1970s within the context

of a greater fluidity in international economic relations. The fact that the Latin American conception of economic integration had placed such emphasis on its capacity to contribute to the balance-of-payments problems of the region, and its very limited capacity to do so, was largely responsible for the waning of the hopes placed in the enterprise. At the same time the degree of development reached by a number of Latin American countries, and the challenge of strengthening their capacity for growth and external projection presented by this process and by the new international situation, induced them to seek new forms of economic complementarity which would help them to achieve the said goals through non-traditional modes of operation. The origin, importance and perspectives of these new modes have not yet been sufficiently analysed within the context of the traditional theory of Latin American integration.

What role could Latin American integration and cooperation perform in the future? For one thing, the heavy burden placed on the Latin American economies by the extremely high external indebtedness they incurred in the unusual conditions of international financial permissiveness already referred to within a global context markedly recessive and uncertain, is an indication that Latin America has once again entered a period of severe external restrictions which will call for more inward-looking development strategies than in the recent past. This should give a new impetus to regional economic cooperation.

At the same time, however, we must not forget that the international linkages of Latin America have been profoundly transformed and that even the nature of its current external restrictions, though these are very serious, has changed. Given the level of development achieved by some Latin American countries and their degree of integration into the international economy, it would be difficult for them to cease to rely to some extent on the recovery of the economies of the North and on global economic activity as an 'engine' of their development. Indeed, one of the most distinguished recent proponents of a strategy based on South-South cooperation to surmount the crisis considers this formula more viable but less efficient and satisfactory than one which relies on a more advantageous insertion of the countries of the periphery into a more open and more dynamic world economy.[19] In the light of the foregoing analysis, we consider that a strategy of South-South cooperation—whether at global or regional level—regarded as an alternative rather than as a complement to a strategy of more active participation by the developing countries in the world economy would not only be less efficient, but also less viable. Regional economic cooperation is called to play a very important role in attenuating the external vulnerability of the Latin American countries, enlarging the bases of its economic development and strengthening its external projection. But any attempt to present it as a panacea for the enormous difficulties that the economies of the region face today in their external sector would be an act of opportunism placed at the service of a just cause deserving of a more perceptive defence.

This defence should begin by recognising that the role of regional economic cooperation will necessarily have to be complementary to that of other policies within the framework of development strategies which are more open, more dynamic and more integrated into the international economy than during the postwar period. Next it should assume that more attention will be given, aside from the commercial aspects of the process, to its ability to contribute to the improvement of the institutional and technological capacity to promote the development of infrastructure and the productive sectors. This in turn will demand that less should be expected of the global and preferential instrument of economic integration used in the past and that more attention should be paid to the new forms of economic cooperation now arising among the Latin American countries, which are generally of a more operational, diversified and specific nature. Paradoxically, the revitalisation of Latin American integration would seem to arise out of its 'disintegration', through concrete actions of economic cooperation, carried out in a more flexible but not less deliberate way.

Notes

1. See Guillermo Maldonado, Eduardo Gana and Armando di Filippo, 'América Latina: crisis, cooperación y desarrollo', *Revista de la CEPAL* (20) August 1983. The authors sustain, in what in our view is an important departure from the traditional thinking of ECLA, the need to 'recognise that the so-called "integration crisis" is in fact a "crisis of development" and of the policies leading to it' and they anticipate that the different schemes will be slow to recover their capacity to contribute to a new strategy 'more in keeping with the international economic outlook and with the national realities of the Latin American countries'. Another analysis concerning the linkage between integration and development can be found in L Tomassini, 'La integración y el cambio de las estrategias de desarrollo de los países Latinoamericanos', in M Wilhelmy (Coordinator), *Sociedad Política e Integración en América Latina*, Santiago, Chile, 1982.
2. For an analysis of this trend made at the time of its first manifestations see, by L Tomassini, 'Hacia nuevas formas de cooperación Latinoamericana', in *Comercio Exterior* (Mexico) April 1975 and also 'Los Procesos de integración y otras formas de cooperación

en América Latina', *Integración Latinoamericana*, Buenos Aires, April 1977. These analyses are connected with a preliminary study made in INTAL on the subject.

3. See 'El desarrollo de América Latina en el umbral de los años ochenta', Santiago, 1980, pp 163–67 and subsequently 'Integración y cooperación regionales en los años ochenta', Santiago, 1982, p 75.

4. The book by William Cline and Enrique Delgado (editors), *Economic Integration in Central America*, Washington, DC, 1978, recognises the emphasis placed on the restrictions of the balance of payments. See Chapter 3 and Appendix C.

5. The works which have been among the first to analyse this phenomenon in the economic field include those of Richard N Cooper, *The Economics of Interdependence: Economic Policy in the Atlantic Community*, New York, 1968. From the viewpoint of the analysis of international relations the basic works are the book by Robert O Keohane and Joseph S Nye entitled *Power and Interdependence: World Politics in Transition*, Boston, 1977, and the work previously published by them: *Transnational Relations and World Politics*, New York, 1972. See also the studies contained in *Globalism Versus Realism: International Relations Third Debate*, edited by R Maghroory and B Ramberg, New York, 1982.

6. This analysis is developed further in L Tomassini, 'Interdependencia y desarrollo nacional', published in *El Trimestre Económico* (200) corresponding to October–December 1983, and in 'El proceso de transnacionalización y el desarrollo de los países Latino-americanos', *Estudios Internacionales* (64) January–March 1984.

7. OECD, *The Impact of the Newly Industrialising Countries on Production and Trade in Manufactures*, Paris; OECD, 1979. The countries included by the OECD in this category—NIC's—are Brazil and Mexico, in Latin America; Hong Kong, South Korea, Singapore and Taiwan in the East and Southeast of Asia; and Greece, Portugal, Spain and Yugoslavia in South Europe and the Mediterranean.

8. IBRD, *World Development Report 1979*, Washington DC: The World Bank, 1979, pp 128–9.

9. Independent Commission on International Development Issue (Brandt Commission), *North South: A Programme for Survival*, London: Pan Books, 1980.

10. Exposition made by the President of Colombia, Sr Alfonso López Michelsen, in Medellín, 17 September 1976.

11. 'Bases para una Respuesta de América Latina a la Crisis Económica Internacional', a paper presented by Carlos Alzamora T, Permanent Secretary of SELA, and Enrique V Iglesias, Executive Secretary of ECLA, to the President of Ecuador, Dr Osvaldo Hurtado, in response to a request from him, p 34. This paper was considered in the Latin American Economic Conference at Quito in January 1984.

12. Miguel S Wionczek, 'Can the broken Humpty-Dumpty be put together again and by whom?', *World Development*, 1978, p 782 and *passim*.

13. 'Integración y Cooperación Latinoamericana: los Beneficios Ocultos', editorial of *Integración Latinoamericana* (6) September 1976.

14. Several studies carried out by IDB/INTAL had reached these conclusions on the basis of the analysis of two hundred cases of joint Latin American enterprises. See INTAL/IDB, 'Las Empresas Conjuntas Latinoamericanas', Buenos Aires, 1977 and Jaime Campos, 'Intercambio Empresarial de Recursos Productivos entre Países Latinoamericanos', IDB/INTAL, Buenos Aires, August 1980.

15. See the studies of the IDB/CEPAL programme on these problems, particularly monograph No. 30 this programme, by Jorge Katz, entitled 'Cambio Techológico, Desarrollo Económico y Relaciones Intra y Extraregionales de la América Latina', Buenos Aires, August 1978.

16. The mechanisms of financial and monetary cooperation in Latin America are the subject of another study at this seminar.
17. As stated above, INTAL, with the support of the UNDP, during that period, embarked on a study of the new trends of Latin American economic cooperation. Although this study did not go beyond its preliminary stage, it enabled some conclusions to be drawn similar to those which gave rise to the creation of SELA. See 'El Sistema Latinoamericano', editorial of *Integración Latinoamericana* (1) April 1976, and 'Hacia el futuro: el pacto constituyente de la comunidad Latinoamericana', INTAL document published in the *Boletín de la Integración*, Buenos Aires, May 1975.
18. An in-depth analysis of SELA is omitted here, partly because the subject would require a special study and partly because this essay has sought to analyse the prevailing trends in the field of Latin American integration and cooperation and its main results, without enlarging on its institutional expressions. For further information on this organisation, prepared from an official standpoint, see Francisco Javier Alejo and Héctor Hurtado, 'El SELA: un Mecanismo para la Acción', México, 1976. Among the existing studies of an academic nature, see Robert D Bond, 'Regionalism in Latin America: prospects for the Latin American economic system (SELA)', *International Organization* 32 (2) Spring, 1978, and Patricio Chaparro, 'El sistema económico Latinoamericano (SELA), como instancia de mediación, representación y acción política ¿destinado al fracaso?', *Estudios Internacionales* (48) October–December 1975.
19. This is the thesis sustained by Sir W Arthur Lewis in his exposition made on receiving the Nobel prize for economics and published under the title 'The slowing down of the engine of growth', *American Economic Review*, September 1980.

13

The role of the university in integration

Iván Lavados Montes

The process of integration has many dimensions—political, economic, judicial, cultural, scientific, technological. All help to determine the social structure. The weight that each carries in people's deliberations will depend on the perspective that is being taken. Nevertheless, there is a tendency to associate the concept of integration with the economic dimension and the juridical implications that this carries.[1] Yet there are the other areas. Indeed, in recent years cooperation in the other areas has assumed an ever-growing importance. It received official recognition with the convening in Buenos Aires of the World Conference on Technical Co-operation Among Developing Countries (CTPD). The action plan approved at that conference views CTPD as an essential element in economic and social development, and includes in its scope all the different dimensions of the development process.

The plan states that in order to affirm the cultural identity of the peoples of the region and to enrich and strengthen their collective consciousness the CTPD must be used progressively to promote educational and cultural links and mutual understanding. This would be done by stimulating exchanges in the realms of social science, education and culture.

The United Nations Conference on Science and Technology for Development, which was held in Vienna in 1979, also affirmed the importance of cooperation among developing countries, especially in the areas of science and technology.[2] It recommended that 'the developing countries should establish a network of scientific and technological institutions or organisations in order to carry out, in a cooperative way, projects related to the whole spectrum of scientific and technological activity—for example, the promotion of technological innovation programmes and of research and development.'

Development depends to a great degree on a country's capacity for absorbing, adopting or creating technologies, and the development of its human resources. That is why the academic, scientific and technological sectors in our countries are so important. It could be said that the academic sector has a fundamental part to play in the task of achieving greater integration between Latin American countries. This paper, therefore, is an examination of the role of the Latin American university in that process and of the mechanisms that are being developed in order to direct and stimulate this role.

The academic role

The past decade has seen the emergence of academic institutions in Latin America whose work is organised on lines quite different from those traditionally encountered. In response to complex social, economic and political pressures, a range of innovative bodies has sprung up cooperating at both national and international level in the search for solutions to mutual problems. They include autonomous private organisations, to be found mainly in the field of the social sciences, technological institutes offering facilities for postgraduate work, and experimental universities and university departments which have been applying the results of their work in their respective disciplines to the problems of development.

These new institutions and mechanisms, whether national or international, have grown up both as a reaction to the limitations encountered in traditional structures and in order to find an effective way of dealing with new kinds of problems. This process has been accompanied by a search for ways in which these institutions can share their knowledge and experiences and coordinate their efforts. Thus, recently, a number of multinational links have been forged which make it possible for Latin American academics to exchange the content and results of research projects and to identify areas in which the academic community can make a more effective contribution to the development process, while at the same time strengthening the participating institutions themselves.

These new structures have contributed substantially to the promotion of academic activity in a variety of fields, linking it more closely with development problems and generating a flow of knowledge, analysis and suggestions that promises to be a great value to Latin American development. They have also helped in the mobilisation of extra resources so that these activities can be expanded and made more effective. Finally, and most importantly, they have made a decisive contribution to the creation of an independent Latin American 'thought process' in regard to the continent's problems and development objectives. As stated above, different forms of academic organisation that have been created, and the networks of cooperation, constitute a significant channel for the promotion of integration.[3]

The universities

Universities have played a fundamental part in the academic, scientific and technological activity of the continent. In recent years they have undergone major changes in their structure and operation. The factor that has most influenced the profile of higher education is the massive growth of the university population.[4] In the 1970s registration in Latin America increased on average by more than 200 per cent, with private universities growing at a faster rate than public ones (at present, they represent 40 per cent of the universities of the continent).

It has to be said that students tend to be concentrated in a few traditional academic disciplines, but there has been a moderate increase in scientific and technological training. In general, too, research in the universities is not directed to the demands of the productive sector, but is mainly of a disciplinary nature.

From an institutional point of view, the universities have some important characteristics. Decisionmaking is now widely based on planning; the departmental structure and the flexible curriculum have become general; teaching and research have been professionalised, and there has been a marked growth in the numbers of full-time teachers and research workers. Efforts have also been made to coordinate the university system more efficiently at national level.

The profile of the continent's universities has been strongly influenced by European, or North American, models. The organisation into departments, or central institutes, the flexible curriculum—and the development of certain areas of study to the detriment of others—are all expressions of this influence. In some universities, however, there are innovations that are interesting pointers for the future. Inter-disciplinary work is developing, with several universities implementing programmes in the fields of education, health, nutrition, regional development and so on. There are also experimental inter-disciplinary programmes of a scientific and technological nature in such areas as energy and maritime resources.

Several universities are also interested in applying their scientific and technological expertise more actively to the needs of the productive sector of the economy. The provision of services of this kind adds an important new dimension to a university's work and also constitutes an additional source of funds for the higher education effort. However, there are difficulties and restrictions in the development of activity in this area that remain a problem.

International cooperation, through advisory programmes, teacher training abroad, and the financing of work centres, has played an important part in the development of the universities. It has helped to consolidate the scientific and technological infrastructure of the continent and to 'internationalise' the knowledge coming into and being generated by our countries. Nevertheless, on a hypothetical level it is possible to argue that the training of postgraduates in other countries has been a two-edged weapon. As well as bringing undoubted benefits, these postgraduates have also adopted modes of thinking and working practices that often do not accord with the needs of the domestic university and are foreign to its environment. In the same way, it could be argued that one of the effects of international cooperation has been to change the original objectives of higher education without regard for national resources and priorities. This has meant on occasion that the interests of the high school student and the undergraduate have been relegated to second place behind those of the academic teacher and postgraduate.

Undoubtedly, most of a nation's technological and scientific resources are to be found in its universities. It is for this reason that they have a fundamental role as in the promotion of cooperation between countries, by increasing mutual knowledge and providing uniquely Latin American answers to problems of development. The university is an indispensable element in the academic dimension of Latin American integration. Universities may be the means by which the transfer of technology between developing countries—a concern of those involved with development— may take place, with a system of inter-university relationships enabling less well developed institutions to learn from the more advanced ones. Many of the universities of the region have already taken part in activities of this kind, both in the pooling of knowledge and the establishment of inter-institutional links.

Cooperative networks

Latin America has various networks of cooperation, which bring together groups from different institutions working in defined disciplines or problem areas. The academic world has its own such links, whose principal function is to promote the collaborative work of the participants through joint studies, seminars, courses, exchanges and publications. This horizontal cooperation is important in stimulating the flow of information and allowing experiences and services to be shared.

These academic links have recently received significant international support. Because of their nature, and their aim of utilising existing scientific and technological capabilities in cooperative programmes, they can play a worthy role in the academic contribution to the integration process.

Although the degree of unity in such relationships varies, along with their usefulness for the institutions taking part, the networks are worth close examination because of their potential contribution in the field of cooperation and, more widely, integration. The principal elements of a cooperative network are:

1) The participating institutions or groups. Their characteristics may be very different, depending on the nature of the network.
2) The central nucleus or secretariat of the network, which coordinates its activities. Here again, there may be very different characteristics. In some cases, one of the institutions forming part of the network may perform its function for a time and then pass it on to another institution. In other cases, a new institution emerges, independent of the other members of the network, although it operates under the direct supervision of a central council or board of directors formed by the latter. Such an institution may work within the confines of an international organisation.
3) The links among institutions that sometimes develop into permanent systems of consultation, with the participants exchanging information, holding periodical meetings, etc. Establishing these links is one of the chief tasks of the nucleus. As long as stable, flexible and reliable links are formed the whole system will run smoothly and efficiently.
4) The flow of information through the network, between the nucleus and the member bodies and between the member bodies themselves. The information may have originated either inside or outside the network. It is sometimes an important task of the nucleus to introduce knowledge from other parts of the world, as well as to assist in the circulation of information generated by individual network members.

The principal areas of interest for CTPD are scientific and technical knowledge and skills, and services such as training and consultancy.

5) The joint activities carried out by two or more members of the network, including research and development; centralised training; the definition of policies for joint action at an international level, and the establishment of codes of practice and common procedures.

A network is initially set up for a number of reasons, which become formal objectives which it is the network's task to accomplish. The objectives usually change with time and circumstances and as new members are integrated into the network and new areas of activity appear. In many cases the objectives are simple: they may consist of a mere pooling of resources. In the better established networks it is possible to find a set of coherent, long-term objectives that will act as guidelines for the network in the short and medium term and that will usually develop into well defined plans and projects.

A key problem for the functioning of the network is the financing of the secretariat, or nucleus, and of the activities that are pursued. Many Latin American networks have only meagre resources, made up of the contributions of the member institutions. Other networks, that have emerged under the wing of international organisations, receive financial support from them.

In some cases a network may come to constitute a 'system'. The conditions for this are that there is a clear definition of the long-term objectives shared by the members; that the links between members are strong and stable; that there is a strong continuous flow through the network; that joint activities are carried out with adequate continuity, and that exchanges with bodies outside the system (in terms of information, knowhow and technology) are not conducted independently by member institutions. The latter need to take place with the full knowledge of the other members and on the basis of a coordinated approach.

It is important to point out that the difference between a network and a system is not simply one of type or degree. There is also a qualitative difference arising from the application of a procedure that regulates the input and output of the system. In a network, each institution remains autonomous and the role of the nucleus is fundamentally one of co-ordination. In a system, on the other hand, the organisation is much more structured and the nucleus not only coordinates but also makes sure that the functioning of each member institution accords with the system's norms.

If these conditions are fulfilled, and a system is organised rather than a simple network, there is a greater probability that the resources and efforts that are injected will produce more substantial returns through a significant improvement in the efficiency of the institutions forming the network. It will also be possible to achieve a higher degree of inter-institutional integration.

The academic networks whose activities may be most useful to the integration process are described below:

a) The Inter-University Development Centre (CINDA)

CINDA is an international academic institution whose aim is to involve universities in the fundamental problems of development. Operating through a permanent network, it promotes contacts between Latin American universities. An important group of Latin American higher education bodies take part in the activities of CINDA either as full members, associates or universities enjoying special membership. The central controlling body is the Board of Directors, made up of representatives of each full member university and of elected members. It meets once a year. An executive board, appointed by the Board of Directors, is in charge of the organisation and implementation of the different programmes. Its headquarters are in Santiago, Chile.

The various research centres and academic units of the member universities take an active part in the programmes of CINDA. Research projects are carried out by work teams made up of specialists from the member universities and co-ordinated by the executive board. The activities of CINDA are organised around the following programmes:

1) *Science and technology.* The objectives of this programme are to help develop the technological and scientific capabilities of Latin American universities and promote their use by government bodies and the productive sector. The areas on which the programme concentrated in the 1983–84 period are technology, the management of scientific and technological activities in the universities and the execution of interdisciplinary development projects.

2) *University and development.* The purpose here is to promote the maximum use of university resources in the development of the con-

tinent and its individual countries. Areas of activity are regional development, international relations and cultural development.

3) *University administration and teaching.* The main aim is to develop the universities' administrative and managerial capability through the exchange of information, and to acquire, and promote, the use of new teaching tools and techniques. Activities centre mainly round administrative problems in connection with postgraduate studies, the provision of services, extra-university relations, teaching methods and international cooperation with other universities and teaching improvement programmes.

4) *Academic cooperation and development.* The main objective of this programme is to enable members to benefit from each other's experiences through the sharing of information on forms of organisation, working methods and personnel and through the exchange of publications.

5) *Diffusion and publications programme.* Under this programme the centre ensures the dissemination of all the written material generated by the various activities that it carries out. To achieve this, it edits and distributes a quarterly bulletin, and also research documents and books covering its activities. Various studies and the results of the projects that have been undertaken are also published.

CINDA's programmes thus include research, training and the dissemination of information. Furthermore, the centre promotes the organisation of meetings and seminars for both members and non-members. By means of these meetings, the results of various programmes are made known and there is an exchange of experiences and information that may be relevant to regional university development.

b) Programme of Joint Studies on Latin American Economic Integration (ECIEL).

ECIEL is an independent, non-profit making, non-political and scientifically oriented institution whose object is to plan, initiate and develop studies that will be useful to Latin American integration and economic development. It was founded in November 1963, on the initiative of the Institute of Economics of the Getulio Vargas Foundation in Brazil, the Economic Research Centre of the Torcuato di Tella Institute of Argentina, the Institute of Economics of the University of Chile, the US Planning

Association and the Economic Growth Centre of Yale University. These institutions formed a team with its headquarters at the Brookings Institution in Washington DC. In 1974, the programme was transferred to its new headquarters in Rio de Janeiro and developed until it became an inter-institutional network of comparative research which associates with an ever growing number of research institutions, both public and private.

Its basic components are as follows:

● The member institutions, who are interested in the advancement of research projects on Latin American economic integration and development. There are three kinds of member. Full members participate on the decisionmaking bodies and carry out research. They form the Assembly of Delegates with the power to appoint the Board of Directors, approve the membership of new institutions and ratify the appointment of the programme's general coordinator. The second kind is the participant who carries out research without taking part in the decisionmaking process; and there are associate organisations, which, without taking part in research or decisionmaking, cooperate with ECIEL in the achievement of its aims.

● The Board of Directors, a collegiate body made up of seven members, which is responsible for the appointment of the general coordinator and technical coordinators and for approving the research projects proposed by the institutes and the Co-ordinating Committee.

● The Co-ordinating Centre, responsible for the methodological technical, administrative and financial support of participant institutes in all areas related to the research projects of ECIEL.

● The Co-ordinating Committee. This proposes, analyses and discusses the study projects undertaken by the programme.

The most obvious manifestations of ECIEL activities are the seminars that take place once or twice a year. Their aim is to analyse current research projects and publish the results. As far as its working methods are concerned, ECIEL has characteristics that distinguish it from other networks and regional research institutions. These characteristics are principally:

1) It does not carry out research itself but coordinates and integrates research projects performed by member institutes.
2) It is mainly interested in comparative studies between countries, its own role being to define work programmes, develop common

methodologies, offer guidance and integrate the research projects' results.

3) ECIEL does not limit itself to the promotion of academic discussion of the results of completed studies; it also commits itself to financing an important proportion of what is necessary at national level to permit these studies to be carried out.

4) ECIEL is something member institutes can make use of, as they seek new lines of investigation, and to support joint research efforts which will allow fuller use to be made of the infrastructure and the professional and economic resources available in the countries chosen for research.

Given these characteristics in relation to subject of study, works methods and means of financial support, ECIEL does not duplicate the efforts of other programmes being carried out in similar areas, nor does it compete with the national research institutes that are its associates. The inter-institutional network that comprises ECIEL is also a flexible body, which permits the participation of new institutes, the only condition for participation in research being the competence of such institutes to take part.

c) Joint Study Programme on Latin American International Relations (RIAL).

This programme was first proposed at a meeting held at the University of Belgrano, Buenos Aires, at the end of 1977, at which there were representatives from Latin American research centres interested in the study of the international relations of the countries of the region. Since then, the number of the programme's member centres has grown considerably, though the intention of keeping the membership within limits that will allow effective academic cooperation has not been lost sight of.

RIAL is an association of Latin American centres that are interested in promoting the study of the international relations of the countries of the region through research, teaching, meetings, seminars and publications. Its fundamental objectives are:

● To develop a broad programme of research and study devoted to the most relevant aspects, as they are currently presented, of external and inter-Latin American economic relations.

● To help improve existing training programmes for professional personnel in the field of international relations, especially at postgraduate level.

● To make known the results of these efforts through seminars and work groups or through publications.

● To help to define, through these activities, Latin American priorities in the field of external economic relations and in the negotiations leading to the establishment of a new international economic order, as well as to assist in the search for the most appropriate strategies and measures for meeting these priorities.

● To stimulate the interest of Latin American research centres in the principal problems faced by the countries of the region in the field of international relations, and to facilitate the application of the work of these centres to meeting the needs that those problems create.

● To create a network of research centres that will be specially qualified to analyse the region's international relations as part of the efforts being made towards strengthening scientific, technical and academic cooperation among Latin American countries.

RIAL has either full or associate members. The programme's general direction comes from an Academic Board, on which all member centres are represented. The centres periodically appoint a President of the Board, who serves for a two-year term. The day-to-day running of RIAL in the hands of an academic coordinator who is appointed by the centres.

Shortly after its activities started, the programme received assistance from PNUD and CEPAL, through a project designed to develop a joint study programme in the field of international relations. The study programme covers the following areas:

● Structural changes at the international level and their consequences for Latin America.

● Latin American interests in international economic negotiations.

● The evolution of inter-Latin American relations, with emphasis on the regional cooperation process.

● Latin American relations with third countries or with other regions.

● The principal variables that influence the formulation of the external policies of the Latin American countries.

Subjects are selected annually within these areas for joint study by centres or research workers interested in the respective fields. The project provides assistance so that the study can be carried out, covering everything from the formation of a working group and preparatory meetings at which the definition of the study and its programming are decided, to the conduct of the study, a discussion seminar and publication of the results.

d) Council for Higher Education in the American Republics (CHEAR)

This institution was founded in 1958 by a group of North American foundations and the International Institute of Education (IIE). Its aim was to bring together the leaders of the continent for the purposes of exchanging information and sharing experiences in the field of higher education.

The main objective of CHEAR is to promote personal contacts between the US and Latin America and to be a forum for the discussion of priorities in educational development. CHEAR's principal activities are annual conferences, the exchange of specialists, workshops and publications.

e) Inter-American University Organisation (OUI)

This was founded in 1979, at the suggestion of the University of Quebec, Canada. Its aim is to forge links between the university institutions of the Americas, to publish information and to bring universities together for programmes of common interest. OUI is made up of universities and university associations, both national and international, from Canada, the United States and Latin America.

f) Inter-American Council for Academic Co-operation for Economic and Social Development

This organisation was formed in 1981 on the initiative of Florida International University, the Simón Bolívar University of Venezuela, and the Independent University of Guadalajara, Mexico. Its objectives are:

● To promote international academic cooperation with the emphasis on social and economic development.

● To give advice on obtaining financial support for programmes in which members are involved.

● To promote the dissemination of information through meetings, publications, etc., coordinating the work with similar activities carried out by other university institutions.

g) Union of Latin American Universities (UDUAL)

This association of universities throughout Latin America was founded in 1949 and has its headquarters in Mexico. Its activities include conferences, seminars and an information service and it is particularly active at the discipline level.

h) Caribbean Association of Universities and Research Institutes (UNICA)

The principal areas of activity of this regional association of universities of the Caribbean and the surrounding coastal region are: agriculture; the administration of small enterprises; educational technology, and university administration. UNICA was founded in 1968 and its headquarters are at present in San Juan, Puerto Rico.

i) Central American University Confederation (CSUCA)

This institution links up Central America's public universities and was founded in 1948. The chief areas in which it is active are the social sciences; health; geology; chemistry, and veterinary medicine. CSUCA performs an important function by publishing student textbooks. The federation's headquarters are in San José, Costa Rica.

j) Latin American Council of Social Sciences (CLACSO)

This is a non-governmental organisation whose members (about 80 research centres) are Latin American institutions carrying out research in the field of social sciences. The principal activities conducted by CLACSO can be grouped under the headings of: Committees and working groups; Research programmes; Postgraduate studies; and, Publications.

The chief areas in which the institution operates are: science, technology and development; urban and regional development; education and development; rural studies, and labour movements.

CSUCA was formed in 1967 and its headquarters are in Buenos Aires.

k) Latin American Council of Schools of Administration (CLADEA)

This is an international association of higher education bodies that are dedicated to the teaching of administration, both public and private, in Latin America. Its principal aim is to promote the advancement of administrative sciences and techniques and to assist in their dissemination. It is principally active in the areas of financial administration; technological decision-making in the productive sector, and the transfer of technology.

CLADEA has a centre for case administration and teaching units. It was founded in 1967 and at present has its headquarters in Rio de Janeiro, Brazil.

l) Programme of Social Research on Population in Latin America (PISPAL)

PISPAL was established in 1973. It is a network of social research centres whose main purpose is to promote and direct studies into the relationship between population and development. The purpose is to establish a scientific basis for the inclusion of population considerations in the formulation and execution of economic and social development policies. At the same time, the aim is to assess the implications for population of such policies. PISPAL's headquarters are in Mexico City.

Notes

1. In this respect, see CINDA and Catholic University of Chile—ICP (editors) *Variables Políticas de la Integración Andina*, Santiago, Chile 1974; Osvaldo Sunkel (ed), *Integración Política y Económica*, Santiago 1970; M Kaplán, *Problemas del Desarrollo y la Integración en América Latina*, Caracas 1968; Miguel Wionczek, *Integración de América Latina*, FCE México 1964; M Casanova, *INTAL-BID El Proceso de Integración en América Latina en 1979*, Buenos Aires, 1980.
2. Report of the United Nations Conference on Science and Technology for Development, Conference A 8/16, United Nations, New York, 1979.
3. The institutions that conduct important academic activities in Latin America include, besides the technological institutes, some international organisations, and some private institutions. Given that these institutions are less able to be actively incorporated into the integration process they will not be analysed in further detail.
4. See Pablo Lantapí, *Tendencias de la Educación Superior en América Latina*, CPU, 1979.

INAUGURAL SPEECHES

Text of speech by
President Belisario Betancur of Colombia

Cartagena is a microcosm of relationships crystallised in a twofold manner—in underdevelopment and in the fullness of a young, rising and independent nation in search of a more equitable distribution of its fruits. You have come here to discuss an increasingly familiar agenda—that of international economic and political relations—under postulates, which notwithstanding their approval as resolutions of the United Nations 10 years ago (the creation of the NIEO and the letter of Rights and Duties of the States), have been rejected by the industrialised countries.

The action for a better income distribution at the national and international levels shall not be a short-term one. It requires long-term solutions, flexible ideas and political strength. To channel the development process along the expectations and needs of our peoples requires a change in our international relations. A new economic order means that—a new direction. And it could not be the present order, a patch here and there; we would deepen even more the dualistic character of our economies and our societies.

In fact, the predominance of the trade flow in the South-North direction only deepens the internal gaps inside our national economies; it generates externally oriented, efficient, high technology areas, on the one hand, and a vast sector confined to the use of traditional but inadequate techniques whose low productivity is translated into incomes bordering absolute poverty, on the other.

There are some promising areas in South-South trade. To encourage them, we must recognise that the present world is not only a set of economic relationships but also of world power; the weight of our ideas, our prejudices and our legal systems are a red light in the way of our South-South progress.

The policies of the superpowers are not based on a static or abstract notion. For them, the world is a battlefield and the Third World a vital playground of tactics and strategies, of a military rather than of an economic or social nature. In that way we see how large and hardly-earned savings are spent and dissipated into armaments.

For this reason, the search for peace is not a matter of political rhetoric but an essential part of a well-balanced and equitable development process where progress will provide our communities with the fruits of the earth and the work of the mind.

I agree with Zhao Ziyang, Prime Minister of China, who said at the South-South Conference held in Beijing last year, that the international community should do its best to apply the criteria contained in the International Development Strategy, as approved by the United Nations. The ever-widening gap between the North and the South is unsustainable; a development strategy which does not provide for the improvement of 80 per cent of mankind cannot be justified.

The stability of this planet in the next 25 years will depend on the coordination of North-South strategies and the living standards of that 80 per cent of miserable people.

What Latin America needs is a more favourable environment and international institutions that understand its present circumstances. The world is in need, for example, of an International Energy Bank. This initiative was strongly supported by the international community but was put aside by some industrialised countries, in spite of the mutual benefits that could be derived for the North and the South. The world needs to speed up the flow of exports of developing countries, among other reasons, to expedite the servicing of the debt. But the Gatt is impotent before the current protectionist trends. The international economic system requires long-term credit lines for developing countries. But there is reticence to strengthen the World Bank and the Inter-American Development Bank. It is also urgent to re-vitalise the compensatory Fund of the International Monetary Fund and create a compensation mechanism to enable developing countries to cover that portion of the interest rate that has already exceeded its normal historical level. But no one seems to understand that.

These adjustments would be necessary to reactivate both the North and the South economies. But there is a serious failure in the decision-making mechanism at the international level. As former Prime Minister Edward Heath recalled at a conference held recently in Bogotá, the decisions to start the plan of reconstruction of Europe took three weeks. In the first year, the US Congress approved the equivalent of US$15-billion today. General Marshall and President Truman acted swiftly and saved Europe with their astonishing courage. Why not, then, design a plan suited to Latin America, the Caribbean and developing countries? Is it because the arms race leaves no time or energy or resources for anything else?

The gross national product of Latin America could be equivalent to 40 per cent of the GNP of Western Europe, instead of 20 per cent as it is today. Or, in other terms, Latin America and the Caribbean could generate about 10 per cent of the world production of goods and services by the 2000, instead of the present 5 per cent.

The human and natural resources of the region would be sufficient to reach such a goal. What is needed is a strategy to conciliate the policies of the oil producing countries, the socialist countries, the developing countries and the highly industrialised countries. Adequate terms of trade and reasonable financing conditions would be required, as well as encouraging selectively the production of capital goods since many of these countries have made significant progress in the substitution of intermediate goods and machinery.

The last point is essential since it is the basis for industrial development in the coming decades. Latin American and other developing countries must persuade multilateral credit organisations to accept a margin of tariff protection of at least 25 per cent to enable the production of such goods. Otherwise, external credit will be in serious conflict with the industrial policy of several countries.

We are facing a growing disillusionment with integration processes. The lack of political will, territorial disputes, the differences between their plans, high transportation costs, the lack of commercial data networks, and the lack of incentives for intra-regional trade are some of the reasons for this setback.

And yet, as I said last January at the Latin American Economic Conference held in Quito, one of the greatest mistakes of the Latin Americans and the Caribbean during this crisis has been our rush to close the borders among ourselves.

We are all guilty. But it is now time to adopt a scheme for liberalising intra-regional trade. This presupposes new financing and compensation mechanisms and a margin of regional preference.

One of the objects of this seminar is to submit formulae for a renewed integration of Latin America and to strengthen cooperation among developing countries. We are interested in hearing the opinions of the experts here present on the possibilities of horizontal cooperation among our continents.

In the last part of the 20th Century we are witnessing a spectacular space race and a dramatic race for the conquest of the sea. The great superpowers—Russia and the United States—having distributed among themselves the world in two areas of influence, are now attempting to split the oceans and outer space.

Developing countries cannot stand as mere spectators in the face of this process and it is in this context that Ambassador Pardo's role acquires a new dimension. It was he who gave impetus to the concept that the seabed is the common heritage of all mankind. And this has been the guiding principle of the new maritime law.

While I hand the Third World Prize to Ambassador Pardo of Malta, I would like to express my hope that developing countries shall continue to participate actively in the design of economic rules and legal principles that will lead to a harmonic and sustained development of the world economy.

Text of message from
His Excellency Javier Pérez de Cuellar

Secretary-General of the United Nations

His Excellency the President of the Republic of Colombia, the distinguished chairman of the Third World Prize Committee, Your Excellencies, ladies and gentlemen.

'The Third World Foundation, its efforts and its achievements, and its contribution to Third World interests are universally recognised. It is most fitting that the presentation of the 1983 Third World Prize is being held in conjunction with the South-South Conference on 'the Role of Regional Integration in the Present World Economic Crisis', organised by the National University of Colombia and the Third World Foundation. It is also significant that this meeting should take place in the Republic of Colombia which has played such an important role in furthering regional co-operation among the developing countries of Latin America and which has made such a significant contribution to the work of the Third United Nations Conference on the Law of the Sea.

The adoption of the United Nations Convention on the Law of the Sea and its opening for signature in December 1982 were the culmination of perhaps the most significant and successful collective effort of the community of nations in recent times. It symbolises the goal of the United Nations to promote peace, justice and progress for all the peoples of the world. For well over a decade nations dedicated their efforts to the negotiation of a treaty which would be widely acceptable and which would respond to the aspirations of all States, developing as well as developed. That it was possible for a Conference of more than 160 States to eventually adopt a Convention which would regulate more than 70% of the earth's surface was a remarkable feat. The Convention, which has already been signed by 133 States, is perhaps the most important achievement of the United Nations since its Charter was adopted. At a time of eroding multilateralism it serves to remind us that the United Nations can be used successfully as a forum for multilateral negotiations—a role which its founders had intended for it.

The Convention stands out as a significant achievement of the international community as a whole. It has special significance to the countries of the developing world whose particular interests and needs it takes into account. It establishes the area of the sea-bed and the ocean floor beyond national jurisdiction as the common heritage of mankind—a completely new approach in international relations which points towards a new order.

It introduces the novel concept of the exclusive economic zone which recognises the rights of coastal States over the resources to be found in areas adjacent to their coasts. At the same time it preserves many important legal principles of benefit to all States and ensures the peaceful and orderly use of the oceans and the equitable and efficient utilisation of their resources.

It is appropriate that the Third World Foundation has given important recognition to the Law of the Sea Conference and the United Nations Convention on the Law of the Sea. It is also appropriate that the participants who laboured so hard for it and who were so deeply involved with it have been similarly honoured.

Dr Arvid Pardo, whose initiative in 1967 brought the item to the attention of the General Assembly, has been given the signal honour that is due to him. Similarly, the recognition of the contribution of the late Ambassador Hamilton Shirley Amerasinghe as Chairman of the Sea-Bed Committee and later the first President of the Conference symbolises the appreciation of the efforts of all those participants who worked for its success.

As Secretary-General of the United Nations, I note with great personal satisfaction the recognition given to the Secretariat of the Conference for its contribution to the successful outcome of the Conference. This Secretariat was led from 1974 up to the signing of the Convention by my Special Representative for the Law of the Sea, the late Dr Bernardo Zuleta. This illustrious son of Colombia will be forever associated with that extraordinary accomplishment of the United Nations, the new Law of the Sea Convention, to which he devoted the last ten years of his fruitful life. It is doubly significant, therefore, that we should be gathered here in Colombia, in the delightful city of Cartagena, for the purpose of receiving this award.

The decision of the Third World Foundation to make a contribution towards the Hamilton Shirley Amerasinghe Fellowship Endowment Fund is a generous one. It will enable the Fellowship to become operational in 1984. The Fellowship itself will contribute to a better understanding of the Conference and to the promotion of the Convention by providing opportunities for the further study of the results of the Conference and of the Covention that it adopted. I believe that I could do no more than fervently hope that the Third World Foundation and other institutions like it will continue to promote the acceptance of the Convention and its ratification so that it can soon enter into force and give meaning to the objectives of all those who contributed to it.'

Text of speech by Sir Shridath Ramphal

Commonwealth Secretary-General and Chairman, Third World Prize Selection Committee

The Third World Prize honours service of excellence to the Third World. Colombia is a nursery of such service; for, did you not nurture Simon Bolivar, whom you rightly honour as 'The Great Liberator,' not only of New Granada, but of all Latin America: Bolivar who was in truth the 'Liberator' in a more ultimate sense of the Third World beyond this continent.

The physical liberation of Asia and Africa came later in time; but it was the spirit of freedom into which Bolivar had breathed life that was to infuse their later struggles for freedom.

Were Bolivar engaged today in the struggle for liberation that the Third World must continue to wage, would he not have been urging on us a vision of oneness of the states and peoples of the Third World. His memory challenges us to keep aloft the torch of freedom and justice that he lit.

And it is being kept aloft. What more splendid example could be given, Mr President, of such continuity than Colombia's inspired and inspiring leadership of the Contadora Group's noble mission to find Central American solutions to Central America's problems—regional solutions that strengthen the independence of the region, not interventionist solutions that can strengthen only the region's dependency.

Today, the Third World Prize honours the world of Dr Arvid Pardo, who more than any other single person, has made it possible for our global society both to extend its horizons of human cooperation and enlarge its frontiers of human endeavour.

When Arvid Pardo rose in the First Committee on 17 August 1967 and proposed to a sceptical international audience a new regime for the seabed and ocean floor beyond national jurisdiction, when he proclaimed the concept that there were resources of our planet that we must now acknowledge to be 'the common heritage of mankind,' a Third World man from a small island in the Mediterranean was urging the world's states to reach beyond their grasp. When, 15 years later, the Law of the Sea Convention was opened for signature and signed by 138 states in Jamaica—another small Third World island in another sea—Pardo's bold and visionary act of intellectual innovation had extended that grasp to lengths unimaginable in 1967. He had served the Third World with unusual excellence, and in so doing, had served all mankind as well. The Third World Prize could not have been more worthily earned.

Others, of course, took up the cause Arvid Pardo had launched, and in a special way today we honour those contributors also: on the recommendation of the Prize Selection Committee, a contribution is being made to the Shirley Amerasinghe Memorial Fellowship Endowment Fund. The Fund was established by the UN

General Assembly to commemorate Ambassador Amerasinghe's contributions over many years as Chairman of the United Nations Conference on the Law of the Sea—the process that brought Pardo's ideas nearer, if not yet fully, to fulfilment. This was another Third World contribution of which with many others—like those of Ambassador Koh of Singapore and the late Bernardo Zuleta of Colombia—we can all be proud. This contribution will make the Shirley Amerasinghe Memorial Fund fully operational this year under the aegis of the United Nations, which will use it to promote Law of the Sea scholarships.

In the symposium that follows this special Prize ceremony we will, all of us, have an opportunity of living up to the beliefs which have inspired the Third World Prize, and none more so than the precept that the Third World must be true to itself. This is a South-South consultation; we are talking among ourselves and with friends, not negotiating with the North. Self-examination is not an indulgence but a necessity; we will not be true to ourselves unless we are honest with ourselves.

This is 1984. The Third World is in distress and disarray. Its governments are demoralised; its people despair. Human suffering has not diminished, but hope of relief from it has. What began as an era of negotiation after the post-war period ended is developing into a time of inertia and studied resistance to change.

Internationalism is in decline, crude power is ascendant, international morality is in retreat. As this Orwellian year began, Western commentators were unanimous in their refrain that George Orwell's prophecies had not materialised; that their societies, and it was of Western societies that Orwell wrote, had not developed into the fearful parodies of brotherhood Orwell had predicted. Perhaps they were right. But the Third World has no reason for contentment or complacency.

If you think of Orwell's society of 1984, not in terms of a single nation state but of a world society of nations, it is not so difficult to identify a hierarchical international community run by a small superpower directorate with an 'Inner Party' of rich countries dedicated to permanent power through an apparatus of economic, cultural, political and military interventions, and a residue of poorer states relegated to the role of Orwell's proles, under constant surveillance by Big Brother. The world's rich and powerful states can have little real basis for self-satisfaction if, while avoiding 1984 at home, they sustain a global system which secures it abroad.

But there are other elements of 1984 that have their roots within some Third World countries: denial, often under egalitarian labels, of basic human rights; authoritarian rule under which deviation from party paramountcy or the leadership cult is treason; political environments in which uniformity of opinion and taste is a national virtue cultivated and imposed to the point of elimination of any freedom of choice and, therefore, of dissent. This is not the reality in most of the Third World. But in 1984, too many people in too many countries of the developing world live, if it can be called living, with the fulfilment of George Orwell's prophecies. We will be false if we pretend otherwise.

Unless South-South consultations face up to these difficulties at home no less than to those in the wider world that is our universal home, they will fall short of the values that inspired the Third World Prize. To face up to them with frankness may be painful; but, only out of such integrity will come eventual release.

Text of speech by Dr F Sanches Torres

Rector, National University of Colombia

We are half way through the eighties, yet this continues to be a decade of great concern about the world's economic situation. This situation which for most countries, particularly those of the Third World, is a clear crisis, not only has repercussions within borders, but also looms as a threat to the stability and to peaceful co-existence to certain geographic regions.

There is no doubt, also, that the life of the Third World countries is closely conditioned by the measures adopted by the developed nations, given the narrow subordination of the economies of the former to those of the latter. Economic dependence, which is a politically odious phenomenon and therefore rejected, has come to constitute something of an inevitability and almost accepted as a legitimate subjection. For that reason, unfortunately, the economic emancipation of the weak is still an utopian concept. The power of the developed and the opulent, and the lowliness of the humble, reach such extremes that the phrase 'international economy,' in the language of the specialists, refers to the economies of the first and exclude the last. It is not difficult to understand the constant pre-occupation into which have fallen the governments of the countries where the crisis is felt more intensely, because besides being mortgaged they lack the necessary resources to face the harsh reality that results from hunger, illiteracy, unemployment and insalubrious conditions. As a result of this, in some parts of the world, institutions, official and private, have been formed which are interested and dedicated to studying the complex problem in the hope of finding solutions. One of them, which is private, is the Third World Foundation for Social and Economic Studies, founded in 1978 and based in London. Thanks to its initiative and support it has been possible to organise this conference which today opens with great promise. As universities are centres for study and consideration of the problems that distress countries, regions, and the world, the Foundation kindly proposed that the National University of Colombia should support the Conference as co-sponsor. The University, which understands its responsibilities, accepted the invitation and through the School of Economic Sciences, has taken an active part in the organisation. As Rector of the University, I must therefore thank the Foundation for allowing us to share the credits which are given by the holding of such a prestigious meeting, which is to be the South-South Conference, Cartagena 1984.

As it is known that the economically weak countries cannot face the crisis alone, regional integration is a course of mutual convenience. This is the subject which will occupy the attention of those at the Conference. To guarantee the best results of the meeting, a list of leading experts has been drawn up who surely will study in depth the main aspects of the world crisis, and will stop to consider principally the role of regional integration. It is to be expected therefore that the conclusions and recommendations of the conference will constitute a positive contribution towards overcoming the serious situation which has put the world on a knife edge.

Distinguished guests: as the legal representative of the National University of Colombia, which co-sponsors and is host to this conference, it is for me an honour to welcome you.

Thank you.

Text of speech by Mr Altaf Gauhar

Secretary-General, Third World Foundation

Your Excellency President Betancur, Mr Governor, Mr Mayor, Chairman and members of the Prize Selection Committee, Mr Arvid Pardo, distinguished Delegates and Observers, Excellencies, Ladies and Gentlemen.

May I offer you all a very warm welcome on behalf of the Board of Trustees and my colleagues in the Third World Foundation.

Your gracious presence amidst us, Mr President, makes this occasion a moment of historic importance. At the conclusion of SOUTH-SOUTH ONE held in Beijing last April it was decided that a summit of Third World academics should be convened every three years and the intervening period used for a thorough examination of specific regional issues and problems.

This is the first regional Conference under the Beijing programme and marks an important step towards SOUTH-SOUTH TWO scheduled for 1986. Mr President, the choice of Colombia as the venue was a tribute to your enlightened leadership and courageous commitment to democratic principles and an acknowledgement of the valuable contribution that this country has made towards Third World solidarity by joining the non-aligned movement. Your Contadora initiative represents the most decisive and far-sighted move made by the developing world in recent years to establish a political framework for regional consultation, cooperation and peace. Last month in a meeting of Heads of State of Latin America and the Caribbean in Quito, you and your colleagues, while rejecting interventionism and stressing the need for a negotiated solution to the problems of Central America, reaffirmed your belief that the region's problems should and can be solved in its own sphere. A highly propitious environment has thus been created for this conference to consider the role of regional integration in the present world economic crisis and it is our hope that a message will go from Cartagena to all parts of the globe that the people in the Third World representing three-quarters of mankind are united in their resolve to rely upon their own resources and their own creative potential to change an unjust order which consigns them to a future of increasing discrimination and growing disparity. That this order was imposed on the Third World by the industrial nations to serve their interests is now an established fact. A recent study brings out the rate at which differences in international levels of income have been growing since the Industrial Revolution when the richest country in the world was less than twice as well off as the poorest country. Indeed, until the middle of the 18th century the average standard of living in Europe was somewhat lower than in the rest of the world due to the high level achieved by China and reached parity only towards the end of the century. By the 1830s, however, the developed countries moved far ahead of the present Third World. The gap in the average living standards then began to widen: it started expanding by a factor of two in the 1870s, three in 1900, five in 1950, and seven in 1970. Today the real GNP per capita in the most highly industrialised countries is thirty times that of the least developed countries. At this rate the gap will be stretching by a factor of 600 before the end of the century when one out of every four persons will be living in absolute poverty condemned to varying degrees of starvation.

Now this is the fate we are required to embrace with patience and fortitude—words fashioned by the masters to shackle their slaves. The patience of the poor is not inexhaustable, nor is their capacity to suffer limitless. They will not accept inequity and deprivation as their destiny. They will not remain a frozen mass for ever: the glacier is beginning to melt, the icebergs are set on invisible but inevitable collision course. Let us make room, for there is room for all to share, before everything that we cherish is submerged and lost. I communicated to President Julius Nyerere of Tanzania the depressing balance sheet of North-South dialogue. His response was characteristically simple: 'Let us share our sense of frustration in putting too much hope in the rich. And let us share the reasons why we still go on. Why we profoundly believe that in spite of everything we shall overcome.' That is President Nyerere's message to this conference.

We have with us some of the most distinguished scholars from the Third World. My friends from Latin America and the Caribbean join me in extending a special welcome to delegates from the People's Republic of China, Bangladesh, India, Pakistan, Zimbabwe, Ghana and Tanzania. We also have with us eminent guests from the North.

We look forward to sharing our views and experience with them. Delegates are here in their personal capacity and not as representatives of institutions or governments. We hope that these meetings of scholars at regular intervals will become a permanent venue for exchange of opinion and an independent and creative source of ideas which should help the developing countries to evolve genuinely participatory self-reliant and democratic social and political institutions to replace the present authoritarian arrangements.

Mr President, the Foundation owes a great debt of gratitude to the Government of Colombia, to our co-sponsors, the School of Economic Science, National University of Colombia, to the authorities in Cartagena and to the management of this Convention Centre for their warm hospitality and for the excellent arrangements that have been made for the conference. On behalf of all the delegates and observers I wish to thank you, Sir, and senior members of your Government, in particular Mr Hugo Palacios and his colleagues, for all the cooperation and consideration that we have received.

Appendix 2

STATEMENT OF THE CARTAGENA CONFERENCE*

The Role of Regional Integration in the Present World Economic Crisis

Introduction

1. The National University of Colombia and the Third World Foundation for Social and Economic Studies co-sponsored the South-South Conference in Cartagena from 23 to 26 February 1984 to enable eminent Third World statesmen and scholars, mainly from the Latin American region, to meet in their individual capacities, to discuss the present global economic crisis and its impact on the Latin American region with special focus on the role of regional integration.

2. The Third World Prize for 1983 was presented at the Inaugural Session. Present at the ceremony were members of the Prize Selection Committee and Dr Arvid Pardo, the recipient of the prize.

3. His Excellency President Belisario Betancur, President of the Republic of Colombia, delivered the inaugural address of the Conference and presented the Third World Prize to Dr Arvid Pardo; a contribution from the Third World Prize Endowment Fund to the Shirley Amerasinghe Memorial Fellowship Endowment Fund was handed over to Mr S. K. Nandan, Special Representative of the U.N. Secretary-General. The Conference expressed its deep appreciation of the presence of His Excellency President Belisario Betancur at the inaugural session and his stimulating address.

Global Economic Crisis and Latin America

4. The participants noted that the Cartagena Conference was held at a time when Latin America is faced with economic and social difficulties, unprecedented in the last fifty years, resulting from unusual levels of foreign indebtedness and from acute recession in most countries. In 1983, interest payments alone absorbed 42 per cent of merchandise export earnings of Latin America as a whole causing a massive

---

*The participants presented a variety of views and put forward many useful suggestions on the issues under discussion. Not every participant subscribes to each and every sentence of this Statement, but it represents overall the general consensus of the Conference on the issues discussed.

drain of liquidity and rising unemployment. Its present debt servicing burden is greater than during the Great Depression of the thirties.

5. The distressing economic situation in the Latin American region is very much a part of the global economic crisis which equally afflicts the developing Asian and African regions. The situation of the least developed countries is particularly grave. The creditor countries, the private commercial banks, and the international financial institutions are pursuing policies and adopting measures which, far from alleviating the condition of the developing countries, are frequently aggravating their already acute difficulties. The adequacy and even the relevance of the present international monetary and financial system is now in question.

6. These difficulties derive both from inadequate domestic policies as from international causes. It must be recognised that in the large majority of countries, the latter have had a stronger adverse effect. The recessive cycles suffered at present by the industrialised economies have as a background a deep crisis, which has its roots in structural malfunctioning of the existing international economic order and questionable development strategies. This crisis may involve a prolonged period of slow and unstable growth and of uncertainty requiring structural adjustments both in developed and developing countries and in their existing relations.

7. Even though the economy of the United States has recently shown signs of recovery, there are legitimate and widespread doubts about its persistence and durability and, above all, about its capacity to spread to the rest of the industrialised world. This recovery has failed to bring about and even if it did persist it is doubtful if it could bring about, significant improvement in the international position of developing countries, enabling them to reduce their debt burden and resume economic growth, thereby easing their social and political difficulties.

8. A substantial part of the present crisis stems from the high degree of militarisation of the economic and political systems all over the world, which is encouraged by the strategic policies of the superpowers. The world's military spending, together with enormous levels of debt servicing liabilities, represent today the major factors in the persisting high levels of interest rates.

9. Most Latin American countries have been forced to reschedule their foreign debts in extremely precarious conditions, and on onerous terms as a consequence of the lack of cooperation of the creditor countries and of the dogmatic and rigid position assumed by the International Monetary Fund. Because of this, they have also been forced to implement drastic monetaristic adjustment policies aimed at abrupt restriction of domestic demand and imports, in order to generate a trade surplus to help cover debt service. This has caused a dramatic deterioration in the prevailing social conditions in these countries and has put pressure on their political systems, in turn putting at risk the possibilities of maintaining, restoring, and strengthening their democracies. This situation threatens to transgress the limits of economic and social tolerance in these countries.

10. The recent Declaration of Quito is an encouraging step in that it represents consideration at the highest political level of a matter which had hitherto received attention on from finance officials and bankers. Political control of the management of the foreign debt based on adequate information and strong democratic

support should allow countries to secure a better response from the creditor countries.

11. The situation demands that Latin American countries adopt policies of demand reactivation and development based in much greater measure than in the recent past on an expansion of their domestic market, and, therefore, on a better use of domestic resources, and on an improved distribution of income. It also demands a greater flexibility from their creditors in the approach to renegotiation than that offered up to now. There should be greater focus on long term perspective in order to establish compatibility between the debt service and development possibilities in Latin American countries. If this is not done, however painful the effort made by countries to service their debts, they will find it impossible to continue to do so. The greater the understanding by the international community in this area, the less painful will be the adjustment demanded of the Latin American countries and less the chance of their declaring a moratorium.

Regional integration

12. Latin America has had long experience of attempts at regional economic cooperation and integration. The first initiative by CEPAL, as early as 1951 in Central America, was followed by the creation of regional and sub-regional integration schemes, as well as by specific cooperation in the fields of trade, finance, production and infrastructure, as well as in the establishment of a regional juridical framework and regional institutions.

13. Regional economic integration has tradtionally constituted an important component in the development policies of Latin American countries. Faced with the need to reinforce domestic development processes, integration is required to play a role which is perhaps different but more important than in the past. Paradoxically, as a result of the present trends, regional integration and in particular intra-trade has suffered the greatest deterioration, and this has in turn deepened the depression in Latin America.

14. Acting on a short term view, governments have chosen to avoid the immediate cost involved in maintaining reciprocal trade, and risked dismantling an established process, which constituted an important element in a development strategy aimed at reducing external vulnerability. This represents in the long term, greater cost, which could have been avoided. But it must also be recognised that the existing payment system is not conducive to maintaining the flow of intra-trade in present adverse circumstances.

15. It will not be enough to defend the present levels of integration if it is to play the role that is expected of it in the present crisis. It will be necessary to establish new characteristics, adapted to existing internal and international conditions. One of these characteristics should be the adaptation and flexibility of instruments used up to now. Another characteristic would be the attainment of a better balance between trade integration and its complements in the fields of infrastructure, monetary and payment arrangements, technology and productive sectors. Still another refers to the needs for integration to contribute in a greater

degree than before to the strengthening of the external position of Latin American countries. This could be done through joint action aimed at strengthening negotiating power and the capacity to enter more dynamically into the world economy.

16. In the light of experience, it has become necessary to find a better combination between the role of global integration schemes and specific economic cooperation schemes which have recently gained in importance; between the role of the market and the instruments of joint programming, and between the action of governmental and non-governmental sectors involved in the integration process. There must be progress towards more effective forms of integration between ALADI, the Andean Pact, the Central American Common Market, and the Caribbean Community, a process in which SELA could play an important role; it will also be necessary to plan Latin American integration as an important part of a broader process of South-South cooperation.

Reform of international monetary and financial system

17. Two specific proposals were made at the Conference. First, the Latin American countries, where much of the international debt is concentrated, should consider taking the lead in formulating a specific proposal aimed at a substantial reduction of international interest rates and extension of repayment periods. Secondly, the Latin American countries should urgently consider providing active support to the on-going initiatives for the creation of a financial mechanism, such as the proposed South Bank, which would facilitate the intra-trade among developing countries and may ultimately lead to their payments union.

18. The proposals for debt reorganisation and for the establishment of a South Bank are steps in the direction of restructuring and reform of the international monetary and financial system to which all developing countries are committed. The Latin American countries have experienced the inefficiency and harshness of the present arrangements to an unusual degree in recent years. They have been exposed to a simultaneous pressure on the terms of trade, interest payments six times higher in real terms than the historical long-run rate, collapse of their exports, both within the region and to other developing countries, enormous devaluations, and widespread corporate distress of both public and private enterprise. The need for internal and external reforms is overwhelming and urgent. At the same time the productive capacity, human skills and organisational ability now available in Latin American countries places them in a unique position to be forerunners in the efforts at comprehensive reforms.

Regional political cooperation

19. The review of the experience of the Latin American region indicates that if the shared goals of democratic stability and sustained growth are to be achieved, there must in addition to regional economic integration, be meaningful political cooperation among its democratic sectors, embracing not only govern-

ments but also social movements, political parties and the academic world. Such cooperation would be aimed at strengthening democracies and redesigning the role of the armed forces to ensure that they do not assume unwarranted political roles and to check and roll back militarism and militarisation in the region. It would also aim at promoting peaceful solutions of disputes among countries of the region in order to strengthen the independence of the region and pre-empt interventionist solutions that can only accentuate the region's dependency. In this context, the efforts of the Contadora Group, under Colombia's inspired and inspiring leadership, to find Central American solutions to Central America's problems may be commended as an approach to be emulated in dealing with regional problems.

South-South cooperation

20. This Conference has provided a valuable forum for frank and valuable in-depth exchange of views and ideas, for the reaffirmation of principles and goals and the formulation of useful guidelines for future action not only in the Latin American region but within the framework of the South-South cooperation on the global plane.

21. The Conference recognised that the Latin American struggle for freedom, justice and peace and against external intervention and domination is part of a historic process in which the entire Third World—embracing Asia, Africa, and Latin America—is engaged. This points to the need for comprehensive and sustained South-South cooperation aimed at adopting unified strategies, pooling of resources and the sharing of experience and knowledge for the attainment of shared goals. To this end, the Conference supports efforts directed at promoting more effective organisation and technical support machinery for the South to undertake systematic research and strategic planning and to promote constant contact and collaborative research between national, regional and sub-regional institutions, governmental and non-governmental. It, therefore, supports the process of continuing consultation between Third World statesmen and scholars of which this Conference forms part.

LIST OF DELEGATES AND OBSERVERS

Argentina	Dr Alberto Calvo	BCCI, 2903, 44th Street NW, Washington, DC 20016 USA
Argentina	Dr Elvio Baldinelli	Juncal 721 3rd Piso 1062 Buenos Aires
Bangladesh	Dr Kamal Husein	7-C, New Bayley Road Dhaka, Bangladesh
Barbados	Mr William Demas	Caribbean Development Bank Wildey St Michael Barbados
Barbados	Dr Vishnu Persuad	Commonwealth Secretariat Marlborough House, London SW1, England
Brazil	Mr Celso Furtado	11 Rue Guy de la Brosse Paris 5, France
Brazil	Mr Eduardo Albertal	ECIEL, Co-ordinator-General Rio de Janeiro, Brazil
Chile	Dr Osvaldo Sunkel	CEPAL, Edificio Naciones Unidas Avenida Dag Hammarskjöld Casilla 179-D, Santiago Chile
Chile	Dr Andres Bianchi	Director, Economic Division ECLA, Edificio Naciones Unidas Avenida Dag Hammarskjöld Casilla 179-D, Santiago, Chile
Chile	Dr Juan Somavia	Instituto Latino Americano de Estudios Transnacionals Callao 3461, Las Condes Santiago, Chile
Chile	Dr Luciano Tomassini	CEPAL, Edificio Naciones Unidas Avenida Dag Hammarskjöld Casilla 179-D, Santiago, Chile
China	Mr Su Zhenxing	Institute of Latin American Studies, Chinese Academy of Social Sciences, Beijing People's Republic of China
China	Mrs Wang Yaoyuan	Department of Development Economics, Chinese Academy of Social Sciences, Beijing People's Republic of China

China	Mr Xu Wenyuan	Head of Division for South America Research of ILAS Chinese Academy of Social Sciences, Beijing People's Republic of China
China	Mr Ma Jia-Rui (English language) interpreter)	International Affairs Section Chinese Academy of Social Sciences Beijing People's Republic of China
China	Mr Tao Dazhao	Ambassador Embassy of People's Republic of China Bogota Colombia
Colombia	Dr José Antonio Ocampo	Fedesarrollo, Calle 37 No 20–27 Bogota Colombia
Colombia	Dr Miguel Urrutia	Vice-Rector UN University Tokyo 150 Japan
Colombia	Dr Guillermo Perry	Calle 96 No 17–16 Bogota Colombia
Colombia	Dr Jorge Ospina S	Jeff Departmentato de Planeacion Nacional Bogota Colombia
Colombia	Dr Luis Eduardo Rosas	Instituto de Ahorro y Vivienda Bogota Colombia
Colombia	Dr Diego Pizano	Secretario Economico Presidencia Palacio de Narino Bogota Colombia
Colombia	Dr Jesus Antonio Bejarano	Decano Facultad de Ciencia Economicas Universidad Nacionale de Colombia Bogota Colombia

Colombia	Dr Alicia Puyana	Apartado Aereo 17413 Bogota Colombia
Colombia	Dr F Sanches Torres	Rector Universidad Nacional Bogota Colombia
Colombia	Dr Roberto Junguito	Colombian Ambassador to EEC Colombia Embassy Brussels 1050 Belgium
Colombia	Dr Jorge Mendez	Calle 111 No 2–17 Bogota Colombia
Colombia	Dr Hugo Palacio Mejia	Banco de la Republica Carrera 7 No 14–78 Bogota Colombia
Colombia	Dr Alberto Schlessinger	ProExpo Bogota Colombia
Colombia	Dr Harold Calvo	Gerente Banco de la Republica Bogota Colombia
Colombia	Dr Rodrigo Llorente	Carrera 7 No 26–20, Piso 27 Bogota Colombia
Ghana	Dr R K A Gardiner	PO Box 9273, The Airport Accra Ghana
Guyana	HE Sir S S Ramphal	Commonwealth Secretary-General Marlborough House London SW1 England
India	Shri B K Nehru	Governor State of Gujrat Raj Bhavan Gandhinagar 382020 Gujrat, India
India	Mr Azim Husain	Principal Advisor Third World Foundation New Zealand House London SW1 England

Jamaica	Mr George Abbot	University of Glasgow Dept of International Economic Relations Glasgow, Scotland United Kingdom
Jamaica	Mr Richard Fletcher	Manager Economic & Social Department Inter-American Development Bank 808 17th Street NW Washington DC 20577 USA
Malta	Dr Arvid Pardo	Apt. 111 900 Eclid Street Santa Monica California 90403 USA
Mexico	Mr Gert Rosenthal	ECLA President Masaryk 29 6 Piso Mexico 5 DF
Mexico	Mr Cristobal Lara Beautell	Ricardo Castro 49 Depto 602 Guadlupe Inn Mexico DF 01020
Mexico	Mr David Ibarra	CEPAL Presidente Masaryk 29 6 Piso Mexico 5
Mexico	Mr Iván Menéndez	Coordinator de Desarrollo Rural Corl. Porfirio Diaz 50 San Jeronimo Lidice Mexico 20, D.F.
Mexico	Mr Cesario Modales	Mexico
Pakistan	Mr Altaf Gauhar	Secretary-General Third World Foundation New Zealand House London SW1
Pakistan	Mr Humayun Gauhar	Managing Director Third World Foundation New Zealand House London SW1
Pakistan	Mr Rumman Faruqi	333 East 30th Street Apt 10-b New York, NY 10016 USA

Peru	Mr Edgar Moncayo	Co-ordinator Junta Acuerdo, Cartagena San Isidro Lima Peru
Spain	Dr Ramon Casilda	Maldonado 55 Apt 602 Madrid Spain
Tanzania	HE Mr Amir Jamal	Minister without Portfolio State House Dar es Salam Tanzania
United Kingdom	Mr Anthony Sampson	27 Ladbroke Grove London W11
United Kingdom	Rt. Hon. Dame Judith Hart MP	House of Commons London SW1
Uruguay	Mr E V Iglesias	Executive Secretary ECLA Santiago Chile
Uruguay	Professor Luis Faroppa	Diario El Dia Avenida General Paz 1269 Montevideo Uruguay
Venezuela	Dr Sebastian Allegrett	Permanent Secretary Siestemu Economico Latino Americano Caracas 100-A Venezuela
Yugoslavia	Mr Dragoslav Avramovic	UNCTAD Palais des Nations Geneva 10 Switzerland
Zimbabwe	Dr T Muzondo	Senior Deputy Secretary Ministry of Finance, Economic Planning & Development Harare Zimbabwe

NOTES ON CONTRIBUTORS

Osvaldo Sunkel is in charge of the CEPAL/UNEP Development and Environment Programme in Santiago, Chile. He has been Professor of Economic Development, both at the Chilean National University and the Catholic University of Chile. He is a Professorial Fellow of the Institute of Development Studies, University of Sussex.

Enrique V Iglesias is the Foreign Minister of Uruguay. He was Executive Secretary of the Economic Commission for Latin America (ECLA) from 1972 until his appointment as Foreign Minister in 1985.

Celso Furtado is the principal author of the economic platform of the Partido de Movimento Democratico Brasileiro, the majority party in the Brazilian government. He has been Directeur de Recherche at the Institut de Hautes Etudes en Sciences Sociales, University of Paris.

Aldo Ferrer is Governor of the Banco de la Provincia de Buenos Aires, Argentina. He is a long-standing member of the Radical Party and has occupied important posts with various governments, including Minister of the Economy in 1970–71. He has lectured in Economics at Buenos Aires University and in 1970 helped to found the Latin American Council of Social Sciences.

Juan Somavia is the Executive Director of the Instituto Latino Americano de Estudios Transnacionals (ILET) in Santiago, Chile.

Jose Antonio Ocampo is Executive Director of FEDESARROLLO in Bogota, Colombia. He has been a Professor of Economics at the University of the Andes since 1976.

Dragoslav Avramovic was Senior Adviser on Economic Cooperation. Office of the Secretary-General, UNCTAD. He was Director of the Secretariat and an ex officio member of the Independent Commission on International Development Issues (the Brandt Commission), Geneva.

Gert Rosenthal is Director of the Economic Commission for Latin America (ECLA) in Santiago, Chile.

William G Demas is President of the Caribbean Development Bank. He has been Economic Adviser to the Prime Minister of Trinidad and Tobago; Secretary-General of the Caribbean Community Secretariat; Chairman of the UN Committee for

Development Planning; member of the OAS Group of Experts on Inter-American Development Cooperation and of the Commonwealth Group of Experts on *Towards a New Bretton Woods.*

Germanico Salgado Penaherrera is a consultant on economic and financial affairs. He has been Director of the Department of Economic and Social Affairs of the Organisation of American States, Washington DC; a member of the Committee of the Cartagena Agreement, in the first years of the Andean Group, in Lima; Minister of Industry and Commerce in Ecuador; and Ecuador's Ambassador to Spain.

He has also been an adviser to the United Nations and to other international organisations.

Elvio Baldinelli is an economic consultant in Buenos Aires, Argentina. He has been Argentina's Secretary of State for Foreign Trade; Secretary of State for Industry and Mining and Ambassador to the European Economic Community. He has also been Joint Executive Secretary of the LAFTA and President of the Argentine Export Credit Insurance Company.

Luciano Tomassini is President of RIAL (Programa de Estudios Conjuntos Sobre las Relaciones Internacionales de America Latina) in Santiago, Chile.

Ivan Lavados Montes is Executive Director of the Inter-University Centre on Development, and Professor of Political Economy at the University of Chile.

INDEX